BREAK THE INTERNET

BREAK
THE
INTERNET

the power of
online influencers

OLIVIA YALLOP

SCRIBE

Melbourne • London

Scribe Publications
2 John St, Clerkenwell, London, WC1N 2ES, United Kingdom
18–20 Edward St, Brunswick, Victoria 3056, Australia
3754 Pleasant Ave, Suite 100, Minneapolis, Minnesota 55409, USA

First published by Scribe 2021
This edition published 2022

Copyright © Olivia Yallop 2021

At the time of writing, all quotations and information sourced from
web pages were accurate and all URLs linked to existing websites
and social media accounts. The publisher is not responsible for
and should not be deemed to endorse or recommend any website
other than our own or any content available on the internet
(including without limitation, any website, blog post,
or information page) that is not created by the publisher.

Typeset in Minion by the publishers

Printed and bound in the UK by CPI Group (UK) Ltd, Croydon CR0 4YY

Scribe is committed to the sustainable use of natural resources
and the use of paper products made responsibly from those
resources.

978 1 912854 17 2 (UK paperback)
978 1 913348 33 5 (UK hardback)
978 1 950354 87 0 (US paperback)
978 1 922310 20 0 (Australian paperback)
978 1 92258607 0 (ebook)

Catalogue records for this book are available from the National
Library of Australia and the British Library.

scribepublications.co.uk
scribepublications.com.au
scribepublications.com

Break the Internet:

To post something that causes a very large amount of interest, shock, or excitement, with a large number of people sharing or reacting to what you have posted. **Example:** This cute kid basically broke the internet, with his video getting almost a billion views. (*Cambridge Dictionary*)

In 2016, The Webbys introduced their inaugural Break the Internet Award, granted to 'a person with an undeniable talent and natural ability to use the Internet to create buzz, engage with fans and communities, and get the world to pay attention.' The first recipient was Kim Kardashian.

To Mark and Rosemary,
unlikely influencers

CONTENTS

PREFACE

'It's increasingly obvious to me that the teenagers and twenty-somethings who have mastered these platforms — and who are often dismissed as shallow, preening narcissists by adults who don't know any better — are going to dominate not just internet culture or the entertainment industry but society as a whole.'

— KEVIN ROOSE, *THE NEW YORK TIMES*[1]

I can still remember the first time I accessed the internet. I was around seven, and my school's Information and Communications Technology lessons — 45 minutes every other Tuesday in a room that smelt of stale air and static — had reached a long-anticipated crescendo. After weeks spent generating imaginary ClipArt party invites in Microsoft Publisher and practising loading and ejecting floppy discs (the name was misleading: they snapped if you bent them too much) the class was going to learn to 'surf'.

I was dimly aware of the internet: my parents intermittently announced they were off to 'look at emails' and I occasionally liberated a bulky PalmPilot from my dad's suit jacket to role-play an adult with an office job, but I had no idea what being 'on the internet' would actually entail. Arranged in rows, two to a computer, hovering at the edge of infinity, we patiently awaited our instructions. The

1

screensavers displayed a sunlit, pixelated meadow: it was somehow everywhere and nowhere all at once. In the foreground the Internet Explorer icon floated; its cobalt, curvilinear 'e', encircled by a planetary ring, offered intergalactic possibilities.

The strenuous effort required to dial up felt like a full body experience. I cringed at the graunching sound of millennium Dell technology cranking into action and squirmed with every passing minute of expensive bandwidth. The school keyboards made clacking sounds and the beige plastic servers shuddered as they laboured to connect.

What the class discovered, after several agonising minutes, was underwhelming. There was no sci-fi binary code, no sleek dashboard with which to navigate through cyberspace: just a flat grey browser box and a loading bar gradually inching its way into existence. Over the weeks that followed, we learned to scroll Yahoo and AOL, click brightly coloured hyperlinks, tap concise requests into Ask Jeeves' search bar, and watch images slowly unfold themselves.

We also learned what to avoid. The internet was out to get you; hackers and phishers and spammers were waiting to unleash a bug or a thousand-year chain email curse. Danger lurked in chat rooms, on forums, and in unmemorised website addresses. A list of 'friendly' sites hung above the classroom printer, typed in Comic Sans. I can't remember much about my ICT teacher, but I will always remember what she said: never, ever, under any circumstances, share any personal information about yourself on the internet. If someone asks you, say no and log off straight away.

Jump ahead two decades, and she'd be disappointed. Today we share our most private info willingly. Oversharing online has become not just a common pastime, but a highly lucrative industry, making millionaires of its most popular protagonists. Many of these are now household names who communicate en masse with multi-millions, mining their experiences for TikTok clips backed by 15-second trending tracks, breathlessly gesturing into a front-facing camera to broadcast personal milestones and invite unseen strangers into intimate domestic moments.

In the years that have elapsed since I first learnt to 'surf', sharing yourself online has become second nature, whilst the logic of engagement and self-optimisation has begun to permeate every corner of our lives, both on the internet and IRL. Influencers — masters of online attention — are both emblematic of our present moment and a harbinger of where we're headed next. We no longer need to dial up. Increasingly, it seems unlikely that we'll ever get to log off either.

CHAPTER 1

THE MILLION-FOLLOWER POLICY

WHAT IS AN INFLUENCER?

It's 8.45 pm on a rainy Thursday in August, and I'm standing in the marble lobby of an obnoxiously expensive hotel in central London. The sweeping staircase has been cordoned off and the air is still. Sleek-haired staff hover, pawing at their iPads and shooting intermittent glances towards the revolving doors and the gloomy street beyond. A chandelier casts a champagne glow over the motionless tableau.

Perspiration is condensing in the curve of my lower back. I catch my reflection in a perfectly polished lift door and regret wearing trainers. We are not waiting on the arrival of an A-list actor, chart-topping popstar, minor royal or political leader. There are no paparazzi outside, nor will there be any press coverage in the tabloids come the morning. But the evening will be livestreamed in full 360-degree glory to over 100 million viewers waiting in breathless anticipation all around the world.

We're waiting to welcome a new kind of celebrity: the stars of social media. A Who's Who of top fashion and beauty influencers are congregating tonight for the UK launch of an LA-based fast fashion label — let's call them Babe. The company — or more accurately, empire — has built a billion-dollar business from the power of social media influence. You may not know their name, but if you've accessed Instagram at any point over the last three years you will have probably come into contact with their particular brand of glossy, impossible aspiration.

Babe have come to be synonymous with influencer culture, and their feed is a feast of conspicuous consumption: branded swimming pools, candlelit Parisian dinners, hot air balloons, lavish trips to tropical locales, a private festival with performances from Grammy-winning rappers. Babe are more like a cult than a clothing brand: for many attendees, a partnership with them — including attendance at tonight's event — represents their arrival in the upper echelons of influence.

Instagram has over a billion monthly active users across the globe[1] — an eighth of the world's entire population — and over 100 million posts are uploaded on the platform every day. In 2018, it hosted more than 3.7 million sponsored posts[2] — by 2020, this number was estimated to have reached 6m.[3] Instagram reports that 87 per cent of its users have been 'influenced' into buying something by a creator.[4] The scale and speed of social media makes it impossible to pin down how many influencers there are exactly, but studies suggest there may be more than 50 million around the world: 2m full-time professionals — approximately equivalent to the entire population of Slovenia — and the rest amateurs uploading in their spare time.[5]

That may sound like a lot, but the vast majority of participants are minor players — micro-influencers — with an audience of merely tens of thousands, hustling hard to generate re-grammable content and court brands in exchange for freebies and PR packages; vlogging and posting and streaming to a small audience of dedicated fans.

As influencers' view counts and audience statistics tick upwards, they begin to attract more lucrative sponsorship deals with better brands, and savvy agents keen to capitalise on commission. The path to success becomes increasingly strategic: content cycles become ever more demanding, cliques form between creators, competition heightens, cancellation looms. Only 0.14 per cent of Instagram users make it to the top tier of social media stardom, achieving the magic million-follower count.[6] With 1 million followers you're not just an influencer any more: you're a media empire and lifestyle brand, boasting fan accounts, a behind-the-scenes team, and lines of merchandise bearing your name.

The most successful creators represent a new class of the super-rich. Kylie Jenner, the highest earning influencer on Instagram, is reportedly paid around $1.2 million per post.[7] In 2019, *Forbes* reported that the ten top gaming streamers — all unlikely looking, Monster-drinking millionaires in their teens and early twenties — had a combined 270m followers and earned a collective $121m.[8]

When Shane Dawson and Jeffree Star — a controversial conspiracy-theory vlogger and an ostentatious beauty guru, both of whom have spent over a decade accumulating their audiences on YouTube — collaborated to release an eyeshadow palette together in 2019, it sold out instantly, crashing Shopify[9] and making $35 million in mere seconds.[10] 'Kidfluencer' Ryan Kaji, a bubbly Texan who has attracted over 45 billion views to his upbeat videos unboxing brightly coloured toys, was the highest-paid YouTuber of 2020, earning $29.5m from advertising revenue and $200m from his merchandise line:[11] not a bad salary for a nine-year-old. After that, the zeros start to blur together.

Tonight is for the 0.14 per cent. Tonight, the internet glitterati will congregate offline to gossip and gawp and 'gram for an online audience that will easily outnumber the entire population of the UK. But the industry is both cynical and cyclical, always on the lookout for the next big thing: the guestlist also includes a mix of ambitious smaller influencers snapping at their heroes' strappy Missguided heels. Influencing is a reputation game, and attending tonight's event could convert to contacts, contracts, and an influx of followers. At past influencer events I've tagged on my Instagram Stories, I've had DMs from strangers begging for entry or asking to buy my branded gift bag, presumably to post on social media and pretend they were there too.

It's 9 pm and I'm jolted from my thoughts as, Uber by Uber, the members of the new media monarchy start to arrive and mill about excitedly in the foyer. There's just one problem: so far, nobody's going in. 'What's going on?' I ask, battling to the front of the queue where voices are beginning to be raised. 'Why aren't you letting people through?'

'Sorry,' comes an West Coast drawl from behind an iPad, from a woman whose chunky gold hoops and silky blouse mirror the uniform of the crowd she is attempting to control. 'We're operating a follower policy on the door tonight. Only girls with a million or more are allowed in before ten. Do you wanna show me your Instagram, babe?'

I knew tonight was for the influencer aristocracy, but I wasn't expecting the pecking order to be so explicitly policed. Neither, clearly, was the increasingly flustered crowd gathering at my back. Eyelash extensions are rolled, and bitter glances shot at the few who start to move towards the front of the queue. A voice over my left shoulder mutters after a passing figure: 'What a joke. I'm nearly at 800k. I bet half *her* followers were bought anyway.' I decide against pulling out my cracked iPhone to reveal my 568 Instagram followers.

At this point you are probably wondering who I am and how I've ended up here. I'm in the influencer business, working for one of the hundreds of digital agencies that have sprung up in response to what is often referred to as 'the social media revolution'. My agency doesn't represent influencers directly, but acts as an intermediary between them and brands, curating, casting, and engaging social media stars for marketing campaigns, launch parties, and photoshoots, organising elaborate brand trips to Iceland or Ibiza, showering them with freebies, creating customised and Instagrammable 'brand experiences', or helping them develop campaigns of their own. It sounds like a glam way to get paid, but parties are generally the exception; I'm more often found sitting on a beanbag in our office, 20 tabs open, hypnotically scrolling TikTok.

Although I've been in the industry over half a decade, when I first started, influencer marketing didn't formally exist. Communities of online hobbyists had been accumulating since the dawn of the social internet, and commercial relationships between bloggers and brands had begun to formalise in the late 00s, but for all but the most forward-thinking brands, working with influencers was still considered experimental and risky until the mid-2010s. Brands were still learning to navigate the budding social media landscape, and those prepared to take the plunge grew swiftly.

Founded in 2012, the agency I work for got in early, in the days before we had the language to describe what we were doing or the regulation to tell us when to stop. Since then, we've shifted with the landscape, moving fluidly with trends and platforms, and watching as successive generations of influencers have risen to fame and fallen from it, made millions, launched businesses, or eventually burnt out.

Like most in the social media space, the company I work for is small and agile, staffed by fresh-faced creatives unencumbered by the wisdom of experience or the accepted ideologies of the traditional industries we are up against. We say things like 'disrupt' and 'democratise', 'thumb-stopping' and 'older target audience', usually meaning anyone over 25. We share reaction GIFs and influencer gossip on any one of several open channels of communication until the early hours of the morning; my phone rattles and battery saps with near-constant notifications.

We unite behind a gently rebellious manifesto: attention spans are shrinking, mainstream media is dead, content is king, and we represent the future. Brands come to us to understand this future and for help to get there first, or to sell their sports bras or sneakers or make-up or CBD-infused tampons to youthful demographics in the interim. No matter what they're selling, the brief is usually the same: brands want to engage young customers, drive hype, go viral. They want to be woke, but not political; aspirational, but still authentic; to speak as if they are your friend and not a subcommittee of overworked social media managers reworking Twitter copy in a Google Doc for the seventh time that week. For them, influencers are a useful marketing vehicle: a digital proxy, a spend-efficient way to reach a generation permanently glued to their phones.

'Influencers — the good ones at least — hold a strong combination of popularity, aspiration and authority,' explains Marina Mansour, Global Head of Beauty Partnerships at Kyra Media, a Gen Z media company at the forefront of the social media revolution, who represent and incubate top TikTok talent. 'Combine this with frequent visibility across multiple channels and the nuanced understanding of how to connect with their own audience deeply and powerfully, and it makes influencers arguably the most powerful marketing tool there is.' Creator influence, she notes, extends beyond just selling. 'The content and communities on social platforms are the hotbed of where trends are shaped, ideas are hatched and challenged and movements are sparked,' Marina continues: 'Creators ARE pop culture.'

The influencer industry of the early 2020s is, in many ways, reminiscent of the tech industry of the early 2010s. Though it's been developing for over a decade, it's still seen as a relative 'wild west', attracting a ragtag bunch of technologists, marketers, entrepreneurs, investors, and opportunists, all keen to capitalise on the rapidly developing landscape and relative lack of regulation. The industry still remains largely unstructured, un-formalised and un-legislated, leaving ample space for ambitious individuals to experiment, mirroring the 'move fast and break things' philosophy that originally underwrote its host platforms.

In 2014, five UK YouTube vloggers were reported to the Advertising Standards Authority (ASA) by a BBC journalist who had suspicions about a series of innocuous challenge videos in which people raced to lick the middle of an Oreo.[12] It transpired that this wasn't a neat piece of creative synchronicity, but an ad campaign briefed and funded by Oreo's parent company Mondelez. The ASA banned the videos and introduced the world's first influencer regulation, but new and innovative methods were soon springing up as fast as rules could be introduced: disappearing posts, brand trips, gifting, or simply sneaky wording that skirted around legality. Other markets take a more relaxed attitude: the US Federal Trade Commission (FTC) issued its first complaint against social media influencers for failing to comply with its Endorsement Guides in April 2017,[13] whilst Australia only established a Code of Practice requiring influencers to disclose sponsored posts in 2020.[14]

The shiny new 'creator economy' — a slick Silicon Valley rebrand of the existing influencer industry, a spiritual successor to its previous invention, the gig economy — is at the centre of a digital gold rush. We are in the right place at the right time, flush with untapped opportunities, boundless attention, and venture capital (VC) funding. Our sector moves at the speed of algorithm updates and product ships: new avenues for revenue open up, new platforms emerge, and new types of content and operation models develop swiftly. It's not unusual to wake up and discover a new feature, a new restriction, or even a new influencer scandal has blown up overnight, accelerating your progress, recalibrating your strategy, opening up new and obscure marketing channels or business models. Creator economy millionaires — of which there are many — are usually in their twenties, and are just as likely to have developed a winning piece of software, a new creator-based platform, or run a lucrative talent agency as to be social media stars themselves. There is no textbook, few rules, and many fortunes to be made for the fortunate or forward. I have learnt to expect the unexpected.

My job — like all jobs in this space — is a slippery hybrid, somewhere between creative and strategist, marketer and intermediary, helping brands to understand the internet landscape, and work out how to profit from that knowledge. More practically, it requires me to spend up to 16 hours each day logged on to social media, to track and interpret its shifting currents, translating the complexities and contradictions of online discourse into a language that's understandable to brand managers, a set of 'actionable insights' and 'consumer drivers' that give them a commercial edge.

Working in social media is a strange way to make a living; I sit as an interface between the expansive and idiosyncratic landscape of creators, the all-powerful and monolithic platforms, and the corporate world of brands with competitive budgets and lucrative contracts. I'm in a front-row seat at the largest synchronised spectacle in human history unfolding in real time every single day.

It's a position that gives me a unique perspective on the inner workings of the industry, but having a stake in both sides of the influencer game means I can sometimes feel trapped between two lives and two languages — a consumer and producer, a parasite and a host, simultaneously invested in and alienated by the industry's core philosophies. Most of the time, however, I'm too wrapped up in unpacking trending topics or understanding ephemeral internet drama for any of this to register.

Tonight, my agency has curated a group of London tastemakers to attend Babe's event; the mix includes models, DJs, fitness gurus, beauty bloggers, and a former reality star with gleaming teeth and a profitable side hustle in crystal healing. Our job is simple: get the 'right people' down to the party, ensure they have a good time, and make sure they post on Instagram whilst doing it.

The team has spent weeks meticulously orchestrating this evening of fun to appear as spontaneous as possible. They have stalked social media profiles, strategised, set targets. They have conducted audits to identify fake followers and trawled back through timelines to catch any embarrassing Facebook statuses or misguided tweets from 2012. They have sweet-talked managers and agents, pulled favours, booked taxis. I have changed out of my office-appropriate outfit, travelled an hour from our studio in east London to the centre of the city, charged several portable battery packs in preparation. But now we have an unanticipated problem: the million-follower policy.

This industry has desensitised me to any number of outlandish and outrageous requests, but it's the first time I have encountered the mythical 'follower policy' IRL. Babe are keeping several internet it-girls waiting on a technicality. Patience may be short, but Instagram Stories criticising Babe and their party's dodgy door policy to millions of potential customers are shorter: 15 seconds, to be exact. Influencers' ability to propel a brand to relevance with just a few quick clicks is just as effective when executed in reverse: social media managers live in perpetual fear of being 'put on blast'. Keeping these digital doyennes happy is our own personal marketing target for the night.

After considerable time spent skulking in the foyer, and several frantic WhatsApps back and forth, my colleague and I are rescued by the arrival of two friends whose 5.5m combined followers offer sufficient compensation for our lack of clout. Our flock of unimpressed influencers are eventually released from captivity and let into the party. I am desperate for a drink, but they ignore the bar and the dance floor and head first for the WiFi password. Within a few seconds we've all lost each other in the gloom, the bodies, and the noise; neon lights and palm fronds transform the hotel's mirrored ballroom into a dark, throbbing jungle.

This is not my first influencer party, nor will it be my last, but I will never get over the sheer weirdness of it all. It's extravagant, it's excessive, it's engineered for Instagram: it's an event designed as much for the people who weren't invited as for those who were, with photo-op backdrops and lighting that's been carefully calibrated for flattering pics so the party looks as good onscreen as it does off. Semi-familiar faces made up in uncanny valley Instaglam loom left and right, eyes connecting with me for an instant before slipping past. Only having 568 followers might make me a nobody, but it also means I can head for the smoking area unchallenged.

Loitering outside in the relative tranquility of the terrace, I catch my breath. The sun has set, and sirens wail somewhere close by in Soho. It's cold, but nobody seems to notice. Small seats have been thoughtfully placed at intimate, gossip-friendly intervals, planters providing privacy between whisperers. Guests linger, waiting to take pictures in front of a backdrop of pink-neon Babe logos, jostling to align their angles before squinting at playback. In the corner, a woman in a bold, patterned tracksuit is speaking animatedly into a camera held aloft at head height; she gestures wildly with her other arm and enthuses at the rectangle in her hand. We're all watching each other watch ourselves: stealing small sideways glances or gazing expectantly into the middle distance.

I feel a now familiar, but still unsettling, sensation. Amongst a gaggle of impossibly glossy camera-ready stars in the uniform of the fashionably online, I'm scruffy and awkward, conspicuous by my insignificance. As predicted, I'm the only person wearing trainers. I wince as phones flash around me and duck out of sight: the last thing I want is to be caught in the background of a story viewed by hundreds of thousands of strangers. 'She's got 11 million followers ...' my companion comments over her shoulder, warily eyeing an anatomically impossible Brazilian woman in a tight white vinyl dress and pointed sock-boots, who has just appeared. As if by some influencer herd instinct, all eyes have silently swivelled to the largest star in the room: '... and she's *definitely* had her bum done.'

Uneasy posturing, submerged rivalry, and a shared goal of showing off online make influencer parties a bizarre and complex social ecosystem. It is perfectly possible to take each other's pictures and swap Facetuning tips in the toilet queue whilst silently resenting that the person standing opposite has been paid double, or triple what you have to attend. The night unfolds as a semi-surreal performance of a 'really good party' put together by someone who's watched a lot of other people go to 'really good parties' on the internet: the bar is free, the crowd is attractive and animated, and everywhere I look is logoed. Babe's insignia is emblazoned across everything from food to loo roll, ensuring no moment in the partygoer's life cycle remains unoptimised by our omnipresent sponsor.

Two semi-famous DJs remix 90s RnB and take turns filming each other behind the decks. I pull up their Instagram Live streams on my iPhone, dizzied by the inception-like effect of simultaneously watching them in the booth, and the rest of the room from it. A girl in a shiny snakeskin suit bumps into another, identically dressed attendee; they shriek with laughter, snap a picture, and avoid each other for the rest of the night. I am introduced to people by their Instagram handles, which I immediately mix up. The lurid neon lighting makes everyone look vaguely sick; I am disoriented, my developing headache perforated by the snap of photography flash panels improbably produced from the tiniest of clutch bags.

On my way to avail myself of the branded bathroom facilities, I pass through the corridor. The walls are lined with mirrors; the optical illusion is enough to stop me in my tracks. I see myself reflected again and again and again, stretching behind and in front into a non-existent distance; an image of an image of a woman clutching a pink drink framed by vinyl hashtags into infinity. Of course, I take a photo and post it to my Stories.

None of this is real, I think, philosophically emboldened by the three cocktails I have just downed in quick succession. We're just the images of ourselves online, digital impressions on 100,000 phone screens, as many approximations of the original image as I am seeing now. The real thing isn't the party, it's our recording of it; those watching the event through us on their phones at home are more here than we will ever be. The thought is vaguely unsettling and I'm glad to be absorbed back into the endless succession of culinary quirks and visual spectacles put on by Babe's event producers to vie for the attention of 200 distracted guests who go to events like this for a living.

I never planned on working in the influencer industry; I didn't grow up thinking you could make a living from being online. In many ways, this puts me in the same position as my subjects: on a career path that is, to this day, still very much under construction. Originally, I planned to be an astronaut, then a geologist, then a photographer, a bakery taste-tester, the person who named the shades of nail polishes and crayons, then editor of a glossy fashion magazine. At 18, still undecided, I opted for the university refuge of generalists and apathetics, and studied English, but three years of medieval poetry did surprisingly little to clarify my career aspirations. Whilst my peers were planning gap years, filing grad school applications, or submitting to corporate serfdom with varying degrees of enthusiasm, I wavered, still unsure. Eventually, undefined artistic urges and a natural disinclination for risk funnelled me towards an advertising grad scheme, which promised to combine the emotional fulfilment and social clout of a 'creative' career path with the financial stability of full-time employment.

I didn't know it yet, but I was about to graduate into the burgeoning 2010s digital publication industry: an engagement-driven, hyper-individualised, ephemeral landscape of commodified 'content', churned out by a millennial taskforce encouraged to mine the depths of their personal experience for a pittance, producing personal essays and memes and listicles to be published by new digital media houses, editorial platforms, and brands boasting shiny new social media 'newsrooms'.

Advertising was the intersection of culture, creativity, and commerce I gathered from trawling careers sites as I was procrastinating over my final papers. It had been the training ground for Salman Rushdie, F. Scott Fitzgerald, Ed Ruscha, and Hugh

Hefner. It had given us gorillas playing Phil Collins and middle-aged maestros singing 'GoCompare'. It offered, if not untold riches, then at least the reassurance that I wouldn't have to wear a suit to work. I remembered singing along to mattress company jingles on the radio on the way to primary school and dissecting heavy fashion magazines in order to Blu-Tack perfume ads to my bedroom wall as a teenager. I'd read interviews with successful business people in the newspapers, in which fond childhood anecdotes such as these had given their careers a satisfying air of teleological inevitability. Maybe, I thought, advertising was meant to be.

I batch-applied to London agencies identified by a string of interchangeable initials and stumbled through successive rounds of calculatedly quirky questions like 'If you had a time machine, which period would you visit?' and 'How does the colour yellow sound?' The agencies I visited had ping-pong tables and rooftop bars and all the toothpaste or chocolate bars or client freebies you could cram into a branded swag bag. Once there, I pitched made-up products and offered ill-considered criticisms of multi-million-dollar, Cannes Lions-award-winning ad campaigns to the people who had created them. At one interview, we all sat on the floor. I was taken aback when a job offer on self-important letterheaded paper arrived on the morning of my 21st birthday. Along with several others, I had been selected to represent the next generation for the oldest, and one of the most reputable, agencies, the birthplace of advertising and a bastion of creative communications for over 150 years.

In the 1800s, the agency had hired artists and writers to form the world's first creative department and began producing targeted ads specifically for women. In 1915, it had been the first agency to introduce market research, bringing in a department of academics and behavioural psychologists to analyse consumer spending habits. In 1925, it was the first to replace illustrated ads with photographs. With the arrival of TV, it was the first to persuade top film and TV directors to make adverts, spearheading a golden era of iconic 60-second spots for cigarettes, sportscars, and luxury watches that were really miniature cinematic stories of power, sex, status, insecurity, and ambition — in short, the full spectrum of human experience. Along the way, the agency claimed to have invented the grilled cheese sandwich, had broken the Guinness World Record for the largest billboard, and had introduced the world to a lovable puppy with a penchant for toilet roll. Advertising was the agency, and the agency was advertising. And now, the letter was pleased to inform me, so was I.

As soon as I stepped through the door and onto the strip-lit carpet tiles of the head office in central London one morning in September, it was evident that something somewhere had gone wrong. Despite the awards lining the walls of the entrance hall, the flurry of colourful sketchbooks and vintage printouts and 3D models that littered the floors of the creative department, and the presence of celebrated industry veterans who I passed with awe in the corridor, the agency was beset with an atmosphere of perpetual stress and creative malaise. It was the mid-2010s, the media landscape was shifting rapidly, and it felt like we were sinking fast.

The agency had lost several accounts to smaller, more agile digital agencies. It was clogged up with bureaucracy and paperwork: briefs and rebriefs and debriefs, intricate and circuitous strategic processes, hundred-slide presentations that refused to conclude, email threads several hundred missives deep. I seemed to spend my days in meetings, or meetings about meetings, or updating spreadsheets, or doing timesheets that detailed exactly how much time I had spent doing spreadsheets. Every minute of every day was logged, tracked, and billed at rates that made my graduate eyes water.

'Client' — a composite figure of fear and authority — was always annoyed, or threatening to leave, or demanding to know how we had racked up so many hours on their account and produced so little for it. Our budgets were apparently too high, our output too slow, our workflows too rigid. Account management harangued production, production harangued the creatives, the creatives harangued everyone and got away with it. We hadn't won any awards or new accounts for months. I came in hung-over one Friday to find approximately a third of my department crying, one third in the pub. The last third had been made redundant.

The gap between the agency's progressive rhetoric — pioneering and futureproofing and data-driven — and my experience there was widening with every passing day. Though my department colleagues were kind and more than generous with their time, I felt displaced. I would wander the halls with my swipe card and hide in meeting rooms away from bleak cubicles, my unfinished budget sheets, and the desk phone that rang off the hook with the same upbeat account executive always at the other end of the line. These problems, I soon realised by scouring trade publications and conversing with weather-worn creative teams at the coffee maker, weren't contained within our building. Other famous agencies — the one run by the man who owned the art gallery and married a celebrity chef, the one that began the trend for saccharine Christmas adverts for a much-loved British department store — were facing similar problems too.

I had graduated into an industry that was collapsing around me. The internet was eating advertising. The same year I started my job, app usage exceeded hours spent watching TV in the US for the first time.[15] A Pew Research Center study labelled my generation 'cord cutters',[16] as mobile minutes soared and newspapers and televisions were abandoned en masse. Budgets for digital media surpassed TV, and brand spend on social media rose by half within my first year of work.[17] Newspaper publishing passed an economic milestone, as global ad revenue plummeted below circulation revenue for the first time.[18] Traditional advertising — our kind — was in crisis. 'Rats from a sinking ship', a particularly jaded art director would mutter as another producer or account director announced they were defecting for an entertainment brand, new-media outlet, or digital agency.

Eventually, one Monday morning, I joined them, abandoning the old world of billboards and client servicing departments and multi-million-pound accounts for the wild west of social media and influencer marketing: an outgrowth of the very same concept of 'testimonial advertising' that my initial employers had themselves pioneered with celebrity endorsements for Pond's Vanishing Cream back in 1914. It wasn't a particularly poignant last day: I returned my laptop, thanked my department, and swiped one last multipack of sugary snacks from the client product cupboard. Within a year of my departure, the failing agency would be merged with a smaller, newer, more switched-on digital shop: the end of an era, and another historic moment for advertising. None of the trade papers seemed to be surprised. It was yet another sign of the times.

Within a few months, I would wash up at a new agency I'd discovered, and then DMed, on Instagram, where it had made its name and grown a substantial following of its own. It was there that I learned to weave seamlessly between both media worlds, answering experimental briefs for lean and forward-thinking startups, cashing in on this credibility by helping slower household names — with bigger bank balances — to keep up. My personal career trajectory — from institution to independent, old to new, analogue to digital, big to small — reflects a broader arc in media, celebrity, and entertainment. I'd like to pretend it was premeditated, but it's more like lucky coincidence, or at least a subconscious drive for proximity to the things I enjoyed doing: I am part of the generation that grew up being told that hours spent on Reddit, playing Call of Duty, or scrolling Facebook was 'wasted time', only to find these pastimes solidified into a highly lucrative professional industry by the time we reached employment age.

How did we get here? In the years elapsed since I left traditional advertising, influencing has exploded from personal hobby into professional career path, internet curiosity into mainstream conversation. 'I started using Instagram just as a personal thing, to document my fitness journey,' explains Australian influencer Madalin Giorgetta, a blonde, toned workout guru who built her platform in the pursuit of picture-perfect fitness shots. 'At first, I was a little bit embarrassed about my account: I didn't even show my face in the pictures.' Over months, she shared her progress, personal anecdotes, and beginner workout routines as she began to build her strength. 'My account just kind of exploded,' Madalin tells me, still sounding bemused even several years later: 'It was really rapid: I watched as the numbers just went up, and up, and up. In just two years, I had a million followers.'

In 2019, she renounced the 'toxic' Instagram fitness space and joined the ranks of body positivity influencers encouraging self-love and dismantling beauty standards; today, she's one of Australia's best known anti-diet lifestyle influencers, with a fitness app, a cookbook, and articles in *Teen Vogue* and the *Daily Mail*, on a mission to 'practice body neutrality, promote fat acceptance, and reject the health and fitness industry's core message that you need to change your body shape to be valued and have worth.' Her YouTube channel has over 15m views, and her Instagram posts exposing misleading poses and analysing her body insecurities regularly make the news. Madalin's story — an unsuspecting individual rapidly propelled to life-changing fame, carving out space within an industry by challenging prevailing narratives — is familiar to anyone working in the influencer field, and mirrors the trajectory of the industry as a whole.

Over and over again, influencers have proved their ability to break not just the internet, but everything else they encounter along the way. In 2014, gateway vlogger Zoella — a diminutive Brighton-based creator with marketable older-sister appeal, who built a millennial lifestyle empire filming Primark hauls and recommending the best mascaras sub-£10 — made publishing industry history for her bestselling YA novel *Girl Online*. The story of an anonymous teenage blogger who accidentally ends up going viral, the book became the fastest-selling debut novel of all time, outselling *The Da Vinci Code*, *Harry Potter and the Philosopher's Stone*, and *Fifty Shades of Grey* in its first week.[19]

In 2018, financial analysts shook their heads in disbelief as Kardashian sister Kylie Jenner wiped $1.3 billion off Snapchat's market value in a single day after tweeting 'Sooo does anyone else not open Snapchat anymore?' In a few years, she would front *Forbes* magazine as the world's youngest self-made billionaire, a feat achieved by flogging teenagers 'Kylie lip kits' via Instagram. In early 2019, James Charles — a teenage YouTube beauty guru with 17m YouTube subscribers referred to as his 'sisters' and the theatrically sculpted face of a pixel-perfect cyborg — held a meet and greet in a shopping centre and accidentally gridlocked the UK city of Birmingham for four and a half hours, bewildering local news reporters.

In 2019, Logan Paul — bottle-blond YouTube vlog bro and enfant terrible of the algorithm, notorious for his viral pranks and controversial statements — challenged rival YouTuber KSI (Knowledge, Strength, Integrity — aka Watford-born 27-year-old gamer Olajide Olatunji) to a boxing match that whipped the internet into a frenzy. The livestreamed fight generated over 25 million views and £150m in revenue, making it the largest white-collar boxing event in history, and infuriating boxing's old guard in the process. Later that year, KSI triggered a record number of youth voter registrations for the UK general election with just a single, well-timed tweet.[20]

We've reached a pivotal moment for digital influence. After over a decade of progressive evolution, creators have hit scale. The influencer industry is one of the fastest-growing sectors of the digital economy, worth $10 billion globally today and rising to $15bn by 2022,[21] fuelled by a perfect storm of generational precarity, the rapidly increasing role of platforms, and the creeping monetisation of every aspect of our identities. Digital influence appears to be eclipsing traditional forms of fame: it is bigger, quicker, and more powerful than any celebrity generation before it. In 2016, it took Hollywood actress, Disney Channel graduate, and chart-topping singer Selena Gomez three years to become the first person to pass 100 million followers on Instagram, but in 2020, teenage unknown Charli D'Amelio — a 16-year-old from Norwalk, Connecticut with an aptitude for 15-second dance routines — exploded from zero to 100m fans on TikTok in just over 12 months.

Today, TikTok stars are in the front row at fashion week, top Spotify charts, land Hollywood movie roles. YouTubers open sell-out restaurant chains. Twitter's most successful influencer ended up in the top job at the White House. Though it dismantled seemingly everything else, the coronavirus crisis has only accelerated the influencer industry: concentrating online culture, increasing its audience, introducing us all to the digital rituals of influence. In Indonesia, social media stars were amongst the first to receive coronavirus vaccines to encourage uptake amongst the general population. In the UK, the government spent £63,000 paying 42 social media stars to promote the Track and Trace system,[22] whilst in the US, New Jersey and Oklahoma local government departments employed influencers to urge residents to wear masks and enrol for the vaccine.

This is only the beginning: new platforms, new faces, and new forms of influence are all unfolding, as the creator economy exponentially expands and, with each passing day, its audience accumulates. We're facing the next lifecycle of online existence, a world in which influencers will only become increasingly influential. 'The more traditional side of entertainment and media can't deny the power of creators and social platforms any more,' says Marina Mansour, 'and we need to remember how young this industry still is, it's got a long way to go.'

Welcome to the age of the influencer: creators are about to eat the internet.

But for a cohort so concerned with personal branding, it might come as a surprise that influencers are going through something of an identity crisis. According to The 2019 Influencer Survey, 71 per cent of Instagram influencers don't actually identify with the term. 'Influencer is a dirty word,' Lou Teasdale, one of the UK's leading beauty influencers, admitted when I asked her how she defines herself, one sunny lunchtime at a rooftop bar in London's Shoreditch. Having amassed over 5.5m followers, she has branched out into lifestyle and interiors. 'It's still seen as a really negative thing to want to be.'

'We wouldn't ever describe ourselves as 'influencers', agrees Lovisa, one third of millennial collective @LondonFoodBabes, one of the original #foodstagram accounts responsible for popularising the 'foodporn' trend — ever more elaborate street food, artery-defying 'dirty' burgers, and saccharine 'freakshakes' — that dominated news feeds in the mid-2010s. The eponymous babes have since expanded to several cities around the world and review trendy restaurants, pop-ups, and delivery services daily for their hundreds of thousands of followers, but before they went full time, Lovisa kept her side hustle hidden. 'There's a bit of a stigma in saying you work as an influencer ...' she explains. 'Even though it's now becoming more popular as a full-time occupation, I still feel weird saying it.'

What exactly is the issue with 'influencer'? The word itself predates the internet, first recorded in the English language in the mid-1600s with an astrological significance that modern social media stars can merely dream of. Derived from the medieval Latin 'influentia', the term referred to the radiation of an occult power from the cosmos that had the power to alter human decisions and impact destiny down on Earth. Today's *Love Island* stars harnessing their digital influence to flog fake tan is, depending on your perspective, only marginally less sinister.

Perhaps it's the fact that, technically, 'influencer' is a marketing term. Creators carefully cultivate authenticity and intimacy, and the label 'influencer' exposes the persuasive machinery beneath. In 2018, Merriam-Webster expanded its definition from the generalised 'one who has influence' to 'a person who is able to generate interest in something (such as a consumer product) by posting about it on social media'. Satirical slang site Urban Dictionary, by contrast, lists 'influencer' as 'a word Instagram users use to describe themselves to make them feel famous and more important when no one really knows who they are or cares [sic]'. Twitter is awash with alternative, unprintable interpretations.

Social media stars have long been experimenting with other titles — 'content creator', 'brand ambassador', or 'curator' are all popular. Some of these alternatives are torturously convoluted ('peer-to-peer personality marketer'), others toe-curlingly vile — openly referring to yourself as an 'affluencer' would surely only generate online traction of the wrong kind. 'We've never used "influencer" … the invention of that word was the trigger for the race to the bottom of the type of talent that are around', Dominic Smales, Founder and former CEO of Gleam Futures, the OG influencer management agency and veterans of the industry, told me at his headquarters, when I interviewed him on behalf of my agency back in 2018. 'I would be wary of anybody who describes themselves as wanting a career as an influencer. The word is too homogenous and faceless to be meaningful.'

'Digital-first talent' is the term they use instead: clients on their roster are presented as writers, photographers, stylists, or singers — who just so happen to have staggering social media followings. The biggest influencer you've never heard of, Smales is responsible for representing first generation social media stars that ruled YouTube in the mid-2010s, referred to as 'Team Gleam' — Zoella, her tousle-haired *Pointless Blog* boyfriend Alfie Deyes, her best friend, softly spoken beauty guru @TanyaBurr, and bleach-haired comedian-turned-streetwear hypebeast @MarcusButler. Smales recognised early on that a Hollywood talent representation model could be equally applied to influencers.

In the world of influence, these are heritage names, from a time in which growing a channel on YouTube was strenuous: concepting, scripting, filming, and editing videos of up to an hour's length, three times a week or more. By contrast, today's mobile-edited TikTokers or Instagram selfie stars appear to have it easy, so it is perhaps understandable that Smales's stance on this new wave of social media celebrity skews towards the sceptical: be a photographer, writer, or creative first, and then an influencer second.

However, this criticism ignores the thousands of successful creators who make money from long, rambling video streams or snaps of the contents of their bathroom cabinets, and is indicative of a perceived creative hierarchy within the influencer system, in which influencers who consider themselves famous for 'traditional', off-platform talents are elevated above those whose talent is simply mastering the platform. Expecting influencers to fit into traditional categories for fame misses the point: the most successful influencers are, after all, often those whose skill is influence itself.

Not everyone is anti-'influencer'. Some self-identified 'career influencers', like fashion and entrepreneurial influencer Emily Parr defend the term: 'People who had previously called themselves "bloggers" didn't want to own the title, because it was like throwing our hands up and admitting that we have platforms to influence people, and therefore make money off our influence.'

A long-term creator who has upgraded her strategies for self-promotion in line with the shifting media landscape, Emily's entrepreneurial experience adapting from blogger to vlogger to podcaster to influencer makes her less squeamish than most about the commercial element: 'People who don't own the term "influencer" are in denial as to what they are. It's quite obvious that I'm a brand and what we do is a business. There are millions of pounds being earned every week by people like me doing what we do.' Lou Teasdale agrees: 'I think we should just get over ourselves and say it. We're missing a trick to hide it behind a posh word. Influencers are what people want.'

She's right: influencers are what we want. Unlike the celebrity generations before them, influencers are the first directly self-selected, self-elected stars whose success rests solely on their symbiotic relationship with those who follow them, without the mediating structures of the film, sports, music, or fashion industries, or traditional media. Perhaps 'peer-to-peer personality marketers' should drop the pretence.

In 2021, the term 'influencer' is already dated, replaced by grand, Silicon Valley-backed declarations about the 'creator economy' and with it, the broadening of its participants from social media stars to everyone with an internet connection; from advertising-ancillary marketing channels focused on flogging other people's products to independent entrepreneurial powerhouses, unlocking new forms of value and restructuring the labour market along the way.

'In the mid-2010s, the rise of the influencer industry allowed top-tier creators to monetize through advertising,' reads a statement on the 'future of work' published by venture capital fund Andreessen Horowitz, responsible for pioneering investment in the territory.[23] 'Now the ability to make a living off creative skills has trickled down to individuals at scale, helping everyday people to launch and grow businesses.' They call this the 'creator stack', or 'enterprization of the consumer', which has 'huge implications for … what we'll think of as a "job" in the future.' The term 'influencer' is clearly too specific for this vision.

There's a gendered element at play as well: 77 per cent of influencers identify as female, according to research by influencer marketing agency Klear.[24] Male influencers tend to identify as 'content creators' instead. It's hard to miss the traditional, almost biblical associations behind this coding — the influencer is manipulative and feminine, in contrast to the powerful male creator. Whilst 'influencers' tend to sit within traditionally feminised niches — fashion, beauty, interiors, body positivity, lifestyle, and family — 'creators' can be anyone or anything, not confined to a single identity online. 'You associate "influencer" with fashion, Instagram, a perfect feed …' comments @LondonFoodBabe Lovisa: the reality is far broader and more diverse.

So what exactly is an influencer? That depends on who you ask. On Google, they appear by turns as vacant reality show graduates #sponning PrettyLittleThing, gym bunnies in Lululemon leggings flogging flat tummy tea, or wholesome Mormon mummy bloggers from the Midwest. They are rake-thin, Man-Repelling clotheshorses in clashing concept accessories, or glossy beauty gurus teaching pre-teen girls to contour (*link in bio!*). They are a narcissistic digital freakshow or the voice of next-generation media. They are scammers, stars, celebrities, self-starters, savants, or — perhaps most damningly of all, for those whose job is to be known — to many they are simply a mystery. 'For people who don't work in the industry, it's really hard to explain what you do, especially compared to a normal traditional job ...' says Lovisa: 'My family have no idea!'

Neither, it appears, do the wider public. 'What is an influencer', 'how to become an influencer', and 'what do influencers do all day' are some of the most-searched queries relating to the keyword on Google Trends. Whilst the stereotypes of the clean-eating self-promotion machine or gormless, augmented selfie star persist via memes and media headlines, internet creators are just as likely to be chefs, gamers, teachers, artists, activists, politicians, and comedians. There are mumfluencers, travelgrammers, thinkfluencers, thinfluencers, granfluencers, kidfluencers, and a whole host of other influential online personalities whose 'thing' doesn't fit neatly into any portmanteau. The exact image that springs to mind when you picture an influencer will depend largely on who you are and what you're interested in, and of course, that's the point. There's an influencer out there for everyone.

Influencers have expanded beyond traditional lifestyle categories to condense and commodify almost every aspect of human existence into bite-sized, likeable chunks of content. Scarlet-haired 'farmfluencer' @redsheperdess runs an Instagram account documenting the shifting seasons in her sleepy Cumbrian village, complete with pictures of perfectly ploughed fields and freshly laid eggs. Atlanta-based 'faithfluencer' Heather Lindsey, aka @

heatherllove, has amassed nearly 400,000 Instagram followers for her Christian memes and spiritual Stories, and uses her platform to promote Pinky Promise, her branded celibacy programme. Witches, cowboys, and the Amish all have YouTube channels, whilst landlords, lawyers, and lighthouse keepers are all popular on TikTok.

Influencers have democratised elite institutions and illuminated often unseen experiences. Zimbabwean-born student Vee Kativhu — part of the academic StudyTube community — has vlogged her way through degrees at Oxford and then Harvard, 300k viewers tuning in weekly to watch her write essays, sit through lectures, and revise in timelapse. Vee demystifies the university experience to inspire first-generation students and open access to higher education. Disability lifestyle influencer Lauren Spencer uses her Instagram account @itslololove and YouTube channel Sitting Pretty to give insight, advice, and support to the ALS community, whilst 25-year-old blind beauty guru Lucy Edwards fields questions like 'Do blind people dream?' and 'How does a blind person use a hob?' from her 1.5m followers on TikTok.

At the other end of the spectrum, it's not entirely clear what purpose virtual influencers serve, but that hasn't stopped @lilmiquela, @knoxfrost and @shudugram, all CGI celebrities who look and act like real-life Instagram models, from gaining audiences well into the millions.

Not all influencers are trying to share a lifestyle or sell something: just as many are building platforms to influence opinion. Corporate 'LinkedInfluencers' share virally optimised 'thought leadership' posts and over-punctuated status updates philosophising about performance and productivity. Political influencers are well documented: from government officials and presidential candidates using Twitter and TikTok to build their popularity, right through to home-grown content creators from all parts of the political spectrum. TikTok is home to both #MarxTok, a loose group of teenage communists aggregated by a shared hashtag, and the 'Conservative Hype House', an account shared by young Republicans with more than 1.4m followers — each educating their audience with their respective agendas. Leftist political commentator Hasan Piker discusses current affairs and conservative media bias in daily six-hour streams to over a million followers on Amazon-backed streaming platform Twitch.

Activist influencers campaign for social justice, combat misinformation, and raise money for bail funds and charitable causes. 28-year-old Erynn Chambers, an elementary school music teacher from North Carolina, blew up on TikTok in 2020 after she recorded a song about the over-policing of Black communities: her straight-talking, 60-second breakdowns of topics such as cultural appropriation and media bias have since gained her nearly 700k followers and a bio reading 'Verified Angry Black Woman'".

Other ideological influencers are more sinister. Controversial vloggers such as Stephan Molyneux, Stephen Crowder, and Paul Joseph Watson rose to fame hosting talk shows, podcasts, and live-streamed debates as part of the far-reaching alt-right YouTube community that developed in the 2010s, creating a pipeline for viewer radicalisation that has formed the basis of several studies in recent years.

Online influence can deliver an unrivalled access to audience, a sense of status, and scalable potential, leaving it open for adoption by cult-like ideologies; conspiracy theorists, QAnon truthers, and multi-level marketing scammers use the techniques of mainstream influencers to promote their agendas, building large followings and fortunes.

Influence isn't limited to mainstream social media platforms. According to market analysis from SignalFire, a venture capital firm that invests in the industry, half of the world's professional creators are on YouTube, a quarter on Instagram, and a third on Twitch.[25] The remaining fifth congregate on other emerging platforms, including content subscription services such as Patreon, which allow users to donate monthly to their favourite creators; NSFW website OnlyFans, on which influencers and sex workers sell explicit pics; sleek email newsletter service Substack that enables journalists and bloggers to earn via reader subscriptions; audio-only hangout app Clubhouse, beloved of hustling Silicon Valley techfluencers who never seem to need to take a breath; and right-wing Twitter alternative Parler, to which the Trump campaign defected in 2020. Hosting a well-rated podcast, offering a popular online education course on Coursera, having thousands of followers on clothing resale app Depop, or running a meme account all fall under the influencer umbrella.

Influencers are fast approaching global domination. My YouTube recommendations sidebar, Instagram explore page, and TikTok #ForYou feed — the stream of content shown to social media users by the platforms' proprietary algorithms — serve me Korean and Iraqi fashion influencers, Malaysian Instagram chefs, a comedy vlogger in Kenya, and TikTokers from the Caribbean and the Philippines. The most developed markets are those with the most penetrative mobile internet and a culture geared towards consumerism: China, Singapore, Hong Kong, Australia, the USA, the UAE, India, Russia, Brazil, Nigeria, South Africa, and the UK are global capitals of influence, each with a home-grown creator culture of its own.

Behind the Great Firewall, China's creator industry is faster, larger, and more developed than the rest of the world. Influencers — known as Key Opinion Leaders or 'wanghong' — host live shopping streams on platforms such as Weibo, WeChat, and Douyin. To get a sense of scale, a recent survey by Chinese internet giant Tencent found that 54 per cent of graduates listed influencer as their preferred career choice;[26] whilst Ruhnn Holding, a Chinese influencer accelerator, has been listed on the NASDAQ since April 2019. Luxury hauls, fashion fan cams, and handbag unboxing videos are all popular in Hong Kong and Singapore, whilst South Korean creators influence Western counterparts with multi-step skincare tutorials and mukbang videos (live vlogs in which creators consume large quantities of food on camera).

Dubai, the flashy hub of Middle Eastern influence that's practically architected for Instagram backdrops, is home to so many social media stars that the government established an experimental influencer licence scheme in 2018 to take a cut of the high volume of brand deals brokered within its jurisdiction.[27] During the pandemic, Instagram #entrepreneurs, TikTok forex traders, and fast-fashion influencers bearing Louis Vuitton luggage and PrettyLittleThing (PLT) discount codes all flocked to the LED-lit restaurants and artificial beaches of Jumeirah on avowedly 'essential' business — the city's commitment to continuing the influencer lifestyle during lockdown making it a destination for bottle-popping boomerangs and sponsored bikini pics.

Australia is the birthplace of influencer wellness, a kind of ground zero for vegan lifestyle practitioners, taut gym trainers, glowing beauty gurus, and sunkissed mumfluencers. It's also home to one of the influencer industry's biggest scandals: wellness guru Belle Gibson, who was part of the first wave of clean-eating influencers who said they had been healed by a healthy lifestyle. Belle claimed that her cancer had been cured in 2015, but was later convicted of multiple breaches of consumer law by a judge who described her as having a 'relentless obsession with herself' after she admitted she'd made the whole thing up — and made millions of dollars from a branded app and cookbook.

The Belle Gibson incident, along with other similarly high-profile scandals, contribute to a popular impression of influencers as shallow and scammy, fuelling stigma about the industry. This reputation is sometimes deserved. In 2017, 400 high-profile influencers posted a series of mysterious orange squares on Instagram promoting an unforgettable tropical island event by the name of Fyre Festival: none of them declared their post with #ad. Festival attendees who had paid up to $12,000 each for tickets to 'two transformative weekends … on the boundaries of the impossible' turned up to find a makeshift campsite with no electricity, and little to eat other than limp cheese sandwiches.[28]

The festival went viral and made internet history, epitomising the hollow promise of influencer culture and humiliating those who participated in its promotion. The same year, *Ingrid Goes West* — a satirical Hollywood drama about Instagram-driven obsession and the falsity of social media fame starring Elizabeth Olsen and Aubrey Plaza — won at the Sundance Film Festival.

The scandals kept coming. A year after Fyre, vlogger Logan Paul went viral for filming a dead body he had discovered whilst visiting a 'suicide forest' at the base of Mount Fuji; his two-minute 'So Sorry' vlog was viewed over 59m times. In 2019, it was revealed that YouTuber Olivia Jade was at the centre of a US college admissions scandal, creating ads for Amazon about life as a student for a place at the University of Southern California she hadn't earned.

Influencing's negative reputation has since been further

cemented by a catalogue of more generic crimes — pressuring hotels and restaurants for freebies, destroying wildlife habitats in the pursuit of Instagram pictures, misleading consumers, using protests as photo opportunities, and partying maskless through the pandemic.

Instagram call-out account @influencersinthewild, which documents instances such as these, has over 4 million followers. It's no wonder that tea channels — YouTube gossip vloggers who report on the influencer universe with meta commentary and analysis — have become so popular. 'Tea' — a term appropriated from drag and popularised online by a 2014 Kermit the Frog meme — refers to online drama, secrets, shade, and scandal; influencers provide more than enough opportunity for observers to 'sip', 'stir', and 'spill' it.

'Mainstream media tends to have a very negative take on the industry, parachuting in to cover scandals that arise without understanding the culture and context of the space. This leads to most of the coverage of influencers being about them behaving badly, which I think has created a negative perception of the industry as a whole among average people,' Stephanie McNeal, Social News Editor at BuzzFeed New York and author of 'Please Like Me', a weekly newsletter about creators, tells me over email. But beyond negative attention, more damning still is the media silence that surrounds influencers. Coverage remains disproportionate to its size and reach: 'It is a multi-billion-dollar industry that is having profound impacts on society and culture. When you look at how big and influential the space is,' Stephanie says, covering it 'is a no-brainer.'

Even if you consider yourself abreast of culture and topical events, it's perfectly possible to have never heard of half the influencer industry's key protagonists. Beyond a lack of mainstream media coverage, each of us has an individually tailored algorithm and an idiosyncratic experience of the internet; plus there are just too many influencers out there to keep track. Working within the industry itself, I frequently encounter new faces I've never heard of with many millions of followers. Even after the explosive arrival of TikTok in 2020, during which many mainstream outlets fully embraced influencer coverage for the first time, a deep division still persists, fuelled by media ambivalence about covering celebrities that they have not themselves made famous — and over who whom they consequently hold less sway.

'Mainstream media awareness has slowly been growing over the past six years or so and TikTok just happened to pop up at the right time to benefit from an increase in coverage,' offers Stephanie: 'There are a lot of parallels between how mainstream media covered reality stars. A decade ago, the big magazines would barely cover Bravo stars, Kardashians, etc., or treated them as a sideshow. Now, they are covered obsessively. I predict we will see a similar trend with influencers and online creators.'

It's vital that we do. Influencers represent one expression of a macro-level move from employment to gig work, from offline to online; they're an effective microcosm for what's going on in wider culture. Under its aesthetic exterior and ephemeral content, the rise of influence is a story of platforms, power, algorithms, atomisation, attention, decentralisation, and networks, the championing of the individual over the institution and the market over everything.

At the moment, attention towards the influencer space is focused on instances of unprecedented success — key players, star earners, freshly minted teenage millionaires, record-breaking sales, and internet-breaking viral moments — but influencers aren't just the figures at the top. There is a considerable class of creators who aren't making headlines, but who are plugging away at moderately successful content, making a full-time living off monetising their lifestyles and identities. Around them is an entire framework of ancillary influencer professionals: marketers like me, lawyers, management, publicists, creatives, editors, strategists, assistants, and many more who largely fly under the radar.

The term 'influencer' has in many ways become meaningless, a buzzword used to drum up clicks, wrought with overuse and misattribution. It has surpassed itself to become a broader signifier, a synecdoche for a host of modern neuroses, complaints, and aspirations, indicative of a certain type of person, a set of philosophies, and a cultural moment. In many ways, the term 'influencer' has it inside out: it would be more accurate to say that they're the influenced, the product of forces far beyond any individual's control.

It's a lazy cliché to claim that 'everyone's an influencer', but it's fast becoming true. Increasingly, the rituals of influence apply to everyone: appearing vlogger-style on Zoom, reviewing products online, optimising your online appearance in any way. The requirement to build a profile and accumulate an audience around your 'personal brand' is already pervasive in many professional fields, but influencer dynamics are becoming embedded within the workplace more directly: Walmart are training up an army of 1.5 million workers to become TikTokers, creating round-the-clock content for their brand; 'employee influencers' are a growing trend.

Seeing influencers as a siloed industry is short-sighted. Like the tech industry it's built upon, influence isn't vertical, it's horizontal — spanning cultural, political, and social spaces. In the same way that we don't speak of an 'internet industry', one day we won't speak of the 'influencer industry' either. Soon, all companies will be media companies, everyone will be a brand, everything will be subject to influencer principles.

When I tell people I'm interested in influencers, I'm met with reactions ranging from amusement through to disbelief that this new breed of internet professionals, notorious for their compulsive oversharing and shallow mentality, are worthy of any more than a fleeting 15 seconds of attention. But digital influence is much larger, more pervasive, and more potent than our current conception of the 'influencer industry' or its individual participants make it out to be. It's not the isolated act of taking selfies or streaming video games, or posting travel and lifestyle pictures to social media platforms: it's a fundamental restructuring of the way that information is disseminated, power is accumulated, and culture is produced. It's a battle for control of the internet.

Some of the world's most influential online individuals — Donald Trump, Elon Musk, Q of QAnon — have raised share prices, triggered coups, and brainwashed millions with the same playbook that beauty gurus use to flog eyeshadow palettes. US Congresswoman Alexandria Ocasio-Cortez signed up to Twitch to play against top gaming streamers, Andrew Yang ran for mayor of New York on the promise to bring TikTok hype houses to the city. Mastering the mechanics of online influence — and becoming an influencer oneself — is, increasingly, the key to power absolute.

After the reactions come the questions, with outsiders quick to ask: How much do influencers really earn? What does being an influencer actually involve? Why would anyone choose to live their life online? Though I work within the industry, I also have questions of my own. Questions about what takes place behind the most popular accounts and polished vlogs I browse on a daily basis; who influences the influencers. Most people outside the industry don't know how this new world operates, or the ways it is currently transforming our collective future. When I look at the influencer industry today, I see it echoing patterns from the tech industry upon which it is built — move fast and break things; build now, regulate later; by the time you notice, it's too late. We've already seen some of the disastrous consequences those principles can have when left unchecked. I hope, in some small way, this book might challenge them.

Back at the party, whilst the rest of the guests are happily 'gramming Babe-stamped canapés and snapping outfit pictures, I am preparing to leave. Unlike them, I think in a fleeting moment of ill-will, I have a real job waiting for me in the morning. The agency's task will be a party post-mortem: screenshotting the selfies and outfit pictures currently being produced, aggregating each attendee's content and analysing how well it performed for a reactive marketing report.

Waiting for a bus home on the pavement outside, I strike up a conversation with a man I recognise from the bar. He's an influencer, though he introduces himself as a 'content creator slash stylist slash entrepreneur'. He's got another brand event to attend this evening, he explains, then he's home to prepare for a shoot tomorrow which starts at sunrise on the south London rooftops. I ask what he is shooting. 'Nothing major,' he says with a calculatedly casual shrug, 'just my next few day's worth of content.'

I privately retract my snide thought. Influencing is real

work. Influencers are the creative, strategist, art director, stylist, photographer, copywriter, retoucher, editor, and marketing manager all at once. They are an advertising agency of one. They network, negotiate, cut deals, sort contracts and paperwork, run several social media accounts, develop posting schedules, liaise with brands, and manage a frenetic diary, all whilst posting multiple times a day about activities that aren't any of these.

Their job is to seem jobless. The appearance of effortlessness is a sign of success: ironically, that same effortlessness generates vitriol for influencers' apparently idle lifestyles. It's a double bind that speaks to the inherently paradoxical nature of social media celebrity: simultaneously offline and online, private and public, person and brand, authentic and performed; influencers are neither 'just like us', nor 'one of them', occupying the no-man's-land between celebrity and punter.

Like many digital trends that revel in their own 'disruption', influencers invert our expectations about how an influential figure should behave. For traditional celebrities, fame is largely a by-product of another skill, but with influencers, fame-making is both by-product and preoccupation. The former are famous for the extraordinary, but many influencers profit off the reverse. They acquire fame for the mundane or everyday: videos about their morning routines, 'Come shopping with me', a tour of the detritus in their kitchen drawer.

Unlike generations of film-makers, photographers, creatives, and writers before them, they don't always aim to leave a body of work behind — many influencers' output is inherently ephemeral, designed to expire before it can be canonised. And whilst traditional celebrities keep public and private lives distinct, influencers collapse this boundary, the strategic revelation of personal intimacies propelling their professional success. Influencers adapt, collapse, project, shift, switch, and dissemble; they are as fluid, fluctuating, and fascinating as the internet itself.

My bus is a minute away, and I make my excuses.

'Nice to meet you.' the man says. 'Give me a follow.'

I promise him I will. As I get on the bus he calls after me.

'I forgot to ask: are you an influencer too?' he says, 'or just a normal person?'

CHAPTER 2

THE 'INFLUENCER' FACTOR

WHERE DO SOCIAL MEDIA STARS COME FROM?

When I was a teenager, I accidentally became internet famous. I didn't mean to, it just sort of happened, sometime between signing up for Tumblr one afternoon during a monotonous summer holiday and the thousands of hours I subsequently spent online, reblogging low-res galaxy GIFs and self-conscious lowercase poetry, hunched over a bulky Dell laptop, the battery overheating on my thighs.

Tumblr wasn't my first experience of social media — that accolade went to my Neopets account, from which I graduated to Bebo — but it was the first platform on which I had any measure of success, accumulating tens of thousands of followers in just over a year. Offline, I was anxious and insecure, but online I could become a whole new version of myself: the kind that posted hazy vintage-filtered portraits, emotive John Green quotes, and dark screengrabs of arthouse films I'd never seen.

The substance of my blog was nothing special — the derivative moodboard of your average indie-identifying late-00s teen — but it tapped into a dreamy, sad-girl internet aesthetic that resonated with a generation hooked on floppy-haired boybands and Urban

Outfitters individualism. Unlike other platforms, on Tumblr you could customise your 'theme', and I went all in, with an audio autoplayer permanently tuned to Crystal Castles, a pixelated 'hit counter' tallying page views, and an animated migraine-hazard header I had installed after a morning teaching myself basic HTML.

Founded in 2007 by a 21-year-old high school dropout, Tumblr. com ('the easiest way to share yourself') was a gateway social network, enabling users to upload and repost pictures, quotes, and videos in a virtual waterfall that preceded Instagram feeds by several years. Like a visual version of Twitter, its interface was engineered for engagement, with a one-click 'reblog' button that allowed popular posts to circulate hundreds of thousands of times, comments and responses accumulating underneath. Most users didn't post original content but reposted and reblogged from other places, feeding new material into the self-perpetuating Tumblr ecosystem.

This self-reflexive nature meant it quickly became an engine for internet culture in the late 00s and early 2010s, churning out in-jokes at viral speed: memes, slang, reaction GIFs, moustache tattoos and vintage-outfit pics, lyrics from amateur bands, and the overexposed contents of disposable cameras. The most popular accounts — blogging under expressive, nonsensical pseudonyms like 'studs-and-peaches', 'dreaming-of-lonely-lovers', or 'broken-mermaid-memories' — had hundreds of thousands of devoted followers and a formidable presence on the platform, earning them the enviable title 'Tumblr famous'. A platform metric known as 'Tumblarity' combined data about how frequently users were posting, which topics they posted about, and how many people were engaging with each post to generate a score for early internet influence.

My blog wasn't popular enough to warrant dedicated fan accounts, nor a feature on aggregator thetumblrfamous.tumblr. com, but it still bestowed more attention on me than I was used to receiving IRL. The tiny 'notes' number at the bottom of each post, which measured the internet's resonance with my ramblings, was like a Geiger counter for self-gratification: my posts occasionally gained upwards of 50,000 notes, and I began to steal away from the dinner table to check how many I had accrued.

To this day I'm still not quite sure exactly how I became Tumblr famous: most likely a particular set of algorithmic conditions that had coincided with dumb luck to circulate my handle hundreds, then thousands, then hundreds of thousands of times. I watched in mild surprise as, over months, the followers began to flock, each new post triggering a chain of responses and reblogs that linked my small world — a bedroom with Blu-Tacked posters and a leaking beanbag, bookshelves crammed with dog-eared copies of *Gossip Girl* — to the boundless internet.

As part of the 'zillennial' generation — not quite Gen Z, not quite millennial, a portmanteau as awkward as I felt — I grew up spending countless hours of my teenage life logged on: to Lookbook.nu, Wordpress and Blogspot, BuzzFeed, then later Facebook, Tumblr, and Twitter, my own adolescence developing in tandem with the pubescent internet. Today I try to cut down on time spent staring at a screen, but back then the internet felt like a refuge.

Offline, the world was limited by our direct experience, but online, we could live vivid digital lives: writing long, illogically punctuated blog posts, designing outfits for cyber dolls or tending to virtual pets, curating moodboards for the lives we wished we had, and tentatively tapping emoticon-littered messages into chatroom boxes and online forums away from the prying eyes of friends and parents. I was one of many millions who felt the same.

'I remember being super excited, almost immediately, by the possibilities of the internet,' Jane, who was 'low-key MySpace famous' around the same time and is now 29, recalls. 'I must have been ten when I first began sneaking onto our shared computer after dark, praying that my parents wouldn't cut me off. The internet was this restricted, time-limited thing that felt elusive and untapped.' The idiosyncrasies of our first online experience — a decentralised web of independent sites with kooky names like dollzmania, miniclip, funnyjunk, and lolcats, discovered through older siblings and passed around by word of mouth — was part of the early internet's investigative appeal, as Jane describes: 'It felt like such a goldmine of random shit.'

'Growing up queer and neurodivergent, I often felt slightly out of place IRL,' says Dani, now a journalist covering internet culture for *VICE*, *i-D* and *Dazed*. Online 'I could speak to strangers with similar interests and be whoever I wanted to be, away from the restraints and pressures of conformity and my own accompanying social anxiety,' which came with 'the added bonus of it being from the comfort of my own bedroom. It was on these platforms that I felt validated, probably for the first time in my entire life.'

In 2012, musician Frank Ocean came out in a Tumblr post that gained 109,000 notes. 'Whoever you are, wherever you are ...' opened his wandering, poetic paragraphs, formatted in a screen-grabbed MacBook window in the introspective, aesthetic style of Tumblr lit: 'I'm starting to think we're a lot alike.' His declaration was the ur-text for a generation of online teenagers.

Though Tumblr had a considerable fanbase — 73 million users or 5 per cent of the global internet population in 2013, before being acquired by Yahoo for a billion dollars[1] — it didn't feel mainstream in any cultural or commercial sense. The platform consisted of a series of memes, fandoms, and microcommunities linked by reblogs and question boxes, and its users spoke in a hyperbolic, lowercase language that was impenetrable to outsiders: 'bamf', 'gpoy', 'otp', or simply ';alksjdf;lksfd' — a stylised keyboard smash — when you didn't know what to say.

Tumblr culture was so obscure, cryptic, and platform-specific that the company officially employed a 'meme librarian', internet analyst Amanda Brennan, to document and catalogue its lore: the most reblogged 'ships' (imagined pairings of fictional characters from TV shows and YA literature) or viral GIFs of cats that looked like Hitler. There were Tumblr accounts dedicated to hentai, haikus, hung-over owls, men in red trousers, ugly babies in Renaissance paintings, sad office desk lunches, Wetherspoons pub carpets, and shoplifting. Tumblr girls — goth alter-ego Felice Fawn, who dressed in latex and worshipped Satan, or pink-haired hipster Aly Antorcha, known by her handle daughterofhungryghosts — were quirky alt icons. 'Tumblr always has been the home of the most unique weirdos on the internet,' Amanda tells me over email, 'and the people who became Tumblr Famous were just as weird as the people who adored them.'

Tumblr had no direct means of monetisation, nor was the environment exactly what my agency would deem 'brand safe'. It had a reputation for explicit content — a long-running meme animated a Tumblrer's panic at accidentally flashing their dashboard to a non-user IRL ('*slams laptop shut*'). Unlike many other mainstream internet platforms, Tumblr provided a safe haven for a vibrant NSFW community of camgirls, furries, and fetishists without fear of shadowbanning (suppressed visibility in search results, the feed, and the explore page) or suspension — although the admission of 'adult content' would later be overturned in 2018, after which one fifth of users would leave.[2]

The platform's longest-running meme was centered on profanity: the 'fuck yeah' format, dedicated accounts set up to express niche interests: fuckyeahsharks.tumblr.com, fuckyeahchicago.tumblr.com, or fuckyeahasianfashion.tumblr.com, all curated by — what else — the fuckyeahfuckyeahs.tumblr.com directory. By April 2009, 25 new fuckyeah accounts were being set up daily.[3] When Tumblr's Yahoo deal was announced, its 26-year-old CEO pledged his continued allegiance to the grassroots community he had created with the flippant signoff 'fuck yeah, David.'

Though we couldn't know it at the time, Tumblr was an early exercise in influence. 'The reblog changed the way people thought about content, added a new layer to the way we share with each other,' continues Amanda. 'To know when to build on one another? That was definitely a great way to learn how to build your brand.' The platform's unstated aim was for users to curate a coherent and expressive aesthetic in line with one of its specific subcultures — pastel goth, soft grunge, vaporwave, or seapunk — labels that were half-real and half-manufactured by its obsessively self-identifying community. The text posts, quotes, videos, looping GIFs, and audio clips that all meshed together in a chaotic tapestry of tastes were like mini building blocks for personality; trying on identities was as easy as updating your page's theme and applying the relevant metatags.

I would stay up late, eyes burning, scouring the dashboard for abstract images of abandoned malls, tattooed hands, American Apparel tennis skirts, crushed roses, and brutalist architecture

— whatever happened to be trending. 'Sure, there had been bloggers prior to Tumblr,' says Amanda, but the influencer's understanding of 'aesthetic' — a collection of visual signifiers showing an affinity for a particular look and lifestyle, transient artefacts to be reblogged and then forgotten — 'was built in the early years of Tumblr'. It taught me to curate, to render myself legible, to adopt and replicate the language of the system and be rewarded for it — skills that have since become second nature to social media stars.

Being Tumblr famous back in 2010 wasn't exactly like being an influencer today. One of Tumblr's defining features, lost in subsequent iterations of social media, was a built-in invisibility. On Tumblr, 'the follower count has always been hidden', Amanda reminds me: 'Without the numbers game of follower counts, the type of content you post counts a lot more. Not having a public follower count truly makes Tumblr one of the purest places on the internet when it comes to fame. It puts the person's content first.' It was overwhelmingly anonymous, more like an interactive scrapbook than a personal profile. Though thousands knew my handle, my followers knew little about me, other than what I chose to share in cryptic text posts or the occasional unsolicited 'face reveal'.

Being 'big on Tumblr' had, as a result, very little relation to my offline life. 'Internet fame wasn't something that people spoke about, like, ever,' Jane recalls, 'even to hear the word "MySpace" in real life felt taboo.' When an introvert in our year had been discovered to be 'big on Wattpad', printouts of their fanfiction had made their way onto hallway message boards and been left in changing rooms. Spending lots of time on Tumblr, like being really into online gaming, or tending to a tediously detailed blog, wasn't something cool kids did in 2010. 'I remember, in high school, hearing a MySpace famous girl shout "Excuse me, MySpace royalty coming through" as she pushed through the crowded lunch hall with her equally MySpace famous friend,' Jane remembered with a shudder. 'They'd never been particularly popular IRL.'

Though my Tumblr was my pride and joy, a teenage sense of self-preservation meant it remained private — a best-kept secret between me and several thousand people on the internet.

Whilst I was whiling away Saturday nights alone with a laptop, my more sociable peers were engrossed in *The X Factor*. The show dominated entertainment in Britain for over a decade, and even I could be persuaded to unplug from my computer for the final. Watching it had become a weekly ritual: cushions plumped, allegiances pledged, friends assembled around the flatscreen with Motorola Razrs at the ready to ring contestant phone lines charged at triple rates.

Under the eyes of millions each week, candidates were plucked from obscurity via the infamous open audition format. They stumbled through Celine Dion or Adele, sobbed during long-winded, calculated personal anecdotes and bantered with compère Dermot O'Leary, eking out each broadcast minute in pursuit of a lucrative contract from Simon Cowell's record label.

A rotating cast of judges passed verdicts that quickly assimilated into our vernacular. 'It's a no from me,' Simon, the panel's perma-tanned patriarch, would typically declare, 'quite frankly, that was absolutely dreadful.' 'You've got it!' Girls Aloud graduate and nation's sweetheart Cheryl Cole would exclaim in a raspy gasp, tears filling her eyes: 'You've blown me away. You've got it, pet.' 'You look like a star, you sound like a star,' enthused Louis Walsh, the eternal optimist, to a wide-eyed hopeful and a captivated nation; 'You are a star!'

In many ways, watching the evolution of celebrity was more compelling than its end result. Raw talent and commercial potential — the eponymous 'X Factor' — was identified and then cultivated by a team of entertainment professionals, transforming an unlikely crop of punters into popstars in a process that took 14 weeks. We watched, enthralled, as teeth were bleached, t-shirts swapped for Topman suits, and accents mysteriously neutralised to a transatlantic twang.

The X Factor had glamour, eccentricity, and talent, each to varying degrees, but what it really offered was a golden showbiz promise: that anyone could become a star. During the 00s, talent shows and reality TV contests had become the clearest route to fame for the ordinary person, synonymous with a democratised shot at celebrity success: *Big Brother*, *Pop Idol*, *Weakest Link*, *Who Wants To Be A Millionaire?*, and later *Britain's Got Talent* all gave the man on the street the opportunity for 15 minutes of prime TV airtime.

The X Factor made stars of Pizza Hut waitresses from north London and recruitment consultants from Essex, churning out chart-toppers and upbeat Christmas hits with alarming alacrity. In 2010, episodes averaged more than 14 million viewers in the UK;[4] that year, four tousled teenagers who went by One Direction came third before going on to sell 50 million records worldwide. In 2015, to nobody's surprise, *Good Morning Britain* announced more young people had voted in *The X Factor* than were planning to vote in the general election.[5]

Little did we know that within a decade, the tables would turn. UK TV viewership amongst my age group dropped from an average of 169 minutes per day in 2010 to just 70 minutes in 2019.[6] Meanwhile, social media usage soared: in 2007, Ofcom reported that 54 per cent of UK 16–24 year olds had a social media profile; by 2016, this was 96 per cent.[7] And overall time spent on social platforms was rising, too. By 2019, Ofcom noted that one in every five minutes spent online by UK adults was on social media, and that 'children and young adults spent much more time online than they did watching television'.[8]

The multi-million-pound TV franchise — and the apparatus of fame it represented — had begun to peter out, and my covert online hobby had replaced it as the ordinary person's pathway to fame and fortune.

One afternoon in 2019, an unexpected invite slid into my inbox. At some point I had registered my email address on the mailing list of a TV production company who had subsequently spammed me with invites to join the studio audience of daytime TV game shows and dramatic, courtroom-themed familial disputes that usually filed directly into my junk. This email, however, caught my attention. It was an enticing offer of teenage wish fulfilment: a backstage pass to a live recording of *The X Factor* taking place that Saturday night. I had no idea the franchise still existed.

In the age of social media, TV contests are losing their magic touch. With the means of self-promotion in the hands of the individual, we no longer need talent shows to pluck us from obscurity, to 'discover' us as the 'next big thing'. The ubiquity of online oversharing has put an end to the sob story or the makeover; for the curious, it's all already out there on the internet. These days, if you want to be a star, you can do it yourself with the help of a smartphone and a social media handle: you don't need Simon Cowell to click his fingers. When teenagers are gaining millions of followers uploading make-up tutorials to the internet, who wants to stand in a thousand-strong queue for a slim, singular shot at success?

This shift is merely underlined by our most popular contemporary contest formats. The flagship TV competition of our current moment — *Love Island*, a marathon reality show in which tanned and toned 20-somethings sequester themselves in a villa and attempt to 'couple up' with strangers under 24-hour surveillance — is essentially a finishing school for influence; the real prize isn't being on TV or the prospect of winning £50k, it's emerging with a huge social media following and lucrative fast fashion partnerships in the pipeline. Twenty-one-year-old *Love Island* graduate and uber-influencer Molly-Mae Hague, who spun her 2019 season into an impressive empire, encompassing multiple sell-out PrettyLittleThing partnerships, a fake tan brand bearing her name, and a going rate of £13,000 per sponsored Instagram post,[9] informed her 2m YouTube subscribers in a vlog that she had originally entered *Love Island* as a 'business move'.[10] For her and countless others, TV is now a vehicle for social media fame, rather than the other way around.

The email in my inbox lingered: 'You are now officially invited to join us at *The X Factor*,' read the breathless blurb, 'but it is not as we all know it …' Like its judges, the format had had a facelift. Series 16 — *The X Factor: Celebrity Special Edition* — had a premise recalibrated for a modern entertainment landscape, a desperate attempt to revitalise the flagging franchise. Instead of inviting the public to an open audition, the show selected famous figures to compete against each other. The contestants stretched the definition of celebrity, with a lineup of hereditary hopefuls that included gangster actor Vinnie

Jones and BBC journalist Martin Bashir along with an eclectic mix of lesser entertainment figures: a 'quiz genius' from daytime game show *The Chase*, Megan McKenna from reality series *The Only Way is Essex*, and Hayley Hasselhoff, model daughter of the 80s TV icon. Transplanted from our iPhone screens were TikTok teenagers Max and Harvey (twin brothers from Surrey sharing 7 million followers and a joint account), a band formed from last summer's *Love Island* influencers, and V5, an artificially curated group of Instagram stars flown in from South America by the show's producers. TV talent and social media creators were vying for public attention; a show struggling to stay relevant had been forced to collaborate with its competition.

The result was not just a singing competition but an end-of-decade contest for dominance between warring channels, formats, and factions of the famous: a battle for celebrity itself. I was intrigued to find out who would come out on top. A morbid sense of curiosity mingled with the powerful nostalgia of a long-held childhood memory. I confirmed my backstage pass. Perhaps I would learn something about the future of celebrity or entertainment; at the very least, I would recover something of my past.

My celebrity field trip was off to an unglamorous start: a queue, a car park, and a corrugated warehouse complex off west London's Hanger Lane bypass. Whilst loitering on the tarmac, it began to rain. Sharing an umbrella, I struck up conversation with the family behind me. They were evangelical about meeting celebrities and getting on the telly, reeling off a catalogue of British broadcast's great and good that would have made the *Radio Times* editor's head spin. *The Voice Kids* was 'really inspiring', Keith Lemon was 'nice, but very small'. 'Next weekend we've got the British Heart Foundation Awards,' the dad said cheerfully, raindrops curving down his forehead, 'so we're packing up the kids and driving up to Wigan for that.'

The hoodied teenage girls hanging out behind me, however, made it clear that they were only here for Max and Harvey. They couldn't care less about the show or any other of its other contestants. 'I will

45

literally DIE if I see them in real life,' one girl, clutching a ring light, exclaimed, eyes shining at the euphoric possibility of this demise. Her friend nodded vigorously: 'I have been obsessed with them since, like, the 20th of November 2017.' As I was soon to discover, they weren't alone.

Entering *The X Factor*'s television studio was like emerging on the inside of a retro-futuristic cruise ship. Every surface was gilt and gleaming, laser beams circulated overhead, video screens projected a rotating display of upbeat 'X' animations across the stage, beneath my feet ran streams of sparkling LEDs. From my vantage point, aloft in the amphitheatre, I could lean against the railing and peer down onto the sparse patch crowning Louis Walsh's head.

The set was intimately familiar and yet novel all at once; I had spent years here via the mediation of a TV screen. Airless, timeless, ageless: inside the studio's hermetic universe, surrounded by chrome and screens and steel, it could have easily been 2009, 2019, or 2090.

Though the surfaces were sleek and shiny, the lights and disco balls dazzling, what I hadn't been prepared for was the smell: hundreds of perspiring strangers rammed together, the racehorse tang of backup dancers warming up, a lingering scent of sweat and desperation undetectable to those at home. Viewing figures for *The X Factor* had sunk below 3.5 million, according to watchdog TellyMix, making its 16th season the least-watched live show ever in overnight ratings — down from its record high in 2010.[11]

When I went to share a picture of the stage on Twitter, I saw the online tide was turning too. 'I hope Vinnie Jones wins and it destroys this shit show once and for all,' someone had tweeted, 'Simon Cowell is so out of touch with what viewers want.' 'Simon doesn't care if these boys can sing, all he cares about are their millions of followers £££,' another said.

'Give *The X Factor* a cheer guys, you're going to want to be as loud as you possibly can!!' bellowed the production host, a swaggering man in a shiny black suit and designer stubble who kept the crowd engaged before the cameras rolled and he changed places with on-screen compère Dermot O'Leary in a practised bait and switch. 'If we don't see you cheering we can swap you out!'

The enforced enthusiasm — the lights, the screens, Dermot's glazed smile, the vaguely threatening instruction to turn the volume up or risk being exchanged for one of the hundreds of hopefuls still queuing in the dark outside — seemed so forced and false and futile. What were we cheering for? Ourselves? The show? The 'stars'? The concept of celebrity itself? We roared on regardless, as if by our voices alone we could elevate a flagging media format, regenerate relevance, and reverse the inevitable onslaught of attention-grabbing algorithms and *X Factor* apathy.

After lukewarm performances by an ex-cast member of *Glee* and a trio of unharmonious rugby stars, an adolescent bellow shook the studio to its core. Max and Harvey were up next, and if the shrieks and screams were anything to go by, my queue companions would have competition. In matching tracksuits and baseball caps, two teenage boys exploded onto the stage on BMX bikes to the opening bars of Macklemore and Ryan Lewis's 'Can't Hold Us'.

Outside, in the queue, I'd watched their TikTok videos — dancing in the overgrown garden of a mock Tudor semi-detached, teaching tricks to a gormless-looking labrador, pranking their long-suffering little sister — and against the apparatus of broadcast television, surrounded by a crowd of energetic backup dancers, they looked suddenly small.

But despite their age and size they seemed perfectly relaxed; moving with the confidence of a duo trained on TikTok tricks and accustomed to stunting in front of an iPhone. A giant green-screen video they had shot, edited, and amped up with effects and filters looped behind them as they sang and leapt and swung around the stage. I wasn't the only one impressed; mere seconds after the song ended, Simon Cowell slid off his booster seat to smash the golden button that would grant them a protected passage through to the next round of the competition. 'You two are the whole package,' he said, pound signs reflecting in his wire-framed glasses as he beamed towards his teenage fame-machine. The fans continued to yell as they were ushered off the stage.

It was nearing midnight. The studio had crystallised into jagged migraine shapes and my head pounded with the syncopated rhythm of canned pop sounds. I had begun to fantasise about submerging into the dark void of a quiet Uber. Tuning out the bright lights and upbeat showbiz voices, I made it through the final act of the night — the sing-off — by clinging to the railing with my eyes closed.

When the cameras cut, the studio deflated: Dermot's shoulders caved inwards, an army of runners materialised to sweep the glitter from the stage, and ushers began an instantaneous evacuation of the audience, shuffling towards the doors. I lingered in the amphitheatre longer than I should, hesitant to leave the set that had embellished itself upon my retinas in my childhood. With the house lights turned up and the pounding sound system powered down, I could finally see *The X Factor* spectacle for what it was: illusionary LED panels, a scuffed stage marked with masking tape. Everything looked smaller with the lights on.

My reluctance was rewarded when, having been pushed out by harried production staff, I ran into a second spectacle taking place outside by the portaloos. 'If you're at X Factor we're coming outside I'm just trying to find Max' tweeted @maxandharvey. Over one and a half thousand fans had amassed in the replies. 'Harv mate he's already out there,' commented one, 'WERE WAITING' said another.

The twins had emerged from the studio complex via a fire escape, still in their costumes, and slipped past their security detail. Like pied pipers with iPhones, they were leading a swelling crowd of young fans to a strip of concrete between the production office and the makeshift toilets. Bewildered parents who assumed the show was over followed in their wake, attempting unsuccessfully to extricate their offspring and begin the midnight journey home.

Little did they know, outside under the inky sky, away from the lights and the cameras and the crew, it was only just beginning: Max and Harvey were pulling pranks, acting out skits, shooting selfies and quick TikTok videos with their fans, in a crowd that was fast becoming hundreds deep. As the other *X Factor* contestants retreated back into their private lives, whisked away by cars with tinted windows from the other side of the studio, a second performance was starting: this show — the real show — was off-stage, outside, amongst the fans and followers, and the cheering was real.

The professional expertise and camera rigging of the extensive *X Factor* production team had nothing on a sprawling mob of frenzied teens: iPhones held aloft were livestreaming the twins to Snapchat, TikTok, and Instagram from every angle simultaneously. I was caught up in the crush, packed in between gleeful fans clutching merch to sign, a physical manifestation of a mere fraction of the twins' 7 million followers. The normally disembodied experience of influence — physical presence abstracted and elided through a phone screen, fandoms fragmented and asynchronous — was overcome by the static cling of the crowd, the friction of our bodies and voices, moving in unison towards a single centre.

Online, Max and Harvey were flattened and packaged: out here, they were real people. I joined the line to meet them almost automatically. Why, late at night, with aching legs and rain-soaked trainers, was I queuing patiently for a 30-second selfie with a 16-year-old who posted lip syncs? 'This is giving me feelings I never knew I had!' shrieked a young boy standing next to me, eyes shining. I was secretly inclined to agree: though it was dark, cold, and drizzling, the atmosphere was somehow more electric than anything I'd witnessed inside the studio.

When I eventually reached the front of the queue, Max was polite and professional. By now, the crowd had taken on the rhythms of a ritual; step, hi, duck, arm, smile, snap, thanks, moving in an effortless, entrancing dance repeated for each fan with a fresh smile and a reset of his cap. I stepped forward towards him, into the gaze of 360-degree crowd scrutiny. Max grinned at me, face inches away. I raised my arm, he leant in for the selfie. I wasn't sure what to say. 'Thanks,' I managed, and by then it was too late; I had been displaced, pushed backwards by the desperate pressure of the bodies squeezed behind me.

I left with the feeling of having just been smoothly processed by a machine much larger than any of us could envisage, the fading embers of proximity still clinging to my clothes, a fragment captured in three blurry selfies in my camera roll.

It was hard not to compare my adolescent experiments on the

internet with Max and Harvey's professional, intentional approach to fame. At 16, where I had been awkward, they were strategic and self-aware, adept at handling their fandom. My online world had been anonymous and abstract, theirs was highly public; they were just as comfortable on the stage as they were on the screen. Influence had moved on from the amateur quirks and self-conscious eccentricities of late 00s Tumblr. Extracting myself from the parking lot, I uploaded my selfie to Twitter and went home, wondering who the 'celebrity' *The X Factor*'s 'Celebrity Special Edition' had promised really turned out to be.

If *The X Factor*'s 16th season was an end-of-decade competition for celebrity couched within a competition between celebrities, it was not entirely clear who came out on top. The producers or the contestants? Influencers or their mainstream media equivalent? Max and Harvey would go on to come second to reality TV cast member Megan McKenna. Putting social media stars on a big screen hadn't resolved a power struggle but merely further convoluted the means of celebrity production: just as Simon Cowell was keen to leech teenage audiences from TikTok stars, the power of broadcast was propelling Max and Harvey to new heights; *The X Factor* needed to move forwards, but social media stars also look back for validation.

Influence is iterative and the relationships between platforms is messy, fluid, and fluctuating, there's no neat line between the end of one era and the beginning of the next; channels bleed into each other; fame blooms, falls back, adapts to its host platforms. In collapsing the techniques of TV broadcast and social media influencing — 'reality' and 'spectacle', documentation and self-documentation, the manufactured and the real — *The X Factor* had produced a less stable understanding of celebrity than before; promising its audience insight into the formula for fame whilst struggling to form a coherent narrative of fame itself.

My visit to *The X Factor: Celebrity* had confirmed that the broadcast apparatus was losing its grip on fame, and I found myself wondering where it had all gone wrong. How had the show which once consumed my classmates lost its showbiz sheen? When did two teenagers with an iPhone eclipse a multi-million-pound TV franchise? What changed during that decade, between its peak in the 2000s and its demise during the 2010s? Internet fame had somehow managed to move from the margins to the mainstream, to transcend traditional celebrity and the institutions that upheld it.

'Early generations of the internet famous were kids who were not 100 per cent popular or confident in real life,' remarks Jane. 'Influencers are the popular kids now.' In the years since my first brush with Tumblr, online influence would shift from a fringe activity for alt kids to the widespread desire of one in five, as progressive platforms and cultural cycles made internet popularity more commercialised and desirable: 'The MySpace scene weirdo became the Tumblr indie girl became the basic blogger or vlogger,' Jane explains, 'who eventually became the influencer.'

It's difficult to pinpoint exactly when online self-promotion became cool — taking place as the social internet solidified around us. In her book *Trick Mirror*, Jia Tolentino describes this gradual process as one which, largely, took us by surprise: 'The call of self-expression turned the village of the internet into a city, which expanded at timelapse speed, social connections bristling like neurons in every direction … the curdling of the social internet happened slowly and then all at once.'

Perhaps it was inevitable that the online spaces which first started as a means of self-expression quickly became a competition. The rise of Facebook — the social network on which my generation first began to congregate en masse — had dovetailed neatly with an adolescent preoccupation with popularity. Facebook's functionality added new dimensions to the classroom contest for clout: the 'family' feature, which became an index of social allegiance, the public wall and event page, through which you could gauge who was hanging out with whom, and the poke feature, whose exact function remained tantalisingly vague.

Coming of age on the internet felt strangely synergistic: my generation were developing self-perception whilst systems for self-perception were developing around us. As we matured, the internet was offering up new ways to express and identify via the avatar, the handle, the bio, and the carefully curated feed. Our initial enthusiasm for batch-uploading pictures to expansive Facebook albums became a race to detag embarrassing posts as we learned to optimise our online presence and understand ourselves through the lens of platform metrics. Over time, I began to develop curatorial consciousness: to count the likes that rolled in on a profile picture update, refresh my profile to view it through external eyes. 'Where we had once been free to be ourselves online, we were now chained to ourselves online,' Tolentino writes, 'and that made us self-conscious.'

Previously hazy methods of evaluating one's social standing were soon surpassed by the cold calculations of social media metrics, as Tolentino writes: 'online reward mechanisms beg to substitute for offline ones, and then overtake them.' 'Some people had 1,000 friends and that was mad,' graphic designer Hannibal, now 24, recalls: 'Having a number in front of your face at that age was quite stark. People would be firing out requests to people they had the most tenuous connection with to boost their accounts. It quickly became a mindless competition over numbers.' Eventually, I crossed the coveted 1,000-friend threshold, only to find my feed was filled with family holiday albums and inside jokes from people I couldn't remember adding in the first place.

New platforms, increasingly engineered for scale, were imminent, swapping personal feeds for more generic explore pages, shifting intimate 'social networks' into aggregative 'social media'. The sense of privacy that we had so valued in the early days of the internet began to dissipate, replaced by performativity and public infrastructure. Timeline algorithms adjusted to prioritise branded posts; individuals began to blend with advertising in the newsfeed.

In 2010, YouTube had 15,000 creators in their Partner Program, which enabled users to take a cut of advertising revenue on their videos — by 2013, this figure had soared to over a million.[12] In early June 2012, Tumblr featured its first major brand advertising campaign in conjunction with Adidas, and between 2013 and 2014, Facebook's advertising revenue more than doubled.[13] The internet was crystallising — and commercialising — around us. 'The numbers game flipped over to Instagram and everything amplified,' Hannibal says. '1,000 Facebook friends became 10,000 Instagram followers. These days, it's 100,000 followers on TikTok.'

Eventually, Tumblr faced an exodus. Top Tumblrers began to jump ship for other, buzzier platforms with new features and fast-growing user bases. I didn't join them. By then I was preoccupied with offline occupations — exams and boyfriends — which felt less ephemeral, so I let my following wither out, and forgot my password. I couldn't sense where the internet was heading, but others were more astute. One of my Tumblr contemporaries — a girl I'd never met, but with whom I'd struck up an easy online friendship, leaving expressive strings of consonants and emojis under each other's posts — abandoned her account for Instagram.

I watched with curiosity as, over the years, her audience shot upwards. Awkward, self-shot outfit pictures taken on self-timer in her garden gave way to sultry, professionally snapped street style shots. Overexposed selfies slid into seven-step skincare routines. Her pictures were reposted by the Instagram pages of high street fashion brands, who began to send her freebies to be unboxed on her Instagram Stories. She started a YouTube channel. I watched her chat and put on her make-up in her bedroom, thinking how far we'd come from cryptic poetry posts and elusive, arty selfies with deliberately obfuscated faces.

Soon, she would hit 1 million, and then 5 million followers, be flown around the world on press trips, and buy a matte black Jeep to match Kylie Jenner's. She would sit front row at fashion week and launch a collection in collaboration with a major label that sold out in minutes. Today, she posts selfies from a sunlit London apartment filled with trendy monotonal furniture for which she leaves a swipe-up affiliate link in her stories. 40,000 people like her posts. In a parallel reality, I wonder if I might have been her, telling this story from the other side of the screen.

Though they are inextricably interlinked with social media, the rise of influencers isn't solely the product of their platform's evolution.

Influencers are also the product of their wider cultural context. Shrinking newspaper circulations, rising scepticism towards experts, financial precarity, millennial burnout, and a shift towards viewing corporations, rather than governments, as responsible for solving social problems are all trends that have propelled — and in some cases been propelled by — the rise of influencing.

When did the concept of the influencer first emerge? The Pope declared the Virgin Mary the original influencer in a viral post from his Twitter account @Pontifex, which has almost 19m followers: 'Without social networks, she became the first "influencer": the "influencer" of God.' In more recent history, English potter Josiah Wedgewood is often credited with the first brand partnership — a porcelain collaboration with HRH Queen Charlotte — in the late 1700s. Queen Victoria popularised the white wedding dress and Christmas tree in the UK and USA following circulation of festive family photographs more than 100 years before Kylie Jenner would #spon flat tummy tea with selfies.

Early influencers evolved in accordance with their era and media format: from Hollywood studio sirens promoting cold cream on the silver screen in the 1930s to the fictional 'Marlboro Man' who sold cigarettes in glossy print advertisements during the 1950s. The 1980s signalled the era of flashy sponsorship models, as brands collaborated with celebrities perceived to capture the zeitgeist: Pepsi paying $20m to sign Michael Jackson as brand ambassador, Nike launching their iconic partnership with Michael Jordan. Influencers are simply an evolution of these early pioneers.

Just as no one working in the media of the 1930s could have imagined the unfettered tabloid access that would come later, before the turn of the millennium few foresaw that the internet had the potential to change media consumption habits, let alone make stars. In a now-notorious 1995 *Newsweek* article titled 'The Internet? Bah!', columnist Clifford Stoll declared: 'Electronic publishing? Try reading a book on disc. At best, it's an unpleasant chore: the myopic glow of a clunky computer replaces the friendly pages of a book. Yet Nicholas Negroponte, director of the MIT Media Lab, predicts that we'll soon buy books and newspapers straight over the Internet. Uh, sure.' By

2012, that same weekly news magazine — once a cornerstone of US media — had folded its print edition after 79 years in circulation.

In 2000, the *Daily Mail* heralded the end of the world wide web: 'Internet "may be just a passing fad as millions give up on it"', read the headline of an article, next to a photo of an early internet user, diminutive in front of a squat computer: 'Predictions that the internet would revolutionise the way society works have proved wildly inaccurate.' The clipping — ironically now preserved thanks to the internet — regularly goes viral on LinkedIn.

Despite the *Mail*'s original dismissal of the internet, MailOnline is now the most visited English-language newspaper website in the world; a rare case of a traditional media outlet weathering the digital revolution well. Elsewhere, the shift has been devastating for 'traditional' print news. In 2008, according to a study by the Pew Research Center, more people in the United States got their news for free online than paid for it by buying a newspaper or magazine; at the end of 2019, the United States had 6,700 newspapers, down from almost 9,000 in 2004.

One by one during the 2010s, the lifestyle titles that I grew up reading closed down their print editions and moved online: *Company* (2014), *InStyle* (2016), *Self* and *Teen Vogue* (2017), *Glamour* (2018), and *Marie Claire* (2019). 'Social media hasn't just swallowed journalism,' reported *Columbia Journalism Review* in 2016, 'it has swallowed everything.'[14]

For a time, influencers coexisted in a reciprocal relationship with the mainstream media: magazines and newspapers hosted elaborate street-style spreads and blogger guest edits, whilst fashion editors and the staff of lifestyle outlets were growing online audiences of their own. 'Places like BuzzFeed and *The Huffington Post* were all writing these articles: *the top ten most stylish guys to follow on Instagram,*' recalls New York style star Moti Ankari, a coiffed and curated connoisseur of luxury fashion who was one of the first wave of male Instagram influencers in the early 2010s: 'I was always on them: that's what helped me get my first 100k.'

When Moti began blogging in 2010, the industry didn't exist. 'I always thought I'd have a "real job", and that this was going to be an extracurricular activity,' Moti tells me over video chat from his Manhattan apartment, 'so I got an internship at *GQ*, and I worked there for three years. I was working 80 hours per week, plus on Sunday I would shoot all my content for Monday through Friday, five outfits: bang bang bang.' At the time, the media industry was beginning to buckle to the pressure of digital upstarts: 'I could see it happening because I was in both worlds. I was styling all these big celebrities [for *GQ*,] but I was also getting styled and featured in magazines at the same time.'

Online creators spoke to people in a way that mainstream media clearly didn't. Bloggers were reflecting the looks and needs of their audience, offering new ways to engage with fashion, beauty, lifestyle, and entertainment that circumvented editors and cultural gatekeepers. As a result, Moti was attracting an audience: 'these strong fans that love love love me'. His fans viewed him as one of them, as an extension of their friendship group; he tells me there were 'maybe ten that would message every single day. I'd always respond to every single one of them.' Along with the attention of followers came the interest of brands and advertisers: 'At the end of 2013, I got my first paid [influencer] job. I was like, holy shit, I've made it. I'm rich.'

Whilst his following made him a prominent figure both online and in the *GQ* New York head office, not all of his colleagues were supportive of his side hustle: 'My boss at the time — the creative director of *GQ*, the Anna Wintour of menswear — told me "you should stop, there is no future in this."'

Glossy media outlets attempted to boycott online influencers: in 2016 *Vogue* officially declared war on social media stars, publishing a conversation between top editors in which they took down 'gross' and 'pathetic' influencers. 'Please stop,' wrote Sally Singer, creative digital director at *Vogue*, 'you are heralding the death of style.' 'Looking for style among a bought-and-paid-for ("blogged out?") front row is like going to a strip club looking for romance,' said Alessandra Codinha, Vogue.com Fashion News Editor. *Runway* editor Nicole Phelps commented: 'It's not just sad for the women who preen for the cameras in borrowed clothes, it's distressing, as well, to watch so many brands participate.'

The article was an open declaration of war on these influencer upstarts, who were cutting into marketing budgets, wooing brands, and stealing editors' front-row seats. 'It was so insulting how jealous they were. They would be making fun of influencers,' says Moti, 'but influencers make more than the magazine does now.' It didn't take long for him to leave *GQ* to pursue social media full time.

Though the attitudes of those at *Vogue* appear to have mellowed in the years that followed — social media stars now feature in its pages — the antagonistic relationship between 'mainstream' and 'social' media remains to this day.

Traditional outlets often mis-apply the term 'influencer' to anyone with a social media presence as clickbait, as the *New York Times* internet culture reporter Taylor Lorenz has previously pointed out. Other times, they are too quick to herald influencers' imminent demise. The *Telegraph* confidently reported 'the wane of social media stars' in 2018, two years before Charli D'Amelio's rise would break platform records. 'Are we witnessing the end of the travel influencer?', they asked again in 2019, and in 2021 they pondered: 'Is this the death of the influencer?' — and yet the industry shows no signs of slowing down.

But negative press says less than none at all; it is the relative lack of coverage of the influencer universe, comparative to its impact, that betrays the traditional media's hostility to influencing. 'Journalists and publications are very reluctant to promote the influencer industry … If you scroll down the *Daily Mail*'s Sidebar of Shame,' points out Lou Teasdale, 'it's like influencers don't exist, even though they cover reality TV stars and we have bigger audiences. They ignore us, they won't cover us, they're afraid of us and what we represent.' This silence around influencers — the same silence that may have you wondering why you've never heard of many of those mentioned in this book, despite their millions of followers — speaks volumes.

When teen beauty YouTuber James Charles was invited to attend the 2019 Met Gala in New York — an annual gathering of the glittering elite hosted by *Vogue* editor Anna Wintour — he posted on Instagram that his inclusion amongst A-list actors, fashion designers, and global celebrity powerhouses on the red-carpeted steps of the Met was a significant 'step in the right direction for influencer representation', and that he was excited to be a 'catalyst' for social progress.[15] His remarks — much like the safety-pin bodice he wore on the night — raised eyebrows across the internet.

James is currently one of the world's most popular beauty YouTubers. With millions of subscribers, an iconic sellout eyeshadow palette, and a net worth of $12m, plus a fashion line, a reality TV show, and a team of professionals working furiously for him behind the scenes, he doesn't need a leg-up from *Vogue*. But this invitation, approved by Anna Wintour, validated his status in a way that 17m YouTube subscribers just could not. The Met Gala paradox perfectly captures the complex relationship between 'mainstream' and 'social' media. James eventually landed his *Vogue* cover — for the Portugal edition — in November 2020. His announcement post on Instagram, where he has over 26m followers, received over 1.5 million likes.[16] Meanwhile, Condé Nast lists *Vogue Portugal*'s print readership at 97.5k, and monthly unique visitors at just 900k.[17]

By the mid-2010s, influencing had solidified into a profitable sector and recognised occupation. Bloggers, Vine rejects, MySpace legacies, streamers, Tumblr graduates, and uncategorised creatives had congregated on a handful of centralised platforms. The industry passed its tipping point: between 2015 and 2016, Google searches for the term 'influencer' soared fivefold. The biggest social media stars began to resemble the media behemoths they had left behind. 'All these female influencers were monetising it, getting paid, getting sponsored,' said Moti. 'They were making millions.'

Though online networks gave rise to social media stars, focusing too closely on the platforms themselves is misleading, celebrity academic and sociologist Professor Chris Rojek explains to me over the phone. He has studied the emergence of lifestyle influencers in the 2010s, and cautions against overstating their novelty. 'There's a technological fixation with digital culture and social media networks — a feeling that it transforms everything — and yet when you look at how people emotionally relate to one another, you don't see a revolution, you see a continuation,' he tells me. 'The internet has not created lifestyle gurus, but it has given them a platform to share their views.'

Within the industry, there's a tendency to characterise the rise of influencers as a hero's progress of ambitious individuals, scaling platforms and adopting new technologies with singular ingenuity and pioneering drive. But it's as much about the systems that sustain influencers as it is about them as individuals.'Behind the technology there are power interests,' says Rojek, 'and those power interests are the root of the situation we are in now.'

The story of the influencer's rise is also the story of industrial decline: the attrition of previously dominant industries and institutions, the fragmentation of supporting social structures, and the hollowing out of a generation under splintering mental health and an unstable labour market. Creators were catalysed by crisis.

In *Selfie: how the West became self-obsessed*, Will Storr outlines the 'neoliberal self' as the defining identity of the 2010s: 'an extroverted, slim, beautiful, individualistic, optimistic, hard-working, socially aware yet high-self-esteeming global citizen with entrepreneurial guile and a selfie camera'. What he's describing is, of course, an influencer. It is in many ways the emblematic career choice for my generation: a hustling, posting, self-obsessed, self-optimising internet professional primed to thrive in these conditions.

It is no coincidence that the influencer industry as we currently understand it began to formalise in the period following the 2008 recession. The crash had stunted career prospects for my peers — half of recent US graduates were unable to find work when they left university after 2008 — fostering a rise in self-employment and an imperative to 'make your own work'. In a competitive job market, many young people began starting blogs and using social media to demonstrate their skillset and build a professional presence. Aspiring creative professionals, finding themselves derailed from traditional career paths, were forced to seek alternative routes for self-expression and new avenues for income, directly creating an 'influencer' class; the loss of her job at an interior design firm after the recession was what first pushed watershed influencer Zoella into full-time vlogging.

Even if you were lucky enough to have a job, the way we work also underwent a transformation in this period. 'Capitalism, when a crisis hits, tends to be restructured,' observes academic Nick Srnicek in *Platform Capitalism*, his study of the post-recession landscape that enabled tech platforms to dominate our 2010s economy: 'New technologies, new organisational forms, new modes of exploitation, new types of job, and new markets all emerge to create new ways of accumulating capital'.

The recession facilitated widespread casual self-employment: in other words, the exact economic conditions for influencing. Concrete forms of employment were superseded by 'the gig economy' and tangible forms of ownership by 'the sharing economy', both expressed in precarious social media marketing jobs reliant on rented audiences. Influencers posting about themselves and their interests online — the so-called 'passion economy' — were also participating in a platform-brokered system that linked performance and reward, the creative equivalent of odd-jobbing on Uber or working shifts with Deliveroo. A cohort that came of age in a fractious, fragile economy swapped life milestones — jobs, salaries, or mortgages — for alternative metrics with which to measure success: a follower count or engagement rate.

Millennial wages would not recover to pre-crash levels even ten years later.[18] In the vacuum created by a lack of financial security emerged hustle culture: a competitive lifestyle philosophy that reframed the evidence of economic anxiety — working multiple jobs to make ends meet, converting pastimes into potential sources of revenue, cultivating a corporate-compliant 'personal brand' online — as the empowered acts of a self-starting #entrepreneur.

Hustle culture flourished in startups and WeWork offices around the globe. Not all hustlers were influencers, but all influencers were hustling: demonstrating the logic of self-empowerment through 'grind', a performative obsession with productivity, and the requirement to reimagine oneself as a product to be optimised. Influencers were entrepreneurs of their own identity, 'being themselves' and getting paid for it.

Social media wasn't just a way to show off commitment to the grind, but increasingly the grind itself. Digital influence was becoming a highly lucrative industry. A symbiotic relationship between social media-driven millennial lifestyle brands and the influencer ecosystem emerged during the 2010s: fuelling shopping hauls, lifestyle edits, and millions of unboxing videos. Instagram #girlbosses and 'She-EOs' such as Nasty Gal's Sophia Amoruso, The Wing's Audrey Gelman, Bumble's Whitney Wolfe Herd, and 2010 blogger Emily Weiss — who now leads baby-pink beauty empire Glossier — were building billion-dollar brands and significant social media profiles on the power of digital influence, businesses that were inextricably linked with the burgeoning economy of online content.

'In 2009, in the depths of the recession, consumers were looking for value,' writes Business of Fashion's Alexandra Mondalek in a case study of the evolution of direct-to-consumer (DTC) brands during the 2010s. 'At the same time, consumers became more sceptical of big business. They were less receptive to the marketing and unfulfilled promises made by corporations.'[19] This created the conditions for a new generation of startups with singular product offerings, slick branding, and promises of value and transparency wrapped up in sans-serif packaging: Allbirds, Warby Parker, Glossier, Away.

Flush with venture capital funding, they boomed: the value of global VC deals for DTC companies in the fashion and beauty space exploded from 1.2 billion in 2008 to 10.2 billion in 2015. Mondalek writes: 'An entirely new industry popped up: the direct-to-consumer industrial complex ... which coincided with the rise of social media advertising and brands quickly made this the centre of their marketing strategy.'

As a generation of venture-backed DTC brands with minimal, millennial branding poured money into the influencer industry, influencers helped make them into unicorns in return. Fitness company Gymshark, one of the first brands to take advantage of influencer marketing, amassed over 5.1m followers and a valuation of over £1 billion thanks to its iconic glute-hugging pastel-hued 'influencer leggings', making founder Ben Francis the UK's richest self-made person under 30.[20] By 2016, Instagram claimed one in three users had bought something they had seen on its platform.[21]

In 2019, 7 million exhausted internet users clicked on millennial bible BuzzFeed to read a viral essay entitled 'How Millennials Became the Burnout Generation.' Anne Helen Petersen, a journalist with a PhD in media studies and a reputation for timely cultural analysis, had outlined an experience that clearly struck a chord: slow to answer emails, swamped by indecision, she was perpetually putting off simple admin and overwhelmed by feelings of fatigue. She was burning out. 'It's not a temporary affliction: it's the millennial condition,' Petersen proposed. 'It's our base temperature. It's our background music. It's the way things are. It's our lives.'[22]

Burnout was a sign that something, somewhere had gone wrong. Millennials were statistically more likely to stay single longer, marry and give birth later, and suffer from depression and anxiety than any other generation. They were cut off from traditional forms of community, uncomfortable in social situations, stuck behind the obstructing interface of a screen. A millennial mental health crisis was brewing, and isolation had become an epidemic. In 2019, a YouGov poll found that nearly a quarter of US millennials could not name a single friend.[23] Overworked, underpaid, burdened with student debt, and failing to achieve, as Petersen put it, 'the dream that had been promised', it was unsurprising that her generation had begun to crumble, unable to 'adult'.

Influencers are the product of this psychological landscape; emerging as lifestyle gurus and virtual companions to respond to the emotional needs of an anxious, atomised, alienated generation. Online, overwhelmed millennials could simply sit back and allow themselves to be influenced by an influx of content — fitness routines, meal plans, mortgage vlogs, skincare tips — designed to ease cognitive load, fronted by a relatable face prepared to guide you through whatever life could throw your way, and sell you whatever you need to get it done.

Over time, influencers evolved into an emotional support system; parasocial relationships standing in for authentic friendships. In 2016, data from Google and Ipsos claimed that four in ten millennials said their favourite creator understood them better than their friends.[24] In 2019, a study of 2000 UK 18–25-year-olds concluded that they were twice as likely to take advice from social media influencers than they were to trust the judgement of friends or family when it came to making life decisions.[25]

Influencers offer escape from burnout, too: aspirational influencer content is a form of virtual fantasy, round-the-clock vlogging allowing for vicarious participation in someone else's life. 'Millennials are far less jealous of objects or belongings on social media than the holistic experiences represented there, the sort of thing that prompts people to comment, *I want your life*,' Petersen goes on to explain in her essay. Influencers appeared to represent it all: 'that enviable mix of leisure and travel, the accumulation of pets and children, the landscapes inhabited and the food consumed seems not just desirable, but balanced, satisfied, and unafflicted by burnout'.

Influencers may have emerged as a coping mechanism, but this aspirational element is, as Petersen points out, also a fundamental part of the problem too: 'There is no "off the clock" when at all hours you could be documenting your on-brand experiences or tweeting your on-brand observations … always ready to document every component of your life — in easily manipulated photos, in short video bursts … The social media feed — and Instagram in particular — is thus evidence of the fruits of hard, rewarding labor and the labor itself.'

As both a producer of content in my day job, and a consumer of it in whatever time I'm not spent working, this kind of burnout is something in which I have first-hand experience. Working as an internet professional isn't exactly the most arduous of occupations, but it comes with its own context-specific challenges. Being always-on is overwhelming and disorienting: traumatic world news, live political updates, and internet aggressors mix with memes, pictures of friends and pets, and requests from colleagues to forward emails or read Instagram infographics they have shared. My brain strains from registering and categorising a million digital micro-interactions every day; sifting the important from irrelevant provides an undercurrent of cognitive tension. Every online action triggers a reaction, every post or comment setting off a chain of subsequent responses, infinitely replicating notifications and updates to respond to ad infinitum.

At the end of a long day's work down the algorithm mines, panning for ephemeral internet trends and references to surface for my clients, I don't switch off or 'digitally detox'. My index finger instinctively reaches for TikTok or Twitter. Even as my brain feels decayed and my eyes blur from upwards of 12 hours spent squinting — always too close — at a screen, I find myself craving more of the same. The numbing effects of scrolling down an endless newsfeed are both the problem and its own relief.

Over time, this works to delirious effect. Periodically, after long projects or particularly lengthy binges, I feel saturated and dissociate. No longer able to process information, I let my unread messages pile up in my inbox and notifications from friends accumulate whilst I lie for hours on my sofa during the weekends, unable to do anything, but unable to do nothing either. The flatter I feel, the more I use social media to stimulate myself; stretching out my scroll sessions into the early hours, instinctively stroking my phone screen downwards with one erratic thumb in a desperate quest for more content.

Millennial instability doesn't end at burnout. Professor Rojek links the emergence of influencers to social disillusionment on a macro scale: 'The institutions that society has set up for hundreds of years to help people manage their lives are now seen as defective.' He argues that this collapse in trust is far-reaching: 'Professional experts are speaking a language that nobody can connect with any more, your GP isn't on your wavelength, elections aren't fair, your leaders don't represent your interests, and the police don't exist to protect you.' This distrust, he tells me, is not entirely unfounded.

Since the financial malpractice of the 2008 crisis, a series of coverups and scandals combined to fracture faith in the establishment as an arbiter of truth and justice: Jeffrey Epstein and Prince Andrew, Operation Yewtree, the #MeToo movement, US police brutality, and of course the rise of Donald Trump. 'The same problem keeps on coming back,' says Rojek. 'The main institutions in an established democracy no longer seem to work for the people ... The man in the street is thinking: nothing is ever going to change, and if that's the case, you disinvest in the society around you and look elsewhere for purpose. Once you get that level of distrust, it's pretty clear where people will turn to get some kind of solace ... the internet.'

The hollowing out of traditional forms of leadership created a power vacuum in which influencers — along with other alternative sources of authority — could expand. The 2010s saw a boom in 'lifestyle alternatives' — from health movements such as anti-vax or 'clean eating' to esoteric trends for tarot, witchcraft, and astrology — rebranded for the millennial generation by iPhone-wielding influencers. Alternative movements need maverick actors to position themselves against accepted ideology and share anti-establishment narratives. Influencers, along with populist politicians, alt-right online personalities, and conspiracy theorists have often played that role.

BuzzFeed's Stephanie McNeal has reported on the ideological overlap between influencers, the wellness movement, conspiracy theorists, anti-vaxxers, and multi-level marketing schemes. 'Influencers are seamlessly weaving in evidence-free far-right conspiracy theories that are usually found in the significantly less Instagrammable parts of the internet, such as [notorious troll forums] 4chan and 8chan, in between their usual idyllic family snaps,' wrote Stephanie in a 2020 report. 'While these theories obviously originated on the internet and have been circulating there for years, seeing them pop up in the feeds of previously mostly innocuous parenting and lifestyle bloggers is a strange new development.'[26]

All this was taking place alongside the damage that digitisation had wrought on traditional media. Trust in mainstream media, measured via the Gallup poll, officially reached a record low of 32 per cent in 2016;[27] further fuelling the rise of partisan, individualistic, opinion-driven online content and the emergence of an antagonistic narrative that pitted legacy media against digital alternatives. In 2017, academic Tom Nichols's bestselling book *The Death of Expertise* summed this up as 'a Google-fueled, Wikipedia-based, blog-sodden collapse of any division between professionals and laypeople, students and teachers, knowers and wonderers — in other words, between those of any achievement in an area and those with none at all.'

Influencers, offering native knowledge, peer-to-peer recommendations, and information that claimed to circumvent traditional gatekeepers in their respective subject areas, were another expression of the same trend. In June of 2016, the UK's Justice Secretary Michael Gove declared in relation to the Brexit vote that 'this country has had enough of experts'.[28] The sentiment of his statement applied just as well to the shift towards influencers as away from politicians.

Not only was public focus shifting from institutions to individuals, but from governments to corporations. In 2018, I had been working within advertising for a few years when a global study by Edelman confirmed that for the first time, over half of the world's population believed that brands could do more to solve social ills than the government, and 54 per cent believed it easier to get brands to address social problems than to get government to act: society's defining leadership structure was perceived to be the private sector, not the state.[29]

'Brand purpose' quickly shifted from the abstract rhetoric of strategy frameworks into a widespread marketing tactic. I received an influx of briefs from companies looking to ramp up corporate social responsibility programmes or respond to an increased appetite for 'branded activism'. The industry was tasked with 'connecting to communities', 'amplifying unheard voices', and pitching campaigns centred around feminism, sustainability, and intersectionality.

New marketing models emphasising the role of 'brand personality' personified inanimate corporations. Brands began tentatively, by establishing their social media presence and sending overly-familiar marketing emails riddled with emojis, before descending into bizarre viral one-upmanship on social media with heavy-handed use of slang, bleak memes, and existential engagement baiting. The logical conclusion of this trend? Frozen meat-strip seller Steak-Umm tweeting about anticapitalism and student debt burdens (*Vox* labelled them the 'philosopher-poet of frozen meat sheets'[30]). Orange juice corporation SunnyD declaring it had depression ('I can't do this anymore' — 140k likes[31]). Brands: they have feelings too!

Influencers were the counterpart to this shift. As a digital evolution of the oldest marketing channel — word-of-mouth — they represented a convenient human mouthpiece for corporations now challenged to 'connect' with consumers, to 'entertain' and 'engage' them, to build a 'relationship' based on 'authenticity'. Brands were becoming people, and people were becoming brands.

So much had changed in the time elapsed since I had begun my Tumblr. Sharing irreverent thoughts and filtered photos had gone from awkward to aspirational, from teenage hobby to professional job. Power had shifted. New infrastructure for fame-making had emerged. New platforms had arisen with new faces on them. We had new language to describe it all. I had grown up.

Had I known, when I first signed up to Tumblr, that the outcome of the hours I spent online could have eventually landed me a slot on *The X Factor*, a *Vogue* cover, or an invite to the Met Gala, I might have kept my password somewhere safe. But as well as feeling nostalgic for the elapsed sense of opportunity, I also missed the earlier internet's sense of awkward innocence and adolescent intimacy, absent in the polished teenage vloggers and professional streamers of today.

Given so much had changed over the decade, I also wondered what might have stayed the same. How different could influencers really be from previous generations of the famous? Surely some principles of influence remained fixed, consistent with those that had fuelled celebrities and royalty for centuries? The idea that influencers represent a 'new' kind of celebrity or 'authentic' glimpse behind the traditional apparatus of fame is, after all, simply another kind of spectacle.

Though my experience at *The X Factor* had proven that certain structures for celebrity were now outdated, I couldn't get my one-time Tumblr peer's trajectory out of my head. I wondered if, after all these years, it was time for me to try for fame again.

CHAPTER 3

EXTREMELY ONLINE

HOW DO YOU BECOME AN INFLUENCER?

'Hi guys, welcome back to my channel!' The words sound hollow; I can't get the intonation right. I stop and grit my teeth. It's my seventh take. I start again. 'Hey guys! Livvi here. Before we get started, make sure you've hit the subscribe button below ...'

I'm perched precariously on the edge of the bath in my flat, phone propped between two bottles of shampoo and a wavy-paged novel that's reserved for reading on the toilet. Off camera, I've dragged a chair in from the kitchen; on it sits a series of props and products. A hastily scribbled script is propped up on a cardboard box. I've repurposed a lamp from the living room to counteract the glare from the overhead light; the extension lead snakes dangerously from the bathroom door to a socket in the hallway.

I'm trying — unsuccessfully — to record an intro for 'my morning skincare/make-up routine' vlog — an activity that's actually taking place closer to midnight — which I hope will become the debut upload to my new channel on YouTube. That is, if I ever get that far. Each time I re-record I feel more awkward, and listening back to the video clips brings on paroxysms of cringe. My voice sounds affected, my arm keeps impulsively attempting an embarrassing half-wave, and

I can't stop staring at my face on the screen instead of at the camera. I accidentally drop the face mask I'm holding on the floor. When I manage to regain autonomous functioning, I try again. It's going well until my phone falls over and I let out a decidedly non-advertiser friendly expletive. I decide to leave it in. Vlogging, as it turns out, is really f---ing difficult.

In real life I'm rarely at a loss for what to say. But when it comes to striking up an on-camera conversation with myself, staring down the front-facing lens into oblivion, I stall. The void stares back at me. I can't remember my own name. Monologuing for an invisible audience — sharing personal anecdotes with the glazed screen of an iPhone, cracking jokes to which there is no reaction — is much harder than vloggers make it appear. Bereft of encouraging responses, I feel hyper-conscious about how I'm coming across: am I too earnest? Too expansive? Too animated? Not animated enough?

Struggling with my eighth take, I wonder if — despite my premature success with Tumblr — I'm just not cut out to be an influencer today. I'm a fairly private person, I'm not particularly photogenic, and it often takes me three to five business days to respond to my friends on WhatsApp. Though my Screen Time reports that I often spend up to seven hours a day scrolling through social media, I rarely post anything myself.

To complete this catalogue of incompatibility, I'm also perfectly content to be a nobody. 'Each day on Twitter there is one main character,' goes the axiom, 'the goal is to never be it.' Every time I log on to see some unsuspecting user accidentally trending I shudder and feel grateful for my low profile. I'm not exactly angling for an invite to join the blue tick crew.

Though the idea of being surveilled by hundreds of thousands of people gives me palpitations, I appear to be in an ever-diminishing minority; one in five UK children now say they want to be an influencer when they grow up. YouTubers have even knocked astronauts off the top spot.[1]

With the possibility of one fifth of our future workforce gainfully employed behind a ring light nine to five, it's clearly time to start taking the influencing profession seriously. What does it take for aspiring influencers to 'make it'? What skills or mindset do successful creators have? What's life like when you make it to the top? To fully understand, I was going to have to face my fears and attempt to become one myself.

Everybody has to start somewhere, and for a select few, it's at influencer training camp. Whilst I am in my bathroom agonising over my iPhone, a fresh-faced generation of social media stars are being trained at 'Creating for YouTube: Become a YouTube Influencer' in London, a week-long influencer programme for teens aged 13–17 that sees 70 participants graduate each year. During the long, hot summer holidays, whilst other children are messing around outside or honing the art of irritating their parents, a small cohort of aspiring influencers gather together to 'learn to create eye-catching content, master YouTube's professional tools' and tell 'stories that drive engagement', according to organiser FireTech's comprehensive course literature.

YouTube is arguably the most popular of all influencer platforms for young audiences. According to Pew, 80 per cent of parents of children 11 and under in the US say their kids watch YouTube.[2] It's also given birth to the industry's biggest players and richest influencers, from beauty gurus to gamers, toy unboxers to travel vloggers. Despite the arrival of several successive platforms in the decade-plus since its launch, becoming a YouTuber is still in many ways the Holy Grail of social media success.

The Fire Tech camp first launched in 2018 — the same year PewDiePie and T-Series fought an epic online battle for the title of most subscribed channel, Logan Paul went viral for filming a dead body, and the YouTube beauty community imploded under 'Dramageddon' — a fallout between top influencers complete with shady tweets, hour-long apology videos, and plummeting channel subscriber counts live-streamed in real time. These incidents were viewed by multi millions and generated shockwaves across the influencer landscape, yet passed beneath the radar of most internet users over a certain age.

Fire Tech's influencer camp offers attendees a tantalising

opportunity: to learn the technical skills required to produce high-quality videos and unlock their latent influencer potential. Conscious that I need all the help I can get and hoping to brush shoulders with tomorrow's YouTube superstars before they hit the big time, I decide to sign up.

Beginning the course bright and early on a Monday morning in August stirs memories from classrooms past, as the students — myself, plus a small group of animated pre-teen boys hailing from across the UK — go around and make our introductions: an interesting fact about ourselves, our favourite foods, two truths and a lie. A pandemic-proofed schedule means we are learning remotely, in my case prostrated on my parents' sofa. Once logged on, we meet our course coach Nathan, an upbeat, relentlessly patient Scottish instructor with a homegrown YouTube channel of his own, on which he reviews electronic synthesisers and (he reveals privately to me) vlogs whisky-tasting.

Twenty minutes into our induction, I realise I am already out of my depth: I have accidentally landed in a class of aspiring YouTube gamers. Within the influencer landscape, gaming is a microcosm complete with its own language and lore, each new game franchise spawning an expansive universe of characters, weaponry, codes, and customs. Whilst the students are happily chatting multiplayer platform compatibility, I am stealthily googling acronyms.

Far from the bedroom-dwelling pastime of the shy and socially reclusive, as it has been previously painted, gaming is a sprawling community activity on social media platforms. Over 200 million YouTube users watch gaming videos on a daily basis; 50 billion hours were viewed in 2018 alone, and two of the five largest channels on YouTube belong to gamers.[3] And that's just YouTube — the largest dedicated gamer streaming platform is Twitch, a 3.8m-strong community, which has an average of 83,700 synchronous streams — with 1.44 million viewers — taking place at any time.[4]

Just a fraction of these numbers are users actually playing games themselves. Gaming content usually consists of viewing other people play: pre-recorded commentary following skilful players as they navigate their way through various levels or livestreamed screenshares to which viewers can tune in to watch their heroes play in real time. According to Google's own data, 48 per cent of YouTube gaming viewers say they spend more time watching gaming videos on YouTube than actually playing games themselves.

If, like me, you find yourself wondering why, you're probably in the wrong demographic. My classmate Rahil, a die-hard fan of Destiny 2, broke it down: 'What makes these content creators so good is that they are very confident in what they do in gaming, but they are also funny, they are entertaining to watch. That's why they have so many followers.'

Watching other people play video games is a way to level up your skills, engage with the community's most hyped gaming rivalries, and feel connected to something beyond your console. Being a successful gaming influencer is also a way to get filthy rich. Video game voyeurism is a lucrative market, making internet celebrities of its most popular players, a string of incomprehensible handles that read to me like an inebriated keyboard smash but invoke wild-eyed delight in the eyes of my classmates: Markiplier, elrubiusOMG, JuegaGerman, A4, TheWillyrex, EeOneGuy, KwebbelKop, Fernanfloo, AM3NIC.

PewDiePie — aka 30-year-old Felix Kjellberg, the only gamer noobs like me have ever heard of — has 106m followers and is estimated to earn around $8 million per month, including more than $6.8 million from selling merchandise and more than $1.1 million in advertising.[5] Blue-haired streamer Ninja, aka Detroit-born 29-year-old Tyler Blevins, is the most-followed gamer on Twitch, and signed a $30 million contract with Microsoft to game exclusively on their now-defunct streaming service Mixer.[6] UK YouTube gaming collective The Sidemen upload weekly vlogs to their shared channel in which they compete on FIFA, mess around, prank each other, order £1,000 takeaways, and play something called 'IRL Tinder', living out the fever dream of a million teenage boys across the internet. For many tweens, getting paid to play as a YouTube gamer is a hallowed goal, and each of my classmates is keen to make Minecraft a full-time occupation. I decide to keep quiet about my abortive attempt at a beauty tutorial.

Class kicks off with an inspirational slideshow titled 'INFLUENCERS: FROM 0 TO MILLIONS'. My laptop screen displays a Wall of Fame of top YouTubers smiling smugly to camera: OG American vlogger Casey Neistat, Canadian comedian Lilly Singh, PewDiePie, beauty guru Michelle Phan, and actor, activist, and author Tyler Oakley, each underlined by a subscriber count that outnumbers the population of most European countries. 'Everyone started off where you are today,' says Nathan enthusiastically. 'A laptop and a smartphone — that's all they had. Everybody here started with zero subscribers.' The class is rapt. I try to imagine my own face smiling onscreen between professional prankster Roman Atwood (15.3m subscribers) and viral violin performer Lindsey Stirling (12.5m subscribers). Somehow, I can't.

Nathan hits play on early comedy vlogger nigahiga's first ever upload — a 2007 viral video sketch entitled 'How to Be Ninja' that now has 54,295,178 views — and then a later video from 2017, 'Life of a YouTuber'. 'Look at that — 21.5M subscribers!' Nathan taps on the follower count under the video. 'It didn't happen overnight. It took a year, 12 months of putting up content with 50 views. Don't get disheartened. Take every sub, every view as a ...' he mimes celebrating like the winner of a round of Fortnite.

Thanks to its nostalgic pixelation and condensed frame ratio, watching 'How to Be Ninja' creates the impression that we're sitting in a history class studying archival footage from a distant past: *Late Noughties Net Culture (2007, colourised)*. In a poorly lit, grainy home video that feels like a prelapsarian time capsule, two teenage boys act out a hammy sketch in which they transform into martial arts experts, including off-tempo miming, questionable jump cuts, and a tantalising glimpse of old-school YouTube — running on Internet Explorer — that flies over the heads of my Gen Z classmates. The sketch feels like two friends messing around with a camera at the weekend; it's almost as if they don't know they're being watched.

In the second video an older and now more-polished Higa — complete with designer purple highlights in his hair — breezily addresses his multi-million-strong fanbase in a nine-minute HD monologue that's punctuated by kooky 3D animation and links to his supporting social media channels. 'I am in one of the final stages of my YouTube career,' he says, 'and my YouTube life, so …' The camera cuts to reveal his extensive video set-up, professional lights, and a team of three clutching scripts, clipboards, cameras, and a boom mic behind the scenes, all celebrating exuberantly: 'That means we can get out of here right?' asks one. 'Yeah, it's really cramped back here …' says another, 'I have to poop so bad.'

'What's the difference between these two videos?' Nathan prompts us. 'What changed?' The answers roll in quickly, students reeling off a list of ameliorations with ease: better lighting, better equipment, a better thumbnail, slicker editing, a more professional approach, background music, higher audio quality, and a naturalistic presentation style that at least appears to be ad-libbed.

'What makes a good video more generally?' asks Nathan. 'What are the key elements?' When he eventually pulls up the next slide, it turns out Nathan wants us to discuss passion, fun, originality, and creativity: but the class has other ideas. 'I heard YouTube doesn't like videos lower than ten minutes,' offered Alex. 'There's many things that they don't like,' Lucas corrects him. 'The algorithm is very complicated, and it's always changing. They used to support "let's plays" [a popular gaming stream format] back in 2018, and then they changed it, and a lot of Minecraft channels died.' Rahil pipes up: 'They find as many ways as possible to scrutinise your video … if you do many small things wrong, you get less money, even though YouTube is paid the same money by the advertisers. So you should never swear in your videos.' 'No, demonetisation is different,' corrects Fred.

There is something fascinating and incongruous about watching pre-teens reel off the details of various influencer revenue models with the enthusiasm of a seasoned social media professional. The fluency with which they exchange terms I'm more accustomed to encountering on conference calls and in marketing decks is a startling reminder of the generational gulf between us: though they may be students, they're not exactly beginners on the internet.

As the conversation quickly descends into technocratic one-upmanship, Nathan attempts to steer our analysis back to entry level. 'Once you reach 1,000 subscribers,' he enthusiastically explains to the class, 'that means you can monetise your channel and have ads on it.' A heated debate about the intricacies of YouTube monetisation ensues. Nathan is corrected by one of his students, before another pipes up to undercut them both, and suddenly everyone's talking all at once: 'Most YouTubers make money from sponsorships, not advertising revenue, anyway,' offers one student. There is a pause. 'And merch,' he adds, 'the MrBeast hoodies are really cool.'

'Okay then,' says Nathan brightly, shifting the slide forward to reveal a list of attributes for creating successful content that begins, 'Attitude, Energy, Passion, Smile', 'what about some of these ...'

Looking at my notes, I realise Nathan's original question, 'What makes a good video?', has become something else entirely: what does YouTube consider to be a good video, and thus reward accordingly? It's a small elision, admittedly, but significant; good is whatever YouTube thinks is good, and interpretations outside this algorithmic value system aren't entertained. His prompt about creative possibilities has been heard as a question about optimising the potential of a commodity (the influencer) in an online marketplace. 'It's all about value,' he continues, unwittingly echoing my thoughts, 'what value does your video bring to the YouTube community? How are you going to stand out from all the other people doing it?'

This cuts to the heart of criticism against influencer training courses like this one, and others which have sprung up in LA, Singapore, and Paris in recent years: that it's ethically inappropriate to coach young people to commodify themselves, that it's encouraging children to spend more time online, that it's corrupting childhoods. Influencers and industry professionals rolled their eyes or responded with a mixture of horror and intrigue when I'd mentioned the Fire Tech programme in passing. 'That's disgusting,' said one agent, 'way too young.' (Privately, I thought this was an inconsistent position, given she represented a mumfluencer with a family of four.) 'I respect it,' said a Brighton-based beauty guru, 'but I would never personally make that choice for my kids.' 'Crazy times we live in,' offered a NYC-based fashion influencer, before admitting, 'for real, though, I kind of wish I had had that when I was younger.'

These criticisms misunderstand the current state of digital

culture and misinterpret its dynamics. Far from innocent minds being corrupted by the insidious influence of a training course, the students who enrol arrive preconditioned to understand themselves as marketable objects within a performance-driven system. The boys in my class turned up with algorithm tips and an appetite for self-optimisation on day one. Personal branding is second nature to this generation; it is we who are naïve.

I put these challenges to Fire Tech UK Manager Ed Halliday. The camp's ultimate reason for being, he tells me, isn't necessarily to train the next generation of social superstars but to 'encourage young people not just to consume these technologies that are shaping their world but actually effectively harness them'. The influencer programme is just one of Fire Tech's hundreds of tech education courses: others offer coding, photography and music production.

As of February 2020, UK children spent an average of 75 minutes per day on YouTube, followed closely by TikTok for an average of 69 minutes daily,[7] whilst in the US, teens spend more than seven hours per day on screen media, and tweens nearly five hours.[8] As Halliday points out, 'not all screen time is equal'. He challenges me: 'What is the better of the two: being someone who is on YouTube creating in a responsible way — or idly sitting in front of the screen for hours on end? The dangers of social media and YouTube are real. The answer is to get people who really understand these technologies to teach young people how to have the most positive relationship with it.'

Turning the damn thing off altogether — the default cry of grown-ups during my generation's childhood Game Boy craze — is no longer a viable option. 'Throughout history, there is an inevitability to technology which runs side-by-side with fear about the effects of adopting technology,' Ed continues. 'When there is inevitability, it's irresponsible to not educate people on how to use these technologies. It is a much more proactive and positive thing to say, "This is happening, this is how people are behaving", to educate young people on how to make the best of it, how to have the most positive relationship with it.' He continues: 'We want to lead the way in helping young people to use tech to shape their experience of the world around them, rather than being just consumers.'

Back in the classroom, our first step towards becoming an influencer is developing a personal brand strategy, for which we are supplied with a template of helpful questions. Head down, biro in hand, I study them intensely. I am suddenly back at school again, second-guessing myself, fresh with the terror of the blank test page. To overcome the obstacles standing between me and a Streamy Award I will have to grapple with some existential questions: *Who is my audience? In which genre do I sit? What do I want people to think about me as a YouTube personality?*

Assessing my skills from an influencer perspective is a depressing experience, involving a near-total re-evaluation of my CV. What have I got to offer? My professional qualifications quickly pale. Too sluggish for fitness, not handy enough with a fan brush to be a YouTube beauty guru, too slow to throw shapes on TikTok, too tied to a nine to five to drop it all for #travelstagram. My aptitude for Mario Kart would impress an audience of zero within the gaming community.

'Focus on something you love,' Nathan encourages us, 'something that you're good at.' One by one, my classmates finish their templates. 'It could be bullet points,' he offers helpfully, 'but if you want to write a long paragraph, that's fine.' Plumbing my own inadequacy, I wonder if my lack of influencer potential could, perhaps, become my strength. *Ironic influencer,* I write down, *unwitting debut author attempts to become a social media star.*

I decide to be bolder and manifest my impending success. *Accidentally hits the big time. Goes viral, gains 1m followers, lands a high-paying commercial partnership, and lives off swipe-ups for the rest of her life.* With this brand positioning in place, I can breathe easier: the endless quirks and eccentricities of the influencer industry make it an almost limitless source of spoof material.

Thankfully, I am spared sharing my personal brand strategy with the rest of the group, but my classmates are more forthcoming: they want to be gaming streamers or comedy vloggers like their heroes, self-described 'Jesus loving Texan vlogger' Preston (14m), Minecraft legend Stampy (9.55m), and viral YouTube phenomenon MrBeast

(24m). Everyone, it turns out, is a fan of MrBeast. 'What is it you like about him?' asks Nathan. 'He mashes money and challenges together,' says Max with a grin. James is more blunt: 'He has tens of millions of dollars.'

Having decided on our aims and ambitions, it is time to brand ourselves with a customised channel look, logo and header assets, and the perfect YouTube name. 'It has to sound good when you say it, look good when it's written down, and it needs to be googleable,' prompts Nathan. 'It needs to be a name that nobody else has.' My classmates are busy imagining brash and aggressive streamer screen names, an incomprehensible blend of caps and lower case littered with misplaced punctuation. I decide to keep things simple. For the first time in my life, I am grateful for my unusual surname: after years of misspelt spam mail and trailing in the registers, it could prove to be an asset; practically designed for search engine optimisation (SEO).

Over the next few days, we take notes from slideshows, pitch scripts, and discuss strategies. We tinker with video titles, thumbnail formulas, and back-end analytics. We are inducted into a suite of online software to tweak, convert, customise, and optimise every aspect of our online presence. We perfect the formula for the perfect YouTube opener: 'Hey guys! Subscribe to my [social media links]! Today we're going to [activity] …' We learn how to create our own animated channel intros, lurid clips of self-promotion that bring our personal brands to life. We are introduced to the importance of the jump cut: an idiosyncratic YouTube edit style that eliminates all moments of silence or hesitation to create a seamless stream of non-stop commentary, a technique used by top vloggers to keep viewers glued. My Google Doc of bullet points becomes an incomprehensible string of hieroglyphic notes: *<10k +audience — batch create content??? AdSense 45/55.*

We debate the merits of static streaming cams trained at the player versus continuous full-screen gameplay voiced over by an unseen narrator. We spend a day discussing 'digital citizenship', which Nathan says includes 'how to build up a fanbase, how to have a relationship with your fans, dealing with haters', as well as how to stay safe, make use of privacy settings, and act responsibly online. We discover ways to monetise, from selling branded t-shirts to starting a subscription service on Patreon for our most devoted subscribers. We take turns ad-libbing for one uninterrupted minute to practise the spontaneous on-camera conversation that I previously struggled with. We sit a quiz to test our newly acquired knowledge (*Thumbnails only matter when you have a large audience: True or False?*) and take a day to shoot a premiere video of our own.

All along, Nathan urges us to experiment, to be ourselves, to have fun. He stresses the value of a YouTuber's character and individuality, the importance of 'the person coming down through the lens'. 'You've all got amazing personalities, you're all really nice people,' he says, 'I can't wait to see what you create.' This narrative of ultimate authenticity and self-expression feels at odds with the toolkit of techniques and optimisation tricks in which we are simultaneously being drilled.

'Be yourselves as much as you can be on camera,' urges Nathan. 'It's good to learn, but don't feel like you have to copy anyone else.' But mere minutes later, he is reinforcing the platform's hidden formulas and incentives: 'A lot of YouTubers have a recipe for their introduction … you want an introduction and a preview and then boom, you're into what the video is about.'

The idea that you could 'just be yourself' online and somehow end up with hundreds of millions of followers is key to influencer mythology; the reality is a whole lot more strategic. Although Nathan reassures us that 'what makes YouTube videos more appealing than Hollywood movies' is that they are 'more natural, and come across as more human', it appears to me that becoming an influencer is a whole lot like submitting to a rigorous process of algorithmic conditioning. After a week of high-intensity learning, we prepare ourselves to emerge as lean, streamlined content-creation machines.

On the final day of camp, before our class of digital debutantes reintroduce ourselves to the internet, Nathan has us pause for a moment of reflection. Why did we want to become YouTubers? What was it that we liked about our favourite creators? I had expected the class to simply say they wanted a valid excuse to spend all day playing video games, but was surprised to find YouTube wasn't the vehicle, but the end goal in itself. 'The reason why I like YouTube is it's an open platform, you can find any type of content you want — make-up, gaming, real life, challenges,' offers Lucas.

The appeal of being a YouTube star wasn't the prospect of becoming a mega-celebrity, he says, but the fact that top YouTubers appeared to be just like him: 'Anyone can upload their own videos. It doesn't make other YouTubers special: you can make money from YouTube like they can.' The mindset that, on YouTube, basically anyone can make it is shared by the rest of the class, though they are aware the system isn't completely meritocratic: 'It's not like you need to pay for anything,' said Max. 'You can upload whenever you like, there's no requirements on what edit software you use, what camera you use.' He pauses and corrects himself: 'It will affect how many people watch your videos, but you can still upload it.'

The conversation turns towards community, and the relationship between creators and their fans. It is important for us to cultivate our audience, Nathan informs us. 'You're all connected, you're all sharing your passion. You can ask people to comment down below: it can make everyone feel part of this community.' But this effort isn't just in the hopes of making friends or sparking human connection. 'In regards to the YouTube algorithm, it recommends content that has more activity — it proves that people are engaged. It's well worth getting to know who is watching your videos,' Nathan continues: 'Your channel is for you, [but after a while] it starts to be them, it starts to be for your audience …'

None of the class had ever met a YouTuber IRL — but all were avid social media supporters, liking and commenting on their favourite creators' channels daily in the hope of a response. Only Lucas had ever received a message back: 'It was in a livestream,' he recalls with a wide grin at the memory. 'I asked how's life, the creator said "good".' He mimes his head exploding and breaks into a gleeful smile: 'I was like, oh my gosh, he actually spoke back!! I don't like annoying YouTubers [by speaking to them], but it was pretty unique. He's a smaller YouTuber. If it was a bigger YouTuber it would have been really special.'

Though my classmates are deeply invested in the influencer

universe, well-versed in YouTube trends, and quick to show off their understanding of the algorithm, I feel we've finally bumped up against the edge of their understanding. They can reel off facts, stats, and figures, list top creator names and recall follower counts, but they have far less grasp of influencing's invisible dynamics: the calculated relatability of their favourite creators, the asymmetry of these parasocial relationships, the line where performance ends and reality begins. At one point Max incorrectly identified a creator's staged blooper as an authentic mistake. They know how influencers make money, know what to say and how to say it: but they can't say exactly why. And of course the elephant in the Zoom is that, even after a week of top-calibre coaching, it is, statistically speaking, extremely unlikely that any of us will ever make it.

And just like that, influencer camp is over. The class is ready to unleash their potential on the internet. I am poised to become a social media star. 'Remember, this is just the first step,' says Nathan. 'Go forth and make amazing videos.' I log off Zoom, switch my Instagram account to public, and upload my beauty tutorial to YouTube.

Over the coming weeks, I keep the lessons from the camp lodged firmly in my mind as I begin a relentless publicity campaign for my newly relaunched online personality. It's a far cry from my private hobby on Tumblr. As an accessory to the influencer industry, some aspects of my life already lend themselves readily to digital documentation — a work trip to Paris, a brand launch party, an invite-only influencer wardrobe sale — but others feel distinctly less photogenic — working my way through a backlog of emails in timelapse, or sitting on conference calls.

However, I soon find that, armed with my iPhone and a knack for diplomatic cropping, almost everything is a content opportunity: a miserable morning run becomes a #motivational moment, a trip to pick up milk produces abstract snaps of cloud patterns, an afternoon spent writing in the library offers the opportunity for gongbang (study with me) streams and study-based keyboard ASMR.

It isn't always easy to remember to include my invisible audience.

I'll be halfway through a meal before thinking to document it, hastily reshaping piles of broccoli on my plate. I forget to film social events and am forced to retrace my steps, making me late on more than one occasion. Several times, my battery dies mid-monologue.

Gradually, I find it easier to start conversing on camera, easier to ignore the curious glances of people in the street. The gap between my train of thought and its delivery collapses, and the silences begin to fill themselves: I can lift my arm, unlock my phone, and the commentary begins to flow in one smooth motion, an automatic plug-in to my stream of consciousness. By now, I've worked out my angles: the best place in my small flat for flattering light that smooths my split ends and lifts my skin; the iPhone position from which my wonky sofa back is hidden and the books and pots and vases littering the coffee table transform from a haphazard scatter into artistic asymmetry. I begin to reassess my life through someone else's eyes: does this fit my aesthetic? Is this activity on brand?

My followers — a small cohort of family, friends, acquaintances, and strangers — aren't sure how to take my new-found enthusiasm for oversharing. Some comment enthusiastic support, others skewer my attempts at aspiration: 'lol', replies my former flatmate to an artfully arranged display of fry-up ingredients, captioned 'açai bowl xoxo'. A ten-minute 'my morning glam' make-up tutorial receives a string of cry-laugh emojis from a colleague. My outfit pics largely go ignored. The vlogs are better received: 'iconic', a stranger commented under a montage of shots from a party. 'Love this!!!'

Having overcome my initial inhibitions, I get a kick out of uploading myself, incrementally, to the internet. There is something about hitting 'post' and sending a small piece of myself out into the algorithm; a feeling of momentary weightlessness as I wait for the likes and comments to roll in. I begin to eagerly anticipate the ping of a notification. I tag brands and respond magnanimously to my handful of 'fans'. It is a game of variable returns and fleeting gratification, poring over the pixels in my palm like an anthropological excavator of my own increasing self-obsession. I spend nights googling iMovie hacks or sifting through royalty-free stock track libraries. My laptop overheats. My eyes blur. I upgrade my iCloud plan, and order a clip-on ring light and a backup battery pack from Amazon.

Several months into my influencer journey, however, my confidence begins to stall. I have posted hundreds of times and filmed weeks' worth of vlogs. My follower count has continued to climb, but at a rate that feels nothing more than incidental. With only a few hundred followers more than I started off with, the promised land of brand deals, swipe-ups, and detox teas is still a distant dream. There is no rapturous fandom leaving strings of supportive emojis under my selfies. No protein shake sponsorships lingering promisingly in my inbox. I am still an online enigma and beginning to feel fatigued. It's difficult to sustain this cadence of creation, particularly when it feels like I am posting into a void. Perhaps I need to get my hands dirty.

I had heard rumours circling amongst influencers about 'engagement pods': secret groups of creators who band together with a mutual agreement to like and comment on each others' posts in an attempt to hack the algorithm and artificially inflate their popularity. Not quite purchasing fake followers — I was not yet so desperate — but not exactly legitimate business either; a grey market of quasi-engagement that contravenes social media guidelines and games the influencer system. Few influencers I had spoken to would openly admit to knowing where to find one, and even fewer to taking part. Divulging your participation in a pod isn't just breaking the rules and risking a platform ban, it's something far more serious: admitting to inauthenticity.

As a result, most pods are elusive enclaves, access to which is granted only by a special invite from an active member. Tucked away in various corners across the internet — from private WhatsApp chats and Discord servers, through to groups within Instagram itself, though most take place off-platform for fear of being found out — pods can range in scale from small groups of friends to hidden networks of hundreds of thousands of strangers from across the world, orchestrated and patrolled by anonymous bots and aggregators. Could this fake-it-till-you-make-it method boost me up the newsfeed? Could a pod proxy attract genuine attention and catalyse my online career? At the very least, I'd hopefully meet some other aspiring influencers in a similar position.

To find a pod, I start by looking at public blog posts and hashtag trails, then Reddit threads, private Facebook groups, and closed Instagram accounts. Finally, I end up on Telegram — a Russian-founded encrypted messaging app favoured by journalists, criminals, and adversaries of the surveillance state, which advertises features such as secret chat rooms, end-to-end encryption, and an ability to 'self-destruct' its contents.

I'm in. Joining the pod is like crashing a virtual house party with 11,000 guests, everyone talking simultaneously. Fitness, food, and fashion influencers bump up against meme accounts and Instagram dropshipping brands. Craft accounts, gymfluencers, and beauty gurus mingle with online FX trading platforms and peddlers of soft porn. Links and self-promotion shorthand litter the chat, coded messages in an unfamiliar tongue: 'D24h', 'f2f', 'anti-flood', 'DX5', and 'UTM'.

My pod mates hail from Russia, Italy, Romania, the US, South America, and the Middle East. One user's Instagram bio even locates them within my London neighbourhood. Whilst most pod users are micro-accounts with under 1,000 followers, I notice several larger influencers with 50k, 100k, and 200k followers posting prominently, many racking up fake engagement against posts captioned #ad — partnerships with breath mints, art websites, and fast fashion brands who presumably have no idea that their paid-for post is part of an online engagement Ponzi scheme. One pod participant is using it to drive engagement for an Instagram page belonging to their dog.

My pod runs on 'cycles': a 24-hour period in which members are required to like and comment on an automated list of posts curated by a moderation bot, or risk ejection. Various rooms — concentric chats accessed through referral links — offer different 'packages' of popularity like a menu; I can opt for five original comments on each post, 200 new likes, or 50 story views. Before I'd be allowed to 'drop' a link to my post in the pod, I had to pay it forward by liking five posts from previous participants, like an infinite game of karmic pass-the-parcel.

In the space of a few short days I like vinyasa yoga posts, holiday travel snaps, cookery videos, gym selfies, pet pics, and fashion flatlays. I comment asinine affirmations to people I would never know: 'so great', 'love this', 'wish I was here', or simply strings of emojis when the content is too random for me to form a coherent response. In return I rake in likes and comments from random accounts — an influencer from Florida says my selfie is 'cuteeeeee', a jewellery brand leaves a string of praying hand emojis underneath a picture of some flowers.

The more I learn, the more I realise how much there is to learn: new tactics and traction strategies, follow loops, shell accounts, syncing multiple activity waves with my posting schedule. I am automatically added to new pods and splinter groups, each with their own rules and specialisations. The most professional of pod users employ bots and browser extensions to automatically like posts for them, enabling them to gain hundreds of thousands of manipulated engagements and eliminating the increasing amount of time I am having to spend online to keep up.

It is an odd community to belong to, consisting of a flurry of public activity from a secret set of strangers united by a common desire for fame. Cornering just one member of a pod for an actual conversation is harder than I had first assumed. Though we happily exchange heart-eye emojis under each other's posts in public, my private messages are seen, read, and ignored. I can't blame them for being cagey — what we are doing technically contradicts Instagram's Terms of Service — but it feels strange for my podfellows to be continuously cropping up amongst my real-life friends in my comments without being open to establishing some kind of personal connection.

At last, Giannis, an aspiring travel influencer from Greece with 760 followers on Instagram and 34 subscribers on his YouTube channel, agrees to speak. I'd already 'liked' several pictures on his feed, a moody assortment of snaps from alluring destinations worthy of a travel mag: tangled ivy twined around a red brick building in Dublin, market stalls threading the winding streets of Copenhagen, terracotta façades on the Amalfi coast toasting gently in the sun. Many posts feature the man himself — dressed, no matter the location, in the same sharp jacket, rucksack, and dark sunglasses — gazing pensively off camera. 'Not all those who wander are lost', reads one caption, '#wanderlust #fallvibes #travelgram'. Under each picture, a small cluster of now-familiarly generic comments chirp up 'great shot!' and 'love your feed!'

Over DM and through a language barrier, I learn Giannis is a recent pod adopter, frustrated that he was spending so much time crafting creative videos and posts that 'weren't getting anyone's attention'. 'It's much easier to grow your profile if you are a "bikini girl"', he complains, reiterating a stereotype about 'trashy' Instagram models that's commonplace within the industry's complex class system: 'there's no need for a pod'. After consistently posting his carefully crafted videos and polished travel pictures for months without gaining any traction, he realised, 'I need some kind of help.' On top of the time it takes Giannis to capture and edit his videos, he spends around two hours engaging with 500 posts, in exchange for an average of 549 likes and 41 comments per post. When I ask Giannis whether he thinks the tradeoff works in his favour, he weighs up the time invested into making good material in the first place vs time spent amplifying it: 'It works to a certain point, but I've had to spend a lot of my time and that damages my creativity.'

And yet, he has no plans to give it up. Long term, his aspiration is to be a full-time travel photography influencer like his hero, YouTuber Peter McKinnon, and never need to use a pod again, but for now, he's trapped in a cycle of low-level engagement exchange from which he sees no escape. Nor has he been able to use the pod to meet anyone or network — his attempts to reach out to other small accounts for collabs have been unsuccessful: 'When you use a pod you're not aiming for friends,' he says, 'you just want your account to get exposure.'

Other aspiring influencers I talk to disagree. 'Some people think that pods are a lie,' says Bee, a micro-influencer from Chicago I meet via a Facebook group for aspiring influencers. 'They think that people are just having to "like" you because you're in this thread. But you can ask questions, get help, get insight. Everyone is there for the same reason. It really helps.' Ellie, a Scottish 21-year-old who wants to be a beauty and fashion influencer like her heroes Jordan Lipscombe and Carys Whittaker, agrees. Influencing is competitive, and the industry's inner operations are shrouded in secrecy and guarded by word of mouth, meaning there's little visibility over rates, brand partnerships, or tips for those just starting out. 'Unless you're able to talk to someone who is already big,' she says over Skype, 'there is just no way of knowing how to make it.'

Bee began her influencer journey to spread 'plus size Black girl magic'. 'I want to show people you can live your best life, no matter if you're fat or Black or you have a 'fro.' Her feed is pure millennial magical realism: oversaturated street art bleeds into selfies, lush foliage, sun-bleached bikini portraits, rooftop yoga, frosted bakery treats, mugs of matcha, and hazy peeks into her lush plant-filled apartment. In one of her sunlit selfies, Bee embraces herself, poised radiant and nude, in front of a full-length mirror. 'Fat. Chunky. Plump. Overweight. Obese,' reads the caption, 'these are all words that have been used to describe me, but they will never define me. #blackgirlmagic #goodvibesonly #bodypositivitymovement #microinfluencer.' 1,255 people have liked the post. 'Nothing but a QUEEN 🔥 ' reads one comment. 'Good morning to all this energy 😍' reads another.

Ellie fell into influencing when her life was uprooted by a family relocation from Leeds to a rural Scottish village: 'I'm an only child. I moved and I was all alone, so I started to use social media more and more,' she explains to me. 'Now I post literally my whole life.' A quick scan of her feed proves this to be true: a bright mosaic of latte art, high-street style, fitness selfies, homemade fruit bowls, peachy sunsets, and the occasional skincare routine; she's already filed her life into digestible sections: 'nails', 'travel', 'inspiration', 'food and drink' and 'YouTube'. Though she's quick to claim her interest in influencing is its self-expression and creativity, she eventually confesses to an ulterior motive. 'Everybody dreams of the million, everybody dreams about being a household name like Jordan Lipscombe,' she admits. 'Everybody that starts out thinks yes, I'm going to be her. That's the goal for everyone, isn't it?'

Neither Bee nor Ellie's attempts to become an influencer have gone down seamlessly IRL. 'It's really difficult. A lot of people that used to be my friends have been — not exactly negative — but they think I'm weird,' Ellie confesses. 'Quite a few have unfollowed me. They see it as, "What are you doing with your life? Stop trying to be something you're not."' Perhaps, I suggest, her friends will change their mind if she eventually hits the big time, and she agrees: 'If you try to do it and fail, it's more of an embarrassment: haha, look, that's that girl who tried to be a blogger and was crap. But if you get to 5k, 10k, people start to interact with you more, you're seen to be liked by more people.' Like Ellie, Bee has also had to brush off opposition to her decision to share her life online: 'I've had people tell me it's so vapid, it's so self-centered, you're just posting pictures of yourself online.'

We tend to only hear creator success stories, but for every millionaire influencer with a merch line there are millions of wannabes with only a few thousand followers to show for it. Research in 2018 revealed that 96.5 per cent of YouTubers earn below the US federal poverty line of $12,140, and the bottom 85 per cent of YouTube creators only gain an average of 485 views per month.[9] The forums and Facebook groups I'd visited were full of aspiring creators voicing their fatigue and frustration. At 1.5k followers, Ellie has yet to be approached by brands, and she is dubious about her chances of success. 'If I went to scroll through my likes, 80 per cent of them are people like me. In a way that is kind of terrifying.' says Ellie. 'Everyone can want to be an influencer, but not everyone can be. There's not enough brands and money in the world to go around everyone. In reality you're one in — oh god — 50 million?'

As she approaches 5k followers, Bee has reached a tipping point, where her passion has started to provide the possibility of financial return. When we speak, it's a big day for her: she's just landed her first official brand deal, with a lingerie company. 'At the start I was like, I don't want to monetise my Instagram, I don't want this to be about money, I just want to show women they can do this,' she says, but her growing success has led to a change of heart: 'The more I went on, I'm seeing this is actually a possibility: why wouldn't I want multiple streams of revenue coming in? I can still do sponsored content and be true to myself. The shift in mindset has been really surprising.' Unlike Ellie, Bee remains optimistic: 'There's room for everyone to win.' But she thinks she'd set a limit on her own success: 'I don't think I want to get to 100k followers, I would put a stop to it before I got there. There are certain parts of myself I never want to share, that I want to keep protected and private. After a certain number of followers, people feel like they have a right to your life. People stop thinking of you as one of us, they start thinking of you as one of them.'

To understand the tipping point, and find out more about the grind required to get all the way to the top, I turn to Abby Roberts: at 19, the beauty guru is one of the UK's biggest TikTok stars with nearly 17m followers. When I explain my brain can't wrap itself around that number, she laughs and agrees: 'Yeah, it's just incomprehensible.' Known for her viral make-up transformations, in which her porcelain skin and delicate features are rendered unrecognisable as demonic creatures, celebrity cosplay, and optical illusions, the pink-haired influencer rose to the top of the rankings in just under two years. 'Before I started TikTok, I was just doing my A Levels', living at home with her family near Leeds, Abby tells me over Skype. 'I'd posted two videos that kind of flopped initially, and then the third video [in which she turns herself into a Bratz doll] blew up.' It got 13m views. After that, her rise was rapid. 'I gained maybe like 2 million followers within my first three months of posting … I was like, damn, she's a TikToker now!' she laughs.

Though at first Abby states, 'I blew up so quickly on TikTok,' on reflection she notes that 'it took probably like two years of straight posting every single day to get to this point.' She started uploading online when she was just 11, and had already spent years on YouTube and Instagram, 'grinding' away at her 200k following. Once she started TikTok, 'I was posting maybe three, four videos every day because that was how you got your platform,' she said. 'You have to be super consistent with your content. It was always super intense, crazy looks because that was what made me stand out from everyone else.'

As she grew her audience and reputation for outrageous make-up looks, the stakes continued to be raised: 'I always wanted to make sure that everything I posted was like, "the craziest thing you've ever seen", even crazier than the last — it's a lot of pressure.' Her creative make-up looks take an average of five hours to paint, and the longest

— a photorealistic porcelain face featuring blue fine china details — took over 14 hours to complete for a six-second video.[10] She plans each one by drawing up a digital face chart, before making props, sourcing outfits and creating backdrops. Over a sustained period of time, 'it takes a lot out of you doing that kind of stuff daily'. When I ask her what outsiders don't understand about social media fame, she laughs again: 'It doesn't just take five minutes.'

Clearly, I was going to need to level up my content. To help, I sought out influencer photographer Michaela Efford, the unseen aide behind the perfect street-style shots of many of London's biggest social media stars. She's so sought-after that she's got over 50k followers herself and receives hundreds of messages a day from aspiring influencers angling for a spot on her shoot calendar, alongside beauty guru CC Clarke, luxury fashion creator Amy Neville, and 'twinfluencers' Olivia and Alice. Michaela is as happy snapping high street *Love Island* aspirants in fast fashion tracksuits as she is shooting grungy streetwear portraits against concrete car parks, but it's her cinematic shots of luxury-clad influencers striding down Bond Street that have made her — and her subjects — Instagram famous.

What first started as a hobby quickly snowballed when Michaela's contact details were passed around a group of influencer friends. Now, she's back to back. 'I normally do two to three shoots per day, with different influencers, five outfits an hour, six days a week,' she tells me, trailing across London with a suitcase and a changing tent, from the South Bank to Covent Garden, Notting Hill to Shoreditch. Her top clients shoot with her multiple times per week.

Michaela has been flown to Paris, Cyprus, Ibiza, and Morocco to create content for social media feeds, but Bond Street remains a perennially popular choice: 'I get clients who dress in all Dior, just to stand outside the store,' she tells me, many bringing empty shopping bags to stage pictures. 'Then they change into Louis Vuitton, go across the street, and shoot in front of Louis Vuitton.' I wonder what the retail employees think. 'You can just see them staring at us through the window.'

Occasionally, she's booked to pap influencers outside at fashion week: 'They message me saying, "Can you meet me outside this show, can you take a quick pic?" If I take a picture of them, other photographers will then take a picture of them, because they look important.' Gradually, the techniques for garnering online attention are getting more sophisticated. A few years ago, the preferred style was really 'posey', Michaela recalls, 'now, they want it to be candid, as if nobody's there shooting the picture'.

In preparation for my shoot, I spend hours stalking influencers for inspo. My camera roll fills up with screenshots as I plan and replan my outfits, analyse the angles and props and cues that have become creator cliché. Influencing — and in particular, the lifestyle genre — has developed a visual vocabulary of its own: smooth, optimised, aspirational, likeable, legible for the platform and its algorithm. I trawl feed after feed to forensically dissect the formula — the oversized utility jackets, the streamlined lycra cycling shorts, the chunky trainers that anchor their wearer to the pavement — and the more I look, the more everything begins to look the same.

In 2019, *PAPER* Magazine — the outlet that 'broke the internet' with its Kim Kardashian cover a few years earlier — published a visual composite of 'the ideal influencer' based on images from Instagram's top 100 influencer accounts,[11] something Jia Tolentino later termed 'Instagram face', in an essay for *The New Yorker*: 'one of the oddest legacies of our rapidly expiring decade: the gradual emergence, among professionally beautiful women, of a single, cyborgian face. It's a young face, of course, with poreless skin and plump, high cheekbones. It has catlike eyes and long, cartoonish lashes; it has a small, neat nose and full, lush lips. It looks at you coyly but blankly, as if its owner has taken half a Klonopin and is considering asking you for a private-jet ride to Coachella.'[12]

This is the universal aesthetic of the 'Instagram baddie' as popularised by the Kardashian clan and imitated worldwide and online — a post-racial prettification of filler, filters, contour and Facetune that can render women from the East Coast and the Middle East virtually indistinguishable, airbrushing facial idiosyncrasies into a frictionless, ubiquitous existence.

Homogenous influencer aesthetics don't end at facial modulation: there are Instagram interiors (bright, light, neutral, minimal, deliberately placeless, and arranged with content capture in mind), YouTube vlogger backdrops (stage-managed, flickering candles and fairy lights designed to flatter faces and imply authentic intimacy), influencer fashion 'fits' (part streetwear, part sportswear, part Scandi-driven minimalism, and part luxury, comfortable enough for flexible routines and sleek enough for silhouettes on social media). TikTok's alternative is 'TikTok voice': an upbeat, dreamy, neutral transatlantic accent that's simultaneously therapeutic and lobotomised, narrated over montaged clips with the smooth parlance of a professional presenter, again and again and again.

What emerges from influencer culture is a generic global taste: consciously 'curated' yet somehow still homogenous, turning out an uncanny cohort of interchangeable robots ready to be copied by consumers or regrammed by brand pages.

It was this universal influencer image — the perfect product of its conditions — that I hoped to emulate. One £600 fast fashion haul and unquantifiable environmental guilt later, I had stocked up on my starter pack; an array of vacuum-packed items that arrived in baby pink packaging with an order slip that addressed me as 'babe'.

A few short days later, I was dragging a suitcase through the streets of Notting Hill on what was surely the hottest day of 2020. A mere four minutes from my front door and I was already drenched in sweat, pleather incubating my torso like a burrito in a microwave. Michaela had vetoed my suggestion of shooting on Bond Street on the grounds that stripping down behind Dior isn't exactly entry-level influencer activity, so we settle for a quiet backstreet in Zone 2 instead. The whitewashed buildings and stone-flagged streets of west London are practically an influencer amusement park; from the pastel houses of Portobello to the sandstone building backgrounds perfect for snapping outfit pics, there's something about the architecture of the neighbourhood that lends itself particularly well to Instagram composition: rhythmic Ionic columns, porticos perfect for perching, and an intangible aura of material aspiration.

Michaela leads me to a wide road lined by neoclassical porches and patrolled by yummy mummies pushing weapons-grade BMW strollers. Their eyerolls as I struggle with my suitcase warn me they've seen it all before: in 2019, Notting Hill residents complained to the *Evening Standard* about the invasion of influencers snapping pictures on their doorsteps.[13] We set up our makeshift mobile studio, suitcase abandoned on the pavement, water bottles, tripod, and trainers piled by the side of the road. By now, my body temperature is verging on thermonuclear; squinting into the sun, hair slick on the back of my neck. I warily eye the small gathering of builders smoking and watching us with curiosity from the street corner. If anyone lights up in my immediate vicinity, my polyester outfit will incinerate.

Cars roar past. A siren wails. A Deliveroo rider shoots across the road. I adjust my first outfit — a mock-croc top, cropped tank, and vinyl trousers — and begin to regret my decision to go all in. Though in my day job I attend photoshoots for brand campaigns, directing models and squinting into the monitor, this is my first time stepping out in front of the camera. Heavily layered yet somehow still uncomfortably exposed, I stand stiffly on the pavement, patiently awaiting Michaela's instruction. Without warning, she lifts her camera and begins to shoot.

'Ok — look back at me! Over your shoulder! Look up! Turn around! Now look down!' Michaela's manner is brusque and businesslike, camera rattling in her hand, ducking and weaving like my personal paparazzo. I attempt a half-hearted hand on hip. I try to smile. I pray we won't run into anyone I know. 'Why not lean against the wall?' she suggests enthusiastically. 'Why not get down on the ground?'

'What, you mean like, actually lying down in the road? In the gutter?'

'Sure, why not?'

Around 600 shots in, I begin to loosen up. Though I feel absurd in my Instagram ensemble — like I'm cosplaying a Kardashian — the more I lean in to this fantasy version of myself, the easier it becomes. The staccato rattle of the camera soon fades into the ambient soundscape of a sunny afternoon street in west London. Eventually, I get down onto the ground and stretch out on the tarmac under

Michaela's eager encouragement: 'Yes girl! This is it! This looks so good!' At some point, I begin to enjoy myself, until Michaela tells me she's forgotten the tent and I have to change outfits crouched between a wheelie bin and a parked van.

Our final location is the Most Instagrammable Spot in London, at least, according to *Time Out*, the city's online index of bottomless brunches and picture-perfect rooftops serving equal parts quirky cocktails and insta-envy: a cherry blossom tree on a Notting Hill street corner with boughs that heave in the summer months, influencers lining up to snap themselves underneath its branches with a wait of anywhere up to half an hour at peak season. Standing underneath, diffused light streaming through the petals, gives one a rosy glow akin to an Instagram filter.

By now I had fully coalesced into my assumed identity, emboldened by an afternoon of shooting. I urge Michaela to take another picture, then another; try a different angle, shoot from above and then below. Were my trousers better with the cuffs turned up? Did I need another necklace? Perhaps I should swap my shirt for something more off-shoulder?

We're cut short by the arrival of the owner of the house, who announces herself by reversing her Mini into my suitcase which is sitting in her parking spot. Unloading dog, daughter, and tennis racket, she shoots us a withering look and we decide that it's probably time to pack up. Michaela announces she's off to Bond Street; an influencer needs two new outfits for a brand collab snapped before the end of the day. Traipsing back to the Tube, we cross paths with several other influencers clearly doing the same thing as us: a group of boys in streetwear clutching a micro tripod, two girls wobbling past in heeled boots and Dior saddle bags. United by a common hobby, we eye each other and exchange a knowing smile. I am one of them now.

Back home, legs leaden and surrounded by a sea of polyester packets, I reflect on my afternoon. The unglamorous reality of sweatily lugging suitcases across London on the Tube and dodging CCTV cameras as I squatted behind a bin wasn't how the influencer lifestyle looked on screen. The whole production felt inefficient for what would ultimately be only a few days' worth of ephemeral posts.

For me, the shoot had been a one-off experiment, but Michaela's usual clients are out there on the street three times a week, churning out new looks, outfit edits, and hauls to satisfy their audiences and the algorithm.

Later that evening, Michaela emails me my contact sheets, a 72-page PDF containing tessellated images of our afternoon. Here I am shielding my face playfully from the lens, lifting my sunglasses upwards to speak to some invisible companion, shoulders lifted, back turned, gazing at the ground as if unobserved. Flattened by the uniform of the online, I barely recognise myself: the person in the pictures could be anyone. They could even be an influencer.

Studying the sheet in detail I realise that the most successful images are those that are the least posed. My attempts had only reinforced how hard I had to try — how many thousands of shots we had to take — just to nail the few where it looked like I wasn't trying at all.

When the time comes to post the photos to my Instagram, I suddenly feel shy. My influencer experiment had started out satirically, but the longer I continued, the more I wasn't sure. The gap between my objective assessment of and subjective participation in the spectacle of social media was collapsing with every upload. I wasn't clear where research ended and reality began, lingering in the liminal space between who I was and who I was pretending to be. But perhaps that made me more of an influencer than anything else.

It can be difficult to understand exactly when you've 'made it' as an influencer. It's not a title you're ever officially given, nor one that comes with concrete definition. One significant step is attracting the attention of an agent. In any creative industry, representation is a signifier of status and success, but with influencing — in which status is both occupation and goal in of itself — this rings particularly true. Though it's possible to carve out a career without help, few established influencers are without a team behind the scenes. Operating solo has its limits: try brokering brand partnerships on your own behalf or wrangling alone with the legal department of a major corporation. Traditional talent giants such as CAA or WME now represent top

YouTube stars alongside A-list actors. Other media behemoths are also getting in on the act: Rupert Murdoch's News UK opened their own affiliated influencer agency in 2019.

With only 600 followers, I was still a long way off requiring representation, but I didn't think it could hurt to discuss my future prospects with a professional. I emailed around a handful of London's top influencer agencies in the hopes that someone could help me understand what it would take to make it, and get a better grasp of what exactly goes on behind the scenes. To my surprise, an agent I admired granted me an interview, on the condition that she remain anonymous to protect her reputation. She's got a fierce one, plus a tight schedule and a stellar roster of six-figure stars including YouTube beauty gurus, mumfluencers, and *Love Island* graduates. I was excited to find out how she'd respond to my fledgling attempts at influence.

It wasn't destined to be the perfect pitch: having accidentally turned up at the wrong location, and zigzagged back across Hackney I am feeling extremely flustered — and not particularly on brand — when we eventually meet outside an artisan coffee roastery off the canal. Petite, tanned, and immaculately presented, with a tiny teacup puppy gripped under one arm, she bowls into the cafe past the waiting queue and greets the staff as old friends. We are instantly ushered to a table.

After we order, I clear my throat to pose my first question, but without prompting, she launches straight in, bringing her palm down flat onto the bleached wood table to make her point: 'Look. Every week I get ten to 12 DMs and emails saying, "I want to be an influencer." Most are very young, some as young as 12 or 13. Right now, everyone — and I mean everyone — wants to be an influencer.' She is accosted by teenage girls, unknown cold callers, husbands ringing on behalf of their wives, mums accompanying daughters, people with an 'all right following, actually', by which she means 250k. I gulp. 'What's your hook? What's your niche? What's going to make you stand out from every other fucker that's standing there in front of me?' I'm casting around for an adequate response, but before I can muster the words she's already moved on.

Whilst older generations of social media stars may be in it for the money, she confirms, the incoming wave is after one thing only: 'notoriety, notoriety, notoriety'. In the olden days before social media, back when she used to work in TV, the popular refrain was 'I want to be a presenter on the telly', now being an influencer is the new 'it' occupation. 'There are two defining questions that are constantly asked in popular culture. One: what does Kim Kardashian actually do? And two: how do I become an influencer?' I hope she is about to tell me the answer. But, of course, it's not that simple. 'An influencer is a brand. You can't just go, "I want a brand." You have to build the brand, staff the brand, give the brand a logo and the right colour spec, you've got to give the brand an office, you've got to pay tax on the brand. You can't just say, "I want to be an influencer." How bratty does that sound? How unprofessional?' This, it turns out, is where she comes in.

Sitting across from me, with her tiny puppy peeking from behind one arm, sipping a black Americano and skimming her iPhone with a glossy black manicure, the agent is cut from the same glossy cloth as her Instagram charges. Larger than life, she may sound like a caricature on paper, but IRL I immediately warm towards her wit and candour. She rhapsodises, rolls her eyes, throws shade at brands and other agencies, drops industry gossip with a sly smile and a sharp command: *'Don't write that down!'* Just when I think I've got a grip on the conversation, she cuts me off to change the topic, record a voicenote, or challenge me directly with an indeterminably rhetorical question. It's hard to keep up.

During our conversation she periodically shows me influencers she's 'obsessed' with, thrusting her phone across the table. Everyone on her roster is 'amazing'. Recent signings are 'my new favourite person in the whole world'. She may be effusive, but she's also blunt, as a husband who recently rang her up to ask if she could help grow his wife's following found out: '"My agency is not here to train people. That's not our job … [I told him] I don't care who you are. I don't care who your wife is." He hung up! You can put that in the fucking book, actually.'

If this seems a little callous, then that's characteristic: ruthless judgements and harsh decisions are part of the working end of the industry. Whilst a team works tirelessly to make the surface of influencer life seem fun, beneath runs a relentlessly demanding mercenary operation.

In a world awash with wannabes, how does she choose which influencers to take on? Of course, there are 'the numbers' — she'd never sign anyone without detailed analytics — but ultimately 'it's a vibe, there's no science to it'. Sometimes major brands will refer unrepresented influencers to her, others she already has her eye on and approaches directly. She tells me that she once signed a fashion influencer after she was influenced into buying a jumper she'd seen her wearing on her page: 'I thought — well, if she's persuaded me, there's got to be something there.'

The winning formula is an intangible elixir of attitude, work ethic, consistency, and creativity. It's a balance of past performance with future potential: 'I think to myself, what would a group of gaggling PR girls and gays want to see?' Once you're in, that's when the real work starts. Moving from amateur to agent status is 'a huge transition'. It begins by determining a strict 'circle' of on-brand interests, developing a 12-, 18-, and 36-month growth plan, and matching influencers up against her master document of thousands of brand contacts to reach out to for collaboration. She can then begin negotiating aggressively on their behalf: 'I say, okay. Double the money.' In return for this service, the agent demands total dedication. 'That's what I say to all my talent: if you want to do this job, you have to be obsessed with your job.'

Obsession looks like, amongst other things, commitment to a 24/7 news cycle: 'Every single influencer is their own TV channel. There can be no dead air, you've got to fill it with content. You'd never have *Emmerdale*, *Coronation Street*, then blank for two hours, then the news.' Unlike amateur influencing you can say goodbye to an offscreen social life and forget about phone-free family gatherings: 'When you're with your family and your friends, your phone is in your hand, creating content. There can be no exceptions. That's how you make money.' How much does she require them to upload each day, I wonder? She pauses briefly to consider. 'I'd be concerned if there wasn't something new up every couple of hours.'

The relationship between agent and influencer is also highly personal, you're 'mother, nanny, grandmother, sister, friend'. She rings all her clients at least once every single day, and understands their needs, desires, and fears intimately. It's not just about hyping them up, but also being honest, and knocking them back if they get too big for their boots. 'It's a collaboration, you are not the star of the show, the brand is — respect that or get out.' And, vitally, the agent is also the emotional support line, a capacity which is required 'every single day'. When discussing the pressure the industry puts on individuals, her sardonic mood turns sombre: 'I've seen the criticism, the envy-induced trolling. It's so horrendous, they all have nervous breakdowns. But I've also seen the upside of it, getting paid a huge amount of money for doing not very much at all.'

I tentatively venture that this all sounds pretty full on, and she agrees. 'Look, it's a tough world. When you become an influencer you are signing up to a life of entertaining your followers. You owe it to them. You've signed up to this job. People followed you, they can unfollow you. Plus, the negotiations behind the scenes are crazy.'

As if on cue, her phone rings and she picks up. 'Hey doll, are you okay?' It's an influencer I'd seen on my feed that morning, a mega beauty guru with millions of followers, who is heavily pregnant. The phone call, the agent mouths at me, is probably because she's going into labour right that second. It takes me a moment to fully absorb this, whilst she seamlessly launches into a rapid conversation, dissecting the details of a 'huge' brand partnership currently on the table: 'so I said, absolutely no deal, none at all ...'

I couldn't eavesdrop further if I tried; I'm stuck on the horrifying prospect of this mega-influencer simultaneously closing a brand deal and delivering her baby, all whilst on the phone to her agent during my interview. It doesn't seem to faze the agent at all. This, apparently, is everything you need to know about life as an influencer at the top: far from being free to do whatever you want whenever you want, your life is no longer your own — schedules are hectic, boundaries are fluid, nothing is off limits. You're a business, brand, and individual all at once; a star around which a satellite of employees, managers, agents, clients, collaborators, and followers continuously orbit. When the agent eventually puts the phone down, she smiles apologetically and simply says: 'There you go. The life of an influencer.'

I turn back to Abby Roberts again to confirm this. 'It's very overwhelming when it first happens, especially because a lot of TikTok famous people are young kids that have just been thrust into the spotlight,' she says when I ask her what it's like to 'make it'. 'That can be really difficult to deal with mentally, when you have that much pressure and that many eyes on you. I found it quite difficult to deal with.' Now that she's settled, she spends most of her days not doing the thing that made her famous. 'It's a lot of strategy, planning, the business side of things, sitting in meetings, planning things with management and PR and publicity.' She pauses. 'It's a never-ending schedule to be honest.'

It's only now, with 17m followers, she feels free to take a break from the relentless posting cycle. 'I feel like I've kind of got to the point now where my platform is big enough that I can go a day or two without uploading,' she tells me. 'Now and again, I'll take like one or two days off.' In 2019, in a *Sunday Times* interview, fellow top UK TikToker Holly H revealed that if she went a day without uploading, her followers began to worry she had died.[14] 'My followers understand and accept [me taking a break],' Abby tells me. 'There's been more of a discussion around mental health recently and how that can affect influencers.' She still sometimes struggles to switch off, and create boundaries between her job and life: 'If I'm working, I'm on social media. If I'm not working, I'm on social media.'

When I ask her how her life has changed since becoming social media famous, Abby pauses: 'I mean, in every possible way.' She began by shooting pictures in the fields around her family home — now she's working with A-list celebrities, hosting meet and greets, being flown to festivals, and releasing a merch line bearing her name that regularly sells out. She can't leave the house without pulling a crowd. 'I went out to do my Christmas shopping when lockdown restrictions were kind of eased,' she recalls. 'It was just mental on the high street … It was every shop that I went in, just constantly getting recognised … but because of COVID there's not a whole bunch of people even out to begin with. So I'm like, how crazy is it gonna be when everyone is actually let loose again?' She's currently preparing to move to LA, and looking to release a single. 'I'm kind of trying to diversify out of just being a social media influencer,' she says, before admitting she'll never leave completely: 'I'm always looking for the next social platform to move on to.'

When I do eventually go viral, it's not how I expect. Having spent months crafting captions and chopping up vlogs, it's a six-second video recorded off the cuff that blows up on TikTok. It takes me mere minutes to find the right filter, shoot, edit, and upload my variation on a trending meme, before I put my phone down and promptly forget all about it. A few hours later I pick it up to see a flurry of notifications. My stomach drops. Over 10,000 people have seen my video, and with every refresh the view count flickers upwards. Hours later the figures are still climbing, a steady stream of comments and followers latching on. Then, somewhere around the 24,000 mark, it stops. I paw at the screen, willing the view count up. Rather than feeling anxious about my video being shown to thousands of people, I find myself disappointed that it hasn't gone any further.

There is a different meme circulating on TikTok around the same time: a deadpan voiceover stating 'it was a cultural reset', played over screenshots of iconic pop culture moments — Paris Hilton's 'STOP BEING POOR' t-shirt, Dan Humphrey revealed as Gossip Girl, a viral clip purporting to be Jason Derulo falling down the steps at the Met Gala in 2015 — but this meme could just as well apply to the platform itself. Since beginning my influencer journey at YouTube training camp, the goalposts have shifted and the rules of influence have been reset. A new generation of stars has emerged, disrupting the ranks and rules of influence and undercutting all the painstaking efforts I have made. 'TikTok fame is just so much more intensive, so much more rapid, and to such a larger extent,' says Abby. 'It can literally happen overnight, which doesn't really happen on any other platforms.'

Thanks to TikTok, influencer metrics have been recalibrated, virality itself has been devalued. Nobody's quite certain what makes things go viral on TikTok, but everybody's sure that's the central goal. My 25,000 views barely scratch the surface: far from my dreams of influencer trips and brand freebies, I've managed no more, by the platform's own standards, than a marginally successful post. After all my hours of labour invested in the algorithm, it is vaguely irritating that something so flippant finally proved triumphant. I haven't become an influencer, but in the end I don't need to: my 15 seconds of fame have simply confirmed how slippery and elusive chasing social media clout is.

Influencing implies that anyone — everyone — can be a star. It's this potential and possibility that is central to the industry's appeal. Success often appears, at least from the outside, to be the product of pressing a few buttons on an iPhone. But having attempted to realise the influencer dream myself, I am left with just a handful more followers than when I started and an understanding of the sheer complexity and circumstance of making it; carefully calculated strategies and hours of optimisation balanced against the whims of an unknowable algorithm which makes the results of all these efforts unpredictable. What is becoming clear are the ever-increasing demands of the commercial machinery of influence, and the sheer effort required of those even at the top to stay there. Once you've made it as a professional creator, I was about to discover, the demands on the influencer only increase.

CHAPTER 4

HYPE HOUSES, #RELATIONSHIPGOALS, AND KIDFLUENCERS

WHAT IS IT LIKE TO LIVE ONLINE?

It's a sultry evening on an LA roof terrace, set against a peachy sky and fringed with palm trees. A group of six uniformly dressed teenagers with floppy hair and baggy sweatshirts stand in staggered formation like a 00s boy band, then begin to sway and pump in mesmerising synchronicity. The backing track — a remix of sleazy R&B lyrics that jars with their preppy cheerleading routine — begins to speed up and their dance steps accelerate until the frame becomes a blur of sharp jawlines and rhythmic limbs. Suddenly the beat drops and without warning, the group explode away from each other, laughing and knocking over the phone that had been propped up on the floor to film them. 18.2k likes.

We're outside a sprawling modernist apartment complex, all poured concrete, glass, and 80s ferns. A teenage boy with a half-shaved head, chain belt, and dangling earring is standing in front of an illuminated swimming pool, infinity waterfall looping smoothly behind him. As the music plays, he begins to shake, pop, and twist, jerking his limbs and rolling his hips. He's halfway through the dance, when — out of nowhere — a body clad in bright red swimming trunks crashes through a skylight and into the pool behind him, sending a shockwave of water over both the boy and the camera. Unperturbed, he flips backwards, fully clothed, into the pool, but the video cuts out before we see him hit the water. 53k followers.

In the ornate master bathroom of a sprawling Tudor estate somewhere in the English countryside, a large bathtub sits at the centre of the room, surrounded by fairy lights, whilst an anonymous figure dressed in black tie stands beside it, emptying a gallon of milk into the water. The camera advances towards the bath — it's filled to the brim with milk and strewn with rose petals. From its pearlescent depths emerges a young girl with flowing golden hair, wearing a cocktail dress and a spiked mesh balaclava that covers her entire head. A song by Labrinth — the soundtrack of cult teen TV series *Euphoria* — soars to a crescendo as she slowly removes the mask to reveal her identity, and winks to camera. 55.3m views.

Welcome to life in a TikTok hype house.

The scenes I have described — 15-second videos with a collective total of over 70m views — were all filmed on location at creator houses: large mansions inhabited by adolescent mega-influencers who live, work, work out, sleep, hook up, fall out, and make their fortunes together. The clips were all shot, edited, and uploaded for their many millions of fans on joint accounts that represent a digital extension of their living rooms.

Some TikToks show hype house inhabitants living out the teenage dream — throwing parties, playing beer pong, riding skateboards into the pool, spending money on elaborate pranks or eccentric stage sets — whilst others are more mundane: watching housemates brush their teeth, eat takeout, lounge around, or gesticulate into the front-facing camera.

Scrolling through the videos on my iPhone, I can understand their appeal. Hype houses are social media's answer to reality TV, a human game of Sims staffed by housemates with few concrete commitments and apparently bottomless wallets. Through addictive 15-second snapshots, it's all too easy to get sucked into their daily routines. I'm clearly not the only one: the eponymous @thehypehouse, the first TikTok content house from which the set-up gets its unofficial nickname, has over 20m followers — over four times the viewership of *Big Brother* at its peak. A Netflix show is in the works.

Hype houses have become the *des res* of the digital generation, frat houses for the internet's most popular content creators. They are renowned for making careers, breaking reputations, selling out products, and landing lucrative brand partnerships, as well as providing a bottomless source of gossip for millions of young followers, who are as familiar with housemates' rooms, routines, and relationship statuses as with their own. 'The only friend group anyone wants to be a part of,' reads one of the many thousands of enthusiastic comments under one video of a group of teenagers doing backflips in the cavernous hallway of a sunlit content house in Beverly Hills: 'CAN I GET AN INVITE!!!'

Fans are glued to the goings-on of hype houses and offer running commentary on their inhabitants as if they are a digital extension of their friendship group: 'Omg! Who else saw Dixie walking up the stairs in the background?', 'Wait, I thought you guys hung out already yesterday', or 'Get Noen to move in next.' Other viewers are bemused: 'Do these kids not have school?' asked one commentator under a video of a teenager sliding down the banister of a spiral staircase. 'Does anyone know where the parents are?'

When the original Hype House opened in the Hollywood Hills in December 2019, it made headlines in part because the Spanish-revival mansion became HQ to 20 of TikTok's largest stars, including Bryce Hall, Addison Rae, Charli D'Amelio, and Chase 'Lil Huddy' Hudson, fresh-faced teenagers sporting tie-dye tracksuits and hundreds of millions of followers who together formed a TikTok brat pack.

Soon a host of other copycats — with names that read like algorithmically generated Disney Channel spin-offs — began to pop up across LA: Sway House, Clubhouse, Alpha House, Honey House, The Drip Crib, Girls in the Valley, The Factory, and The Vault. In the following months the phenomenon was exported abroad: the UK is home to ByteHouse and Wave House, Spain has The Jet House, the GOAT ('greatest of all time') House is located in Dublin, a Clubhouse spin-off emerged in Russia, and another group came together in a villa in Mexico. So many TikTok hype houses sprung up in quick succession that they became quickly self-referential: Not a Content House and The House That Nobody Asked For.

Devion Young is the founder and head of The Drip Crib. He may only be 25 years old, but the LA native has nearly a decade of experience in what he refers to as the 'clout industry' already, and hundreds of thousands of followers to show for it. His CV reads like a directory of entertainment; from starting a marketing agency whilst still in high school to founding a boyband and convincing investors to lend him money to open a model apartment to support his growing nightlife promo business.

When he calls me, it's late; he's in Miami, he explains, where he's been busy launching a new house and finalising an upcoming reality TV show about his crew. His voice is warm and convivial, his sentences run together smoothly and celebrity namedrops slide out in seamless showbiz-speak. 'We've got 60 people under the brand now,' Devion enthuses. 'We just opened up a Drip Crib house in Europe. The day we, like, posted about it, it was already on, like, Italian tabloids and gossip sites and stuff. It's crazy.'

Devion founded Drip Crib after observing the success of the Hype House, and the subsequent criticism that its members were overwhelmingly white. He hand-picked housemates 'based on chemistry and vibes and stuff', as well as money-making potential, via a series of ads posted to his 150k followers on Instagram. They moved in straight away. Luxury rental company The Maimon Group listed the Drip Crib property — 3,961 square feet of lateral LA living, complete with hot tub, in-house salon, 100-bottle wine fridge, and bathrooms with chandeliers and golden toilets — at $18,900 per month.[1] Devion personally invested $100,000 in getting The Drip Crib up and running and is courting brands and record labels to ensure a steady stream of income.

The compound has a waterfall that pours down from a mezzanine into the outdoor pool beneath. This helped inspire the name, as well as the fact that, as Devion tells me, 'You know, we're drippy: we have a little bit more swag than everyone else.' In viral videos house members are filmed leaping into the pool from the balcony and often end up flagged with TikTok's safety disclaimer: 'The action in this video could result in serious injury.' Devion's long-term vision is to turn The Drip Crib into a 'Kris Jenner'-style 'fully fledged, 360-degree global entertainment brand', with TikTok houses, model apartments (co-living spaces for employees working in the modelling industry), influencer management, a nightlife promotion enterprise, and an ongoing reality series.

Though some hype houses are independently operated by the creators themselves, most are backed by marketing agencies, management companies, or brands who underwrite the rent and offer spots in exchange for contracted posts. In 2018, US competitive video game giant NRG Esports collaborated with Australian influencer management team Click to establish the Click House, a $15m mansion for Twitch streamers and gaming YouTubers in Sydney's Darling Point.[2] (Despite its stunning location, sunlit pool, and balcony overlooking Sydney Harbour, the housemates reportedly spent 14 hours a day inside, industriously streaming in near-total silence.) The UK's ByteHouse is the product of influencer agency Fanbytes, dropping off a weekly 'care package' full of essentials to its crew, who then spend their days making 15-second ads for card games or fast fashion brands.

'In a world where younger audiences are moving away from linear TV and moving online, more specifically to social, it's ever more important for programming to be created by Gen Z for Gen Z,' Fanbytes CEO, 24-year-old Timothy Armoo, told Tubefilter, with brands 'flocking to be part of the first-ever TikTok show'.[3] The agency I work for was among them. We sent the ByteHouse housemates hair dye for a sponsored series of vivid beauty transformation videos that clocked up hundreds of thousands of views on behalf of our client. Other brands cut out the middleman: Fenty Beauty launched the first branded hype house in March 2020, filling it with make-up TikTokers and a fully stocked 'beauty pantry' to generate content round the clock.

In order to keep the roof over their heads, Drip Crib housemates have to hit a post quota, laid out by Devion in a weekly all-house meeting: 'You have to post whatever I say, wherever I say, anywhere between three to five times a week to keep your place in the house,' Devion tells me. 'As long as you're hitting the deliverables, that's pretty much all I require. That deliverable is paid for by a brand and is paying the bills.' In addition to paid posts or brand partnerships, hype houses offer new opportunities for influencers to monetise their lives, by having brands underwrite every element of the set-up: 'There's a ton of product placement. Brands will pay us to wear their clothes or to have a particular couch in the house. Most of the furniture and stuff in the house is from a brand deal. Even the coffeemaker I have was a brand deal. With a house, there's so many different ways that we monetise.'

Hype houses aren't just effective marketing channels, they're also excellent influencer incubators, working collaboratively to boost individual internet fame. Before moving in, most Drip Crib members had merely tens of thousands of followers on TikTok. 'Everyone in the original lineup has over a million now,' Devion explains. 'The twins [Desmond and Dedrick Spence, often seen in matching Dior tracksuits] had like 10,000 combined and they have 4 million on TikTok now.' When The Wave House was first set up, a series of dramatic mask teaser videos — such as the one in the milk-filled bathtub — meant the account ballooned to 2m followers in just a week, before a single housemate had been announced. By bringing together several influencers into one small space and digitally aggregating their fame into a single house account, they centralise creators on an otherwise atomised and disparate social media platform. 'Think about it,' reads one comment under a video of the Hype House members sprawled together on a sofa that's been viewed over 24 million times, 'they all just met like a month ago and now they live together and are like best friends all of them.' 'It's called business ' corrects another.

Hype houses might seem like a novel phenomenon, but they represent a model for fame-making that has evolved over decades, from Hollywood's old-school studio system to the broadcast sets of *Big Brother* and reality TV hit *Love Island*, where contestants spend eight weeks incarcerated in 'The Villa', a neon-backlit party pad studded with hidden cameras and Superdrug-sponsored decals.

The claim to the first official 'content house' is hotly contested, but YouTubers began experimenting with shared channels as early as 2009. Around 2013, the appropriately named 1600 Vine Street, a 550-unit apartment complex in Hollywood, became a hotspot for Vine stars. Vine Street wasn't an officially organised operation, but as more and more creators began to move to LA, posting pictures and videos from the location, it quickly became a hub for both established and aspiring social media stars. Residents paid anywhere between $2,500 to $15,000 a month for a unit, but more importantly, for the opportunity to network with their neighbours. 'Videos shot there have been watched billions of times,' marvelled *The New York Times* in 2017, 'the common spaces — a spacious gym, walkways lined with beige blocks, and a courtyard surrounded by lush plants — are so recognisable that it's like walking onto the set of a popular TV show.'[4]

As YouTube began to make millionaires of its most popular creators, influencer houses became bigger, bolder, and more brash. Members of The Sidemen had been sharing a flat in London since around 2014, but the purchase of a palatial six-bedroom mansion for £6.8m two years later marked the arrival of a new era. The crew had amassed a modest fortune from brand partnerships, a line of hoodies bearing their logo, and YouTube AdSense revenue both from individual channels and their shared account, which was pulling in an estimated $12,500 per day.[5] Orpington, Zone 6 Greater London may not quite be the Hollywood hills, but the 15,000-square-foot house was appropriately opulent, boasting a sauna, gym, indoor swimming pool, and cinema.

The Sidemen Mansion, as it was quickly dubbed by their followers, became the subject of much speculation, complete with its own fan Wiki page where floor plans were pored over and screenshots dissected. *Had Simon and JJ swapped rooms? How many sports cars were hidden in the garage? What exactly did The Sidemen keep in their fridge?* The mansion opened viewers' eyes to quite how much their idols might be making, as well as offering a glamorous backdrop for a new type of video uploaded to The Sidemen's shared channel: dunking each other in the pool, setting up mini-golf in the landscaped gardens, playing the world's largest game of beer pong on the sweeping walnut staircase.

Though The Sidemen beat them to it, the creator house format — in its most notorious, chaotic configuration — would be established just a few months later by Team 10. Ex-Vine 1600 tenant Jake Paul rented an $18,000-a-month party pad in Calabasas to house the handpicked members of his new creator crew. 'We're all young people aspiring to do big things,' enthused a wild-eyed and baby-faced Paul, in the first video uploaded to the Team 10 channel (now defunct). 'I feel great. GREAT!' whilst other members echoed him, saying 'Team 10 is family,' and 'I love everyone here.'

But life in the Team 10 mansion came with strict house rules: members had to create consistent videos for their own channels as well as for the dedicated Team 10 accounts, and give a percentage of their income to Paul in exchange for resources and his connections. Over time, cracks began to appear in the façade; the pranks got out of hand, members began to drop out, and complaints about Jake surfaced on influencer gossip channels and in tell-all videos. Along with bullying came accusations of unfair payment systems, gruelling working conditions, and harassment between housemates. Eventually, the official Team 10 YouTube page went silent: none of its original members were still in rotation when the channel stopped posting in 2019.

Team 10's failure was largely attributed to Paul, but even without the presence of a bleach-blond megalomaniac as live-in landlord, content houses continue to fracture and fall out. Not every house ends in contentious collapse (the Sidemen's relocation was much more amicable: many of its members simply chose to move in with their girlfriends), but history appears to be repeating itself with TikTok. Members of the Hype House fell out over trademark rights soon after moving in,[6] and Los Angeles' mayor authorised the city to shut off power at Bryce Hall's home following a maskless pandemic rager The Sway House threw for his 21st birthday.[7] I had been planning to visit The Drip Crib in LA once air restrictions lifted, but it wouldn't be there by the time I arrived: less than a year after moving into the mansion, its members were being sued by the homeowner;[8] 18 neighbours had made noise complaints, and the landlord was due a backlog of rent.

But if creator houses are on the edge of permanent breakdown, that precarity is part of their appeal. The fights and drama serve their purpose in building intrigue about their occupants and fuelling engagement. 'Why I left the ___ house' videos — confession sessions from defeated teenagers spilling stories of exhaustion, bullying, and blurred boundaries to millions of viewers — are viral regulars on YouTube. When I ask Devion what makes places like The Drip Crib so addictive to young audiences, his initial answer is unconvincing to both of us. 'Um, because, you know, we're all young people, kind of doing the same thing, and, you know, trying to aspire to be the best thing we could be ...' he trails off. 'And also, there's a little bit of drama.'

Unprompted, Devion catalogues six months of altercations and disputes: 'I had an ex-manager leak my nudes, she embezzled over $200,000-worth of our brand deals, she pocketed three months of our rent ...' I begin an effusive extension of my deepest sympathies, but Devion quickly shrugs me off. 'But all of this is kind of how we got the TV show ... Everyone is watching my stories to see what happens next.' The 'messiness', as he describes it, is the magic formula. 'Stuff always happens,' he continues, in the detached manner of someone for whom events like these represent an average day in the office. 'There was a random fight that broke out in my kitchen, I got robbed, the neighbours called the SWAT team on us ... They came in with a helicopter, a dog, 15 police cars.' But even when the house was stormed, 'everyone's just ... filming TikToks with ring lights everywhere'. He bursts into laughter. 'Every two to three days my mom would be like, "Why are you on the ABC 10 pm news?"'

Online, influencer gossip accounts such as the popular @defnoodles have compiled long threads documenting the problematic behaviour at The Drip Crib. 'Drip Crib has completely destroyed the fully-furnished mansion. The hardwood floors are stained and dirty beyond repair. Furniture has extreme soil, including mattresses that are being slept on with no sheets. Kitchen cabinets and appliances damaged or destroyed,' reads one thread 25 tweets deep … 'Drip Crib is located on a quiet street with a cul-de-sac, and the flow of people and cars at all hours of the day and night has residents up in arms, with many expressing concerns of a devaluation of the neighborhood and damage to adjoining property.'[9]

In The Drip Crib's official trailer, uploaded to their YouTube channel, inhabitants are seen brawling at a maskless party, tattooing each other's buttocks in the bathrooms, and throwing furniture through the skylight into the pool. 'We hate you guys!' screams an irate woman filmed through the open window of a car, assumed to be a neighbour. 'We hate you!' The video hastily shuts off. 'James Charles and Logan Paul were the cool neighbours,' shrugs Devion, 'we had a whole bunch of Karens on the other side of us.'[10]

Pranks and pandemic parties aside, I can't shake the feeling that there's something unstable about the concept of a content house at its core. They are as impermanent as the influencer system itself: houses spring up, splinter, and swap housemates and management as they circulate through TikTok's fame and gossip network. Members can be dropped or poached by other houses in correlation with their online popularity. It's difficult to separate manufactured drama from authentic emotional fallout. 'Everyone grows up and grows apart and kind of just does their own thing and uses the houses as a stepping-stone to get to the next step,' Devion explains. 'Even me, I definitely felt like I was used a few times by a few people. That's just what happens when you're in these scenarios.'

Hype houses dramatise influencer precarity by directly linking the roof over their heads to their media metrics. Exact accommodation agreements vary, but most content house occupants grant management companies a percentage of their revenue in lieu of a fixed-value tenancy agreement, and an industry contact confirmed to me that performance clauses are the norm for inhabitants. Members of the UK's Wave House, operated by management company Yoke Network, claimed they were unwittingly evicted partly for this reason. 'Our management basically pulled us into the office and was just like, listen, you're moving out of the house and you have ten days to move out,' said 23-year-old TikToker Eloise Fouladgar in a 20-minute explanation video that's been viewed over 200,000 times. 'We think that we can bring something bigger and better to the table, so pack up, you're leaving. We were like — what? Are you serious?'[11]

The crew's viral announcement TikToks — it was Eloise in the spiked mask and the bath of milk that had originally garnered the Wave House account those 55m views — was proving an impossible standard to live up to: 'Those numbers you're never gonna reach ever again,' she said, hands circulating, words tumbling out in a cathartic rush: 'We started all putting loads and loads and loads of pressure on ourselves to just like do better, get more views, show people what we're all about. We just all got lost.'

Once out of Wave, she was left with an uncertain future, simultaneously unclear of where she might be living or working: 'I don't know what's happening. They could be getting new members in, the house could be changing, there could be no house — I have no idea. I don't know if I'm involved ...' She looks despairing. 'I don't even know what to do with the flat [her current rented accommodation] anymore at this stage, like, what do I do?'

Although many management companies take pains to ensure codes of conduct are adhered to and healthy working boundaries are in place — Eloise noted that Yoke's concern for the mental health of the influencers in their care had contributed to their decision to terminate their stay — it's impossible to ignore the power dynamics at play within the influencer house system as a whole. The inhabitants of most hype houses are young enough that they would still usually be living with parents, or else renting accommodation with friends and taking their first steps towards independence. Instead, they live and work round the clock with colleagues in an arrangement that might look like a nonstop sleepover party from the outside, but which comes with demanding expectations once you're through the door.

Hype houses work hard to project the image of a fun, carefree co-working-co-living space, but the model is vulnerable to exploitation. By collapsing home and workspace and linking performance metrics to basic human provision, they represent a living model of neoliberal competition. Creator houses are sometimes jokingly compared to a modern-day digital commune where members collaborate on shared content production; but they are more like a hollowed out, ultra-capitalist reimagining of a commune, forcing housemates to compete with each other for a place to stay and undermining the solidarity that might stem from cohabitation.

Hype houses may not be a new concept, but it's telling that the trend really took off in 2020, against a backdrop of widespread lockdowns, strained living arrangements, and a global requirement to stay at home. Hype houses offered a self-contained universe that mirrored our own; its occupants were a reconfigured family unit, the same faces in a shared space finding new ways to amuse themselves. But the explosive growth of hype houses represents more than just a neat piece of cultural synchronicity: they offer proof-of-concept for a hybrid future lifestyle of absolute permeability between the workplace and the home.

The pandemic eroded the boundaries in our lives on a massive scale: conference calls conducted from the kitchen table, sporadic working hours, flexible schedules for parents and carers, viral Zoom toilet gaffes. 'Working from home', we quickly realised, was more like 'living in the office'. As articles and academic studies began to flag the worrying implications of this invasion of our domestic space — an increase in working hours of up to 40 per cent,[12] the rollout of invasive new surveillance software, the pressure for workers to be always online — for influencers, that future was already here: teens in hype houses were, in TikTok vocabulary, 'the blueprint'. With no boundary between work and life, and content creation taking place at all times, with no off-switch, hype houses are the purest expression of bringing your work home with you.

'It was very intense …' recalls Eloise in her exit video. Living in a hype house is being permanently 'on': in the back of TikTok videos with millions of views, you can often see housemates passing with plates of food or laundry baskets. A popular genre of hype house TikTok is taking housemates by surprise: bursting in on them on the toilet, in bed, or whenever they least expect it and look most aghast by the unexpected intrusion of a camera. 'I got to the stage where I was so much in that house, if I had to go out into a public scene I'd panic …' says Eloise: 'It was like *Big Brother* … Towards the last two weeks we all crumbled.' The pressure of constant, round-the-clock performance was corrosive: 'I feel like it was like an act, a scene in a play or something like that,' she explains, eyes wide. 'When you're doing something over and over again that's not you it starts to affect you — and it was affecting absolutely everyone … We weren't the same people that went in there.'

Not every influencer lives in a hype house, but they represent the influencer lifestyle taken to its logical conclusion, the complete collapse of occupation and identity. Many of the issues raised by the hype-house model are an amplified version of those within wider creator culture: an invisible tension between labour and leisure, home and work, private and public; feeling pressure to be always on, blurring boundaries, burning out.

Having watched enough influencers at work and even experimented with becoming one myself, I'm starting to understand what it might be like to view existence as a series of monetisable content opportunities. The influencer lifestyle is a carousel of 'routines', 'challenges', 'tags' and 'tours', serialised in a non-stop documentary of the self. Via social media I have been present at births, adoptions, marriages, divorces, deaths, proposals, holidays, and heartbreak. On YouTube, 'study with me' videos get hundreds of thousands of hits. On Twitch, viewers tune in to 'sleep with me' videos, in which creators drift off on livestream for eight-hour stretches. Perhaps as a result of the demands of this increasingly intrusive lifestyle, influencing is cyclical, with generations of creators burning out and dropping off to be replaced with fresher talent, faster platforms and ever more intimate access. When you're an influencer, is anything ever really off limits?

The term 'Instagram husband' was a slur at first, popularised in 2015 by a viral sketch featuring henpecked husbands lamenting their roles as human selfie sticks: 'Behind every cute girl on Instagram is a guy like me,' complains a forlorn-looking hipster trailing his perky girlfriend. 'My job in pictures is to make her look good.'[13] Five years later, with influence a more developed industry, the relationship between a social media star and their partner has moved on from the reluctant operation of an iPhone. 'Influencer husbands' aren't just romantic companions: they play an active role in their beloved's personal brand.

'Dani is the CEO of the Dani Austin brand,' Jordan Ramirez, husband of Texas-based lifestyle influencer Dani Austin (1.2m followers on Instagram, 800k fans on TikTok), tells me over Skype. You may recognise Dani from the viral 'Christian girl autumn' meme: a wholesome clique of pumpkin spiced latte-fuelled, bible-verse-in-bio influencers sporting identical chunky knits and ombre waves. Dani's posts are all honey-toned interiors and layered outfits — a sleek and seasonally appropriate catalogue of all-American aspiration, complete with swipe-up shopping links. Invisible on the other side of these images is Jordan. He says: 'I'm like her COO: involved in more of the operations and handling a lot of the heavy lifting in the areas she doesn't have the time for.' This encompasses the shooting, production, organising, strategising, accounting, and administration that sustain the Austin universe.

The influencer-husband relationship — a concept that applies to partners of any gender, to creators across any social media platform, Jordan informs me — can be complex, navigating territory between colleague and confidant, lover and line manager; an office romance updated for the online age. In addition to being repositioned as an employee, influencer husbands must be prepared to welcome other workers into their relationship: seven employees have since joined Jordan on 'team Dani'.

Roles and responsibilities are not clear cut. As Jordan puts it on the phone to me, there's 'no line in the sand ... Decisions are typically made together, but at the end of the day, because the brand has her name on it there's a certain level of veto power I have to let her have.' CEO and COO aren't official titles at Austin HQ, it turns out. Nor are formalised boundaries or working hours common practice amongst influencer couples. 'I haven't heard of anyone who has a job title,' he says. The way they prefer to work is fluid and flexible. True to form, throughout our conversation 'Dani' — the brand, business, and person — are referred to interchangeably.

In 2018, Jordan established *The Influencer Husband* podcast to 'own the term, and redefine it in a less derogatory way' and support the submerged, but thriving community of Instafamous other halves he found himself amongst. The episodes, a mixture of anecdotes from his own life, interviews, Q&As, and discussions of life on the other side of the screen, frequently feature other influencer husbands presented as appendages to their partners' social media handles: '@juliahengel: Thomas Berolzheimer' or '@sassyredlipstick: Robbie Tripp'. In one episode, Jordan shares what he refers to as his 'testimony', recalling his transition from civilian life to social media.

He first met Dani back in 2015, before influencing was the booming industry it is today. Her YouTube career was getting off the ground, whilst Jordan had already forged a successful path in tech: 'I was CMO for a tech company in Austin, I had already gone through an acquisition with another app company, I was in my early twenties and I was kind of convinced I was the next Zuckerberg,' he admits to his listeners with a laugh. Two years later, Dani's social profile was taking off. At college, she barely had room in her tiny flat to unbox a gifted Casper mattress — now she was being flown around the world by brands. With over 150,000 fans 'she realised she wasn't creating content from her bedroom any more', Jordan recalls on the podcast, 'she was running a business'.

Both on 'incredibly demanding individual career paths', Dani and Jordan were working overtime shooting pictures and doing admin for her account, staying up until midnight to sift through emails and negotiate brand deals. They were also now engaged and planning their wedding. Influencing was beginning to consume their lives and causing 'burnout, stress, anxiety'. The couple asked themselves: 'Is this really a sustainable lifestyle or even a sustainable marriage?'

Jordan describes this moment — the assimilation of his independent career and identity into Brand Dani — as an 'inevitable fork in the road' that all influencer partners face. Anyone in proximity to a social media star will, eventually, get pulled into their algorithmic orbit, because influencer husbands are 'married to an influencer, but also married to the lifestyle of an influencer', he explains on the podcast. 'Most of the husbands I know in this industry are intricately involved in the business side', he elaborates to me. 'There's not a whole lot of influencers that I know who don't have their [partners] working with them full time.'

Jordan is clear that his decision to go full time came after careful calculation — and a thorough cost-benefit analysis — but the way he frames it on the podcast feels more like ex-post-facto rationalisation: 'This is the general gist of how [partners] realise they are Influencer Husbands ... their wives are doing something that they love and that has become a significant portion of the family makeup: time, energy, effort, cashflow.'

Jordan recounts his transition to influencer husband as not just a change of career or lifestyle, but a fundamental shift in his identity. 'There were a lot of things I had to adjust to', he tells me. 'I felt ashamed at first, I felt I was "lesser than", because I decided to do this.' At parties and social gatherings, he felt judgement from parents' friends and acquaintances: 'There are pressures that I feel as a man to be the breadwinner ... I had to navigate those and be like, this is a much larger conversation around gender roles in society.' He's grown into the role and found fulfilment. 'I had my own career before this, I had my own goals, my own ambitions, that was what I was working towards. I'm still doing that, it just looks different.'

Jordan is clearly both devoted to his wife, who he frequently refers to as a 'genius', and adept at what he does, as together, the pair have created an extremely popular and lucrative lifestyle brand. On Instagram, their posts radiate picture-perfect satisfaction: 'I am proud of Dani, I don't desire the spotlight in the same way that I wanted it in the beginning. Women for centuries have been held down by this glass ceiling, if my wife can be a part of breaking that, I'm not going to sit there and fight it.'

Having been drawn into the internal operations of influence, many partners take a more visible role within the brand. Jordan believes the optimal versions of Instagram husbands are what he calls 'characters' on their partners' channels in their own right. On 19 August 2019, Dani posted a formal introduction on her Instagram page; a pastel snap of her and Jordan kissing against a rustic shuttered villa.[14] They're leaning into each other across an upright bicycle; his checked shirt and gleaming sneakers neatly complement her summer dress and espadrilles. It's a perfect metaphor for their partnership. 'Hey everyone … This is Jordan … My husband … 😊' her caption read. 'Online he's a little more elusive but everyday he's the rock right by my side … 💪 Jordan may not be in the spotlight as much but every once in awhile I like to dedicate something to him on here because he's the one that makes my platform possible in so many ways. 📸 Shoutout to all the #instagramhusbands out there who are able to juggle the dynamics of being an insta husband and a loving husband everyday.'

Since that post, there's been a sharp uptick in Jordan's appearances on her feed. He's dancing in the back of a TikTok video. He's smiling next to her in an ad for Kroger's cookie dough. He hops on Instagram Stories to film Dani when she thinks he isn't looking, or narrate her try-on hauls with sardonic commentary. He's a natural and I find his presence very entertaining, so what he tells me next comes as a surprise. 'I hated being on camera all the time, and I still hate it to this day. I get so shy. It was a really hard transition for me to make.' Despite his personal misgivings, he perseveres for its benefit to the Dani Austin brand: 'The value of it is that it creates a deeper level of transparency, and a whole new perspective.' If she can't talk about her husband, 'Dani's not telling one side of her life … The content can be so much more valuable.' He also points out that greater honesty about the running of the account avoids unrealistic expectations: 'We have tried to do a good job about being transparent about the fact that we're not doing it all on our own. Part of me launching that podcast was to be like hey, there's a lot of things going on behind the scenes.'

Though Jordan has no desire to become an influencer in his own right, many partners who were previously behind the scenes end up that way. LA beauty guru Katy DeGroot's 2 million followers knew of her husband Jon from chatty YouTube GRWMs ('get ready with me's) and tagged Instagram Stories. Jon was initially a hidden collaborator, editing and lighting Katy's videos, but later he cast aside his anonymity, starting a YouTube channel and hanging out with other influencer husbands. Now, Jon has 185k followers on Instagram and a merch line of his own. Ironically, the demands of being an influencer husband meant Jordan was forced to abandon his eponymous podcast. 'There's no time to do both! It was a very ambitious and lofty goal: I'll be the Influencer Husband and you be Dani Austin. We would need ten more people to be able to keep up!'

The flattening of independent identity into an influencer's personal brand presents additional issues when influencer couples choose to part. When beauty influencer Jaclyn Hill announced her divorce from her husband Jon in 2018 after months of subscriber speculation, the couple did so with a synchronous Instagram post: Jaclyn apologised to her followers for the divorce, explaining she felt she'd left them down, and in a later video partially attributed the breakup to the nature of a social media partnership and the pressure of #relationshipgoals. Forget the emotional fallout of a split; as an influencer, you've got the added impact of its damage to your personal brand. 'Jaclyn Hill' wasn't just a person but a brand stamped across millions of eyeshadow palettes — her beauty company later dropped her ex-husband's name to become 'Jaclyn Cosmetics'.

There are issues that extend beyond having to make the announcement and purge an ex from your content, as fashion influencer Peony Lim, who herself once had a 'boyfriend slash agent slash manager slash photographer type' recalls. 'If they've taken pictures, do they have any rights? Do you have a contract in place? All that messiness that people don't really realise.'

This complexity is compounded if you're both influencers in your own right. In 2020, 24-year-old rapper and YouTube personality RiceGum, aka Bryan Quang Le, who had broken up with TikTok star, Clubhouse resident, and Fashion Nova model Abby Rao, tweeted: 'Yo my ex signed a contract before we dated. I own like a % of her. I haven't collected on the money tho but should I? Hmmmm 🙂.' It got 52k likes. The complications of their social media split surpassed shady subtweets and allusive Instagram Stories. On a Twitch livestream, Bryan explained that the contract Abby had signed whilst they were dating pledged him 10 per cent of her future earnings in exchange for the social media boost that being in a relationship with a YouTuber with 10m subscribers would bring. As proof, he posted the contract to his 3.8m followers on Instagram. Le's devoted fans created a hashtag: #RiceMadeAbby. The case never made it to court: just a few months later, they were back together in a selfie on her Instagram story.

If influencers become a power couple, their lives — as well as brand deals, fanbase, and digital engagement — become interlinked. Splits quickly traverse new breakup territory, as they seek to untangle their brands and lay claim to their franchises. The end of a relationship means more than just awkwardly updated Facebook statuses and untagged Instagram posts: newly single influencers are forced to ask, *'Do I demonetise those old videos?'* and *'What about the joint brand deals?'*

Happily, this isn't a problem facing Jordan and Dani. When I come back to their Instagram account, I discover they've just participated in the ultimate form of content creation: giving birth. 'Say hello to Stella James Ramirez,' reads the caption to a black-and-white #birthannouncement post cropped close: Dani in a hospital gown with a tiny bundled baby clasped gently between her arms, and Jordan leaning over her, gazing down at them both in awe. I swipe right to discover they've posted a series of videos documenting the intimate details of her delivery: a spaced-out Dani propped up in a hospital bed declaring to the camera that it's 5.40 am and she's 10cm dilated ('we're about to start pushing ... I'm so sore'), and a series of ultra-close-up videos of newborn Stella herself, eyes closed and softly snuffling as she sleeps against her mother's chest, blissfully unaware of the 333,124 people who have 'liked' her arrival into the world.[15]

As the daughter of a prominent lifestyle influencer, baby Stella can expect a six-figure fanbase before she learns to count to ten. She's one of a generation of influencer children who will grow up under the watchful eye of the algorithm. Family-related content is an influencer 'supersector' along with fashion, beauty, food, and fitness, representing roughly 11 per cent of all creator activity within the UK, according to PR tech company Vuelio.[16] The genre generally takes three forms: parenting influencers, family channels, and kidfluencers.

Parenting influencers — 'mumfluencers' and 'dadfluencers' — post from an adult perspective, for an audience of other parents, sharing proud pictures of their offspring, amusing anecdotes, parenting tips and tricks, and relatable moments from family life, mishaps often bearing the hashtag #momlife or #slummymummy. Insight agency Intellifluence claims there are around 4.4 million mumfluencers online and 18.3 million mums who consume their content every week,[17] in line with a wider cultural surge in 'sharenting'. According to the Pew Research Center, 82 per cent of parents who use social media in 2020 say they have posted photos, videos, or other information about their children online.[18] Many parenting influencers, such as legendary 'parents of the internet' @louisepentland / Sprinkle of Glitter (2.4m) or @father_of_daughters (936k) established themselves within the parenting niche — others, like Dani, shift into it from other categories when they decide it's time to start a family.

Family channels are a primarily YouTube phenomenon, in which sprawling, often American, clans create videos together as a kind of all-ages entertainment. Children vlog holidays and days out, parents invite viewers in on life milestones, and families engage in a host of challenges and pranks, cooking and craft tutorials, family singalongs, toy unboxings, dress-up role-plays, tags, and games together. Family channels are an extremely lucrative enterprise: the most successful channels — The ACE Family (19m subscribers), The LaBrant Family (12.7m), and The Bee Family (9.15m) — have become digital media dynasties to rival the Murdochs or Kardashians, whilst a host of younger families, such as viral father-daughter podcast duo, single dad Zeth and two-year-old Saylor from San Diego, are coming up through TikTok.

Though family-related influencing often focuses on the mundanities of domestic life — school runs, errands, play time, routines, homework — audiences are also invited inside the home to share in special occasions and the most intimate milestones: first tooth, first day at school, first fight, first period, first boyfriend/girlfriend, family holidays and celebrations. Followers stay with families as they mature, watching as children are born, grow up, graduate, start jobs and families of their own, or tragically — as in the case of The Bratayley Family in 2015 or Cam&Fam in 2020 — as members pass away.

Then, there are kidfluencers: children who are social media stars in their own right — although accounts must be officially operated by their parents in accordance with social media platform's terms and conditions. It's a lucrative way to spend your childhood. Top kidfluencers include brothers Vlad and Nikita, aged six and four, whose shared YouTube channel has brought in an estimated $64 million,[19] and three-year-old style icons Taytum and Oakley Fisher who have 3.1m fans on Instagram, a rotating wardrobe of matching mini-me outfits, and their own custom fast fashion discount codes ('TWINS15'). Twelve-year-old 'gaming prodigy' H1ghSky1 (known to his parents as Patrick) dropped out of school to become the youngest ever member of gaming collective FaZe Clan, but this success proved fleeting as his Twitch channel was deactivated a few months later when the platform discovered he was underage. Five-year-old RowdyRogan claims to be the 'world's youngest sponsored gamer', streaming violent 18+ first-person shooter video game Call of Duty under the supervision of his dad.

Influence can be passed on through family connections and inherited by younger generations, with influencers' offspring well positioned to become kidfluencers thanks to their parents' platforms. Successive children provide endless opportunities for fresh and original content, ensuring future streams of revenue. 'Micro-microcelebrities are literally grown (in the womb) and groomed (in the home) to inherit their Influencer mothers' social capital,' notes Dr Crystal Abidin, anthropologist and ethnographer of internet cultures, in a study of family channels: 'Their young lifestyles as depicted on digital estates become vessels that are deliberately curated to maximise advertorial potential.'[20] Content creation has become the ultimate family business, with new relatives and generations opening up content streams and keeping audiences entertained.

Mia Jeal, who recently seems to have deleted her online accounts, first started uploading videos to YouTube when she was 14. It was British vlogging's golden age, when Team Gleam — a cabal of bubbly Brighton-based faces including Zoella, Alfie Deyes, Marcus Butler, and Joe Sugg — ruled the YouTube recommendations algorithm. Posting twice a week, Mia gained a small following of around 8k subscribers with lo-fi make-up tutorials, room tours, challenges, and self-piercing horror story vlogs that document the average interests of many teenagers. Then, at 16, Mia found out she was pregnant. 'One of the first things I did was go to YouTube and put in "teen mum vlog", she tells me on the phone. She quickly stumbled upon the flourishing family channel genre. It was full of helpful advice, but there were few UK channels in her situation. 'At first I was like, I don't know if I want to continue with YouTube,' she remembers. 'It's not exactly great, 16 and pregnant — people can be judgy.' She later reconsidered. 'I looked at all these mumfluencers out there, and I thought, I want to be what they are to me. I want to help someone like they're helping me.' She realised her situation could be useful. 'I said to my mum: *I really want to vlog my experience.*'

Mia posted an announcement video ('I am 16 and Pregnant! | 12 week Bumpdate!'), and her channel blew up. Her subscribers tripled in a week, each video now racking up hundreds of thousands of views. Over the coming months, Mia continued to vlog her pregnancy: weekly bump updates, clothing hauls, pram unboxing videos, a gender reveal. 'I started earning money and realised that this was exactly what I wanted to do with my life.' By the time she reached full term, she had grown both a baby and over 70k subscribers. Mia had become a mumfluencer.

Like many parenting influencers, Mia decided to vlog her birth, an experience she describes on reflection as 'a little bit weird'. 'I went into hospital holding a camera in front of me, and they were like, what is going on?!' The doctors were taken aback, but once the midwives found out she was a YouTuber they were supportive. 'It was awkward at first, but once they knew I had a channel, they were very respectful of it. I was really worried about them not letting me film.' The resulting video, 'TEEN MUM EMERGENCY C-SECTION

BIRTH VLOG!', had over 200,000 views.

'Hi guys, welcome back to my channel,' a bleary-eyed Mia says to camera in the classic YouTube opening style, before explaining why she's not wearing make-up: 'today I'm going to be recording my birth … they're going to be putting the pessary in at three o'clock', before cutting to a close-up of her bump, covered in tapes and wires in a hospital bed, and her spaced-out face as she updates us on her dilation, contractions and and heart rate. 'I didn't get as much content as I wanted to,' Mia admits to me me over the phone, but I find it difficult to understand what more she could have shared. The exact moment of her delivery is captured on camera in high definition, before cutting to a tiny glistening newborn being wiped down by a nurse. I feel weirdly voyeuristic, peering into such an intimate moment: new life instantly evolving into consumable content.

Within seconds the procedure has taken a swift turn: 'My mum happened to be recording when she stopped breathing …' flashes up a caption, as a motionless Mabel is seen up close, still, and struggling to draw breath. For one awful moment, it is unclear if the video is about to take a tragic turn, but a swift montage — and five days — later, following several transfusions and a brush with sepsis, to my relief both mother and baby are home safe. Mia's painful, messy, stressful experience of delivery has been flattened into the climax of a video that, at 10.43, is bang on YouTube's suggested length for algorithm optimisation. 'That was an emotional rollercoaster!' says one commenter. 'And now I'm crying,' says another.

The online parenting community is celebrated as a tool of empowerment, education, and democratisation. 'Having kids is incredible but does drop a lot of your social life,' micro-mumfluencer Hanna, aka The Savvy Mummy and mother to Savannah and Juno, tells me over email. The parenting community on social media 'provides me with my own little outlet. It really helped me through having a newborn as there was always someone online to talk to or give advice.' Though much family material aims to guide viewers towards leading a better, healthier, and happier family life, value is also found in offering the opposite — a space to celebrate the accidents, amusements, and mishaps of domestic life that dismantle expectations set by polished depictions of parenthood in other media. 'I loved sharing our little moments together and helping other parents see it's not all perfect,' Hanna continues, 'but you can have some magical moments amongst it all.'

The bonds that form between influencers and their audiences are strong enough to carry across from online to real life. Through YouTube, Mia is now connected with other teen mums across the globe, many of whom she plans to visit: 'Lots of the people I used to watch and fangirl, I'm now friends with.' Throughout our conversation, she refers to members of family channels Okbaby (1.53m) and Cam&Fam (1.6m) as if they are relatives.

The financial benefits of influencing can also enable parents to create a better life for their families and build a safety net for their children. It's 'hugely profitable if you're willing', says Peony Lim, who had to reassess her strategy when she gave birth to her baby girl. 'The people who have shared huge amounts of family life online have been able to financially elevate their family through it in a dramatic way, in a manner not possible in any other career choice.'

'I'm a single teen mum … If it weren't for YouTube I wouldn't have been able to get my car, my house, new shoes for Mabel,' agrees Mia. 'Without YouTube, I would have really struggled.' Mumfluencers collapse the traditional polarity between 'working mums' who (according to the stereotype) prioritise their careers over caregiving, and 'stay-at-home mums' who are committed to a state of perpetual domesticity. 'My children get to have a lovely time with me,' whilst at work, says Hanna, 'and I can be a "stay-at-home" whilst doing so.' Mia agrees: 'I get to make a job from doing my job as a mum. It's so rewarding.'

Family influencing may be emancipatory for its instigators, but simultaneously problematic for its underage participants, the kids who often don't — and can't — consent to being shared. Pew Research found that 83 per cent of parents who share photos, videos, and information about their children on social media say they rarely or never worry that in the future their kids might be upset about the things they posted,[21] however, a 2016 sociological study of US family technology rules and behaviours concluded that children overwhelmingly 'find this content embarrassing and feel frustrated that parents publicly contribute to their online presence without permission'.[22]

Though Mia is comfortable sharing intimate information about herself (her latest vlog is the enticingly titled 'The WORST PERIOD EVER!! | I was in SO much PAIN!'), she has much stricter boundaries for her daughter, and is vigilant about adhering to them. 'I keep a lot of Mabel's milestones private. I don't want to make those choices for her. When she's old enough, and if she wants to share, then fine.'

'I have rules,' agrees Gail, known online as MumForce, a parenting and lifestyle blogger with two children based in Edinburgh: 'no locations, school uniforms, no nudity, and even no pictures in swimwear. I always ask them if I can take their picture and don't fight them if they say no. As my daughter gets older she appears less, she doesn't want to be on my page and I respect that.' Mia notes it's sometimes pressure stemming from followers, not parenting influencers themselves, to share more of their children: 'People ask me to make an Instagram for her, but it's not safe for her to be on that at this age; that's her choice, for the future.'

Mumfluencers and family channels are trapped in a content catch-22: the transparency that followers long for is also the same transparency they're quick to criticise. Viewers demand information about family life — 'I have to explain and justify everything,' says Mia — but condemn influencers for oversharing when they provide it. If they don't provide it, viewers often dig for it anyway. Posting your child comes with problems, Peony admits, but so does leaving them out: 'Having a child is a huge life-changing thing. To pretend that it's not is really alienating for your audience and yourself. To hide it is just not doable, it's not authentic.' Plus, 'If you share nothing, you're building up this idea that then becomes more tantalising than the reality,' she continues. 'You're creating the elephant in the room. If you share a little bit, and share occasionally, that keeps the wolves from the door. It's a very fine line between reality and curation, to keep that myth of authenticity.'

The result is a compromise: along with her husband, Peony made the decision to share pictures of her daughter, but never to reveal her face or name. This results in Instagram Reels where Peony is pushing her pram along the street in London, demonstrating its features whilst concealing its occupant. Having communicated these boundaries clearly, her audience respect them, occasionally DM-ing her to point out where she's accidentally slipped up and shared too much so she can correct her mistake. I'm surprised — this sense of mutual responsibility runs counter to the narrative of overenthusiastic sharenting and dogged followers that surrounds family influencing.

'There's a certain stereotype of a family channel,' Mia agrees. 'They're doing all this for clout, they use their kids for money, and clearly you can also see that a lot of channels *do* do that. Some are really weird about their kids — one started their period and they made an entire video about it … others, when their kids are hurt, record it.' Australian family The Norris Nuts (5.2m) have hundreds of videos entitled things like 'FAMILY INTERVENTION *emotional*' (4.3m views) 'BIGGY GETS TRAUMATIZED ON CHRISTMAS *gone wrong*' (5m views), and 'OUR FIRST FUNERAL *extremely emotional* saying goodbye together as a family' (13m views) in which their six children, Sockie, Sabre, Biggy, Disco, and Naz sob openly and clickbait thumbnails show them screwed up in agony and red in the face. Comments have been disabled across their entire channel. On YouTube, I've watched uncomfortable-looking teenagers filmed struggling with acne or learning how to shave their legs (both moments #sponsored), tearful toddlers throwing tantrums on livestream, and the gory details of illnesses and heartbreaks and divorce: I can't imagine how I would feel as a family channel member, knowing that these moments were forever floating around on the internet.

Clout chasing can quickly escalate into something sinister: in 2018, YouTube terminated two channels belonging to DaddyOFive parent vloggers Mike and Heather Martin, who were convicted of emotionally and physically abusing their children in a series of engagement-baiting pranking videos in 2017. In one video, Heather and Michael splashed invisible ink on the light carpet of a bedroom, then screamed accusations at their sobbing children, demanding to know why they were lying about having ruined the carpet, before revealing the 'prank'. That video, along with the rest of their posts, was deleted by YouTube after the Martins were convicted following an online backlash and a mass reporting by their concerned followers. The conditions of their conviction barred the Martins from making further content of their children.

The result of incidents like this is a culture in which, Mia complains, 'I instantly get questioned. I want to give Mabel a sibling and people are like: are you doing that for views? No, I'm doing it because I've always wanted a big family. When Mabel broke her leg, people said, "she's faking breaking her leg". She sounds exasperated. 'Do you really think I would fake my own daughter's injury?'

Issues of oversharing, emotional exploitation, and clickbait are further complicated by advertising and the cultivation of a family brand. Mia is extremely conscious about sponsorship. Her birth vlog was monetised — she's surprised YouTube let her get away with it — but when it comes to brand deals and sponsorship she draws a line. 'I've done loads of brand deals for Mabel — clothes, swings, toys — but she's not been in the ad, only the product,' she says. 'I don't want my kid to be the face of the ad, I want people to know she's not just there to be a model.' Family influencing blurs the relationship between protector and employer, and commercial interests can sometimes conflict with what's best for the family.

A particularly disturbing example of this conflict is The Stauffers, a groomed and glossy family dressed in matching button-downs, who were a picture-perfect advertisement for the family vlogging genre. From the early days of Myka's miscarriage videos ('LIVE PREGNANCY TEST! AM I PREGNANT?!!!'), subscribers had watched them move house, give birth, and homeschool their four children Kova, Jaka, Radley, and Onyx across several monetised YouTube channels and Instagram accounts. But the couple were keen to adopt; bringing a non-biological child into the Stauffer clan was 'something that we really want to be part of our story', Myka said in a video. The family posted 27 videos detailing their 'adoption journey' starting in 2016.

It was The Stauffers' most popular series yet — Myka's channel exploded in popularity and landed the family several high-profile sponsorships. 'Huxley's EMOTIONAL Adoption VIDEO!! GOTCHA

DAY China Adoption', the YouTube video in which they travelled to China to pick up their new two-year-old son, an autistic boy who they renamed Huxley, in 2017, has been viewed 5.7 million times.

Huxley became a large part of their life — and their channel. Myka's subscribers doubled in the year after she brought him home, and he appeared in several sponsored posts. But Huxley wasn't as co-operative on camera as she had hoped, and alongside video footage of him playing and smiling came tantrums and tears — and a medical assessment that determined his autism was more severe than had been originally diagnosed. There were upsetting videos, where Huxley appeared to have his thumbs duct-taped to prevent him from sucking them, and another in which Myka followed him with a camera whilst he sobbed, asking him if he 'was done'. Over time, Huxley began to feature less and less in the family's videos, eventually vanishing from their channel altogether.[23]

Concerned followers kickstarted the #justiceforhuxley hashtag. Eventually, The Stauffers uploaded a vlog entitled 'Update on our family'. Huxley's behaviours had been too much for them to handle, they explained, and he had been rehomed with 'his now new forever family'. The couple included one illuminating detail in their decision: James mentioned they'd 'struggled to vlog' because of their son's behaviours, and Myka agreed. 'We would start to vlog and maybe Huxley will go into a full-blown tantrum, and we don't know how to parent that tantrum, because it's just out of control, and then we're just like, I want to turn the camera off because I'm so sad and I'm not doing a good job.' The Stauffers were a family, but they were also a lucrative and polished parenting brand, and a child who resisted that vision didn't fit.

In some cases, influencer children have struck out more publicly. In January 2020, a Reddit post by throwaway account u/finallyanonymous, on popular personal advice subreddit 'Am I the Asshole?' began trending on r/all, the site's front page that aggregates the posts with highest traffic.[24] The OP (original poster) was the teenage child of a woman who was 'kinda famous on Instagram' for sharing pictures and videos of family life, and who had not taken their request to stop well. 'It sucks because there's so much out there about us and it's what's gonna come up when I'm looking for a job, when

I'm dating, when anyone looks up my name,' the poster complained. They had tried to resist, but their persistent parent had a million ways of manipulating them into pictures: 'saying that's how she makes income so if I want money for something, to stop arguing ... Or posting without asking and then saying I thought it would be okay because your face wasn't visible.' The teenager had hit on an ingenious solution: printing hoodies with slogans such as 'No photos', 'I do not consent to be photographed', 'respect my privacy', and 'no profiting off my image' and distributing them to their siblings. The mumfluencer, needless to say, was angry, but the internet unanimously concluded that OP was 'NTA': not the asshole.

Dr Crystal Abidin has studied the ways in which influencer parents 'preempt backlash and continuously justify the digital labor of their children' via clever techniques that dramatise their consent: asking children on camera if they're enjoying themselves, letting them direct the videos, mentioning that they're taking the day off. She calls this process of staging authenticity 'calibrated amateurism'. 'So convincing are these displays that family influencers seldom come under fire for subjecting their young children to hours of digital labor for content production ... followers envy and pine after their craft, unity, and family spirit to the extent of wanting to emulate after them as #familygoals.'[25]

'Even if you take out the moral concept of them working it's the fact that there aren't really any safeties in place online in terms of child work,' says Peony. 'We don't have enough legislation around family content ... That's what worries me.'

Even though minors feature heavily in parenting content, their participation is not legally recognised as labour, nor regulated as child Hollywood stars or junior performers are. In October 2020, France passed a groundbreaking piece of legislation aimed at regulating underage influencers. The law restricted the hours that under-16s can work online, who controls their earnings, and granted children the 'right to be forgotten', meaning that social media platforms must remove posts at the child's request. 'Children's rights must be preserved and protected, including on the internet, which must not be a lawless area,' said Bruno Studer, the politician behind the bill.[26] However, the law was far from a panacea: it didn't apply to all children who appear online, only those who spend 'significant' amounts of time working and who directly generate an income — in other words, it worked for kidfluencers but not family channels or the offspring of sharenting enthusiasts.

Putting aside concerns about children's role in influencing, parenting online can raise challenges for parents too. Online, there is no shortage of judgemental observers quick to critique: it's not for nothing that Mumsnet is sometimes regarded as the scariest place on the internet. 'Getting other people's opinions was really difficult: a lot of people judged me for getting induced,' says Mia. 'It was hard to get used to the fact that I had to stand up for myself.' But it didn't stop at mere criticism. 'People's opinions changed my actions during my pregnancy. It made me feel that I couldn't do things that I wanted to with my pregnancy.' Including, it turns out, naming her own daughter: it 'was originally going to be Ocean, but a lot of people were being really rude on my baby name video, so her name is now Mabel.' Other parenting influencers face resistance closer to home. Hanna's husband 'doesn't get it' and 'hates all the boxes that get delivered.' Gail has found her occupation alienating: 'I have lost some friends through my sharing,' she reflects. 'I look at it as: they mustn't have been as good of a friend as I thought.'

Opting into family influencing — vs formal employment with more safeguards, processes, and perhaps stability — places strenuous demands on parents. 'It was difficult vlogging during pregnancy,' Mia says, not least because she became very ill and was also sitting her GCSEs. 'I went from nothing to something quite fast. I'd come home from school and edit all evening. I pre-prepared a month's worth of videos before going into hospital.' As a parenting influencer, attention is divided between your family and your followers. 'Sometimes I get very stressed,' Mia admits. 'I was a new mum, trying to juggle YouTube. Don't get me wrong, I absolutely adore it: but it's also my job. If I do not upload a video, I do not get paid. So you just have to find the time.'

The pressure of maintaining a perfect brand image for millions of followers can be a strain. The Shaytards — once dubbed the 'First Family of YouTube' — were rocked by scandal when father Shay

Carl Butler (aka 'The Vlogfather') was revealed to have been sending explicit messages to a cam girl. In an apology posted on Twitter, he explained that his alcohol addiction had returned and attributed it, in part, to living life on YouTube: 'It's been impossible to keep up this "happiness is a choice" mentality. I can't do it anymore. I started drinking again three months ago,' he said. 'The reason I haven't been uploading vlogs is because I have slipped back into this horrible state … I will not be on the internet.'

Content houses, Instagram husbands, and family channels are all expressions of a trend that's happening all around us: the collapsing of previously distinct identities, the blurring of boundaries between labour and leisure, and the tendency to share increasing amounts of information about ourselves online. Influencers merely represent a more accelerated, more defined, more visible version of what non-influencers are experiencing every day, as well as what's to come in the next decade: a world in which we're all creators and everything has become content, in which influencer principles become engrained in relationships, homes, and workplaces. Though many creators say they find their always-on routines and lifestyles liberating, frequently describing the hybrid nature of their work as its biggest perk, I can't help but feel slightly anxious about the instability and vulnerability these positions inevitably produce: living at the office, working for a partner, having a parent as an employer, being always on.

As someone who had struggled to become an influencer myself, and who is still in the process of determining my own boundaries on social media, I had been curious to discover what happens to your sense of self when you offer up ever more personal slices of yourself online. Commodifying your identity for the internet didn't turn out to be the controlled, calculated sacrifice of private intimacies in the ruthless pursuit of social and cultural capital I had expected, but something more incremental and passive, as if the personal brand was an autonomous entity whose demands became, over time, more exigent: more watchable content, more authentic narratives, more intimate revelations, a more engaging version of a house or home or family. The ability to make money by packaging up aspects of your personal life means that, once initiated, all activities, interests, and relationships can be viewed as a potentially profit-generating activity, which often ends up, ironically, inverting the very freedom and flexibility that influencing initially appeared to offer.

I look back at family holiday snaps from my own childhood — grainy, faded, sweaty, unphotogenic, happy — and wonder what it would have been like if the person wielding the camera was being paid for it. We never had to wonder if the beach was 'on brand' or the sandwiches were Instagrammable. I fell out with my first flatmates over bin schedules and blaring music, not revenue percentages or personal brands.

Criticism of influencer oversharing tends to focus on the actions of specific individuals, but the prerogative to post feels increasingly like a widespread expectation, especially as the mechanisms that enable online content continue to innovate and intensify. In the race to commodify every aspect of our lives and identities, influencers are merely a step ahead of the rest of us.

In late 2020, a platform called NewNew began to gain traction amongst the influencer community, which seemed to mark the next stage of this evolution. The world's first 'human stock market', NewNew allowed an influencer's audience to pay to vote on any aspect of an influencer's life: what clothes to wear, song to play, food to eat or video game to play, how to respond to a text message or spend their afternoon. As long as the activity wasn't dangerous, illegal, or offensive, it could be posted — and voted for — by followers. Through NewNew, influencers could completely commodify their identities, living lives decided by the highest bidder. 'For Creators, Everything is for Sale' reported *The New York Times*. But it wasn't just influencers who could use it. 'Sure, it's fun to control a famous influencer or celebrity, but it's honestly just as entertaining to control someone you go to school with, or your boyfriend's ex-girlfriend,' NewNew's founder told the *NYT*. 'It doesn't matter how boring you think you are, there's someone out there who would find your life interesting to the point that they're willing to pay.' Is there anything the newly minted 'creator economy' can't sell?

CHAPTER 5

CREATOR ECONOMICS

HOW MUCH DO CREATORS REALLY EARN?

'What's up bitches!!'

Tana Mongeau is screaming into my iPhone camera. The 21-year-old vlogger is pressed up so close beside me that her fuzzy bucket hat nearly becomes entangled with my earrings as we jostle to fit our faces in the frame. Next to her on screen, I look unprepared and slightly panicked, glancing apprehensively left, happy to let her take the lead but unsure where she'll take it next. Around us, the crowd is bumping and jockeying for their places, iPhones held aloft, all eyes turned to their YouTube hero. Even at her pitch, it's difficult to be heard above their screams and the beats of canned pop songs that are being pumped around the Expo Hall. 'Subscribe to this bad bitch!!' Tana yells, stabbing her acrylic talons in my direction and leaning in tight to the camera, face distorting in the screen, eyelash extensions fluttering over the top of her tiny white 00s sunglasses.

'Oh my god, sorry if you have to bleep that out ...' she drawls, not breaking eye contact with my iPhone. She flicks her bleach-blonde hair extensions over her shoulder, eyes wide and mouth puckered in a playful smirk for the benefit of the future audience of my vlog. 'That was literally like a million bleeps.' With a theatrical 'mwah', she throws

135

kisses to the screen, and a second later she's disappeared behind me, enveloped into her fans, hat bobbing between heads and selfie sticks. I'm left standing alone, with a 15-second video recording and the dazed feeling that I've just been 'Tana-ed'.

It's my first day at VidCon, the world's largest annual festival of influence. The four-day convention is the Davos of the digital world: tickets sell out quickly, the line-up is the subject of widespread speculation, creators fly in from all around the world, and fans queue to see them from the early hours, riding the hotel lifts in the hope of glimpsing their heroes. Representatives from monolithic social media platforms let down their corporate façade to mingle with sponsors in swagged-out breakout spaces. Industry professionals such as myself observe, network, and eye up the competition, hoping to be introduced to the biggest stars of the moment or — even better — the next big thing.

VidCon is more than just a convention. It's a unique IRL moment for a virtual community, a celebration of creator culture, and a massive fandom meet-up. The event was founded by first-generation vloggers and 'big brothers of YouTube' Hank and John Green, aka the Vlogbrothers, who began their YouTube careers in 2007 as a New Year's resolution: announcing to the internet that in lieu of all private communication with each other they would substitute daily diary vlogs uploaded to their public YouTube channel. Their stunt proved popular: one viral Harry Potter cover, a few years, and several hundred hours of relatable rambling to camera later, the Vlogbrothers had secured a sweeping international fanbase, a *Forbes* profile, an Emmy, and a virtual Hangout with President Barack Obama on swiftly defunct social media platform Google+.

The Greens were at the forefront of the first generation of mega-creators, able to spin their fame into an empire of lucrative new-media projects as the industry expanded, shaping the YouTube we know today. As they — and the industry — have grown, so has VidCon. The first ever event, held in an LA hotel in 2010, sold 1,400 tickets. A decade later, it hosts 75,000 attendees at the Anaheim Convention Center,[1] and the brand has undergone a rapid international expansion, popping up in London, Abu Dhabi,

Singapore, Australia, and Mexico to match the global rollout of the influencer industry. To this day, the festival remains a testament to self-made YouTuber success, a legacy event that was founded — and is still fronted — by one of its own.

VidCon's London iteration, held in the sprawling complex of east London's ExCel Centre over a bleak February weekend, is every bit as overwhelming as the hours of vlogs I watched in preparation had promised it would be. Outside, grey rain lashes the Docklands, inside lies a technicolour alternate reality. Spanning four floors of stages, auditoriums, and exhibition halls, my laminated pamphlet informs me, VidCon has a set schedule of talks and lectures, intimate influencer meet and greets, scheduled photo opportunities, and a series of climactic mainstage events. There are keynote speeches, interviews with top YouTubers, and a Saturday evening party known as the 'Night of Awesome'.

Banners bearing the handles and faces of some of social media's biggest stars hang like medieval tapestries in the cathedral-like convention centre; teenagers pose for selfies, film TikTok dances, and eat sandwiches beneath them. Abby Roberts's gigantic face beams down at me, distant and totemic. Thousands of fans wearing matching vlogger hoodies, with hair dyed pink and blue and green, stream between rooms with a frenzied energy. I stand at the centre of it all clutching my cooling coffee, swallowed up by the crowd and the chaos.

Shuttling industriously between conference rooms, breakout spaces, and auditoriums, I plunge straight into VidCon's intensive creator curriculum. After my unsuccessful attempt to become an influencer, I am curious to find out what I might have missed. I battle to the front of a packed-out hall to watch Rich Waterworth, the newly hired General Manager of TikTok, struggle to describe exactly what the platform does. I join a group of anxious-looking parents clustered around the father of a famous Irish kidfluencer to learn how his son's 'wee hobby' has become the family business.

I slip into the main stage to watch a carousel of creators dispense wisdom in swift, 30-minute iterations: pink-haired streamer Plumbella recalls starting YouTube as a child growing up in a working-class Northern town; gaming, comic, and movie review channel The Cyber Nerds enthuse about a Black British 'creator renaissance'; growth hacker Matt Gielen boasts that he's 'cracked the algorithm'. Fans hang on their every word, streaming panels straight to Instagram and punching notes into their iPhones.

The scholastic atmosphere inside the lecture halls contrasts sharply with the chaos going on outside. Groups skulk outside the auditorium doors, ready to pounce on their favourite creators for signatures on handle-branded hoodies. Stands hand out branded selfie sticks and call out offers for free trials of their influencer auditing software. Everywhere, attendees are shooting videos, scrolling their phones, pulling stunts and tripping over the tangles of white charging cables that snake from plugs studding the skirting boards. The mood is volatile: in an instant the crowd surges as a semi-famous creator is spotted down the corridor, causing me to duck for cover in a break room until the frenzy has died down.

In the basement, an Expo Hall houses a bustling marketplace dominated by merch stands, experiential activities, and interactive pop-ups. YouTube is hosting a 360-degree booth with branded backdrops. Spotify invites passersby to shoot personalised 3D music videos. A wall of salon stations manned by stylists primp aspiring beauty influencers into camera-ready perfection, hairdryers drowning out the monologues of vloggers recording themselves as they pass by. Young gamers are taking turns to battle it out on TV screens that hang above a cheering crowd.

In the lounge, I swap beauty tips with Holly H, one of the UK's top TikTokers. In the corridor, I spot a school friend, since turned successful body positivity influencer with a bestselling book and viral TED talk to her name. At a panel, I strike up conversation with style star Stephanie Yeboah. On the stairs, I take a selfie with LA-based beauty guru MannyMUA, who embraces me warmly and tells me my jacket is 'sickening'. The mythical 'VidCon experience' has delivered: these encounters are every bit as bright and bold and buzzing as I was promised. But somehow, I feel hollow and unsatisfied.

Perhaps it's me, perhaps it's the anodyne airport atmosphere of the ExCel Centre, but being at VidCon feels like a strangely liminal experience. I am perpetually waiting for something to start or something to be over. I wander aimlessly between the floors: foyer, auditorium, booth, bathroom, and back again, treading the geometric carpet tiles in concentric circuits, scaling multiple escalators in pursuit of my next destination. Twice I catch the eye of someone I know across a corridor only to be swept away by the bodies pressed around me and resort to awkward, wild-eyed gestures, mouthing, 'I'll try to catch you later!' only to never run into them again.

It's too loud to strike up a proper conversation, anyway: the air is filled with lights and flashes and chatter and the tap tap tap of plastic against chip-and-pin machines. More than once, I've assumed I am queuing for the toilet, only to later realise I am standing at the back of a snakelike line for merch by Markiplier or TheOdd1sOut. Pushed out by the sheer number of tat-laden sales booths, TikTokers have been forced to meet their fans in the foyer, dancing by the revolving doors under the watchful eyes of security.

Eventually, I collapse in a corner behind a 'family lounge' of bored-looking parents and abandoned buggies, vlogging my disconnected impressions against the pounding sound system and occasional explosions of cheers from a nearby Fortnite gaming stand. I feel drained. I am developing a headache.

When the weekend is eventually over, I have clocked over 27.3km on my pedometer, and am not quite sure I found what I was looking for. Where was the 'VidCon magic' happening, exactly? In the commercial world of brand pop-ups and merch stalls, or in the guerilla meet and greets and DIY dance challenges being captured in the foyer? What — or who — did VidCon really represent?

The last session I'd dropped in on was Hank Green himself; more out of curiosity about the man who had set the whole thing into motion than any enthusiasm for the title of his talk, 'The Art of Collaborative Creating'. It was the graveyard slot on a Sunday afternoon, and I slid into the third row of fold-up chairs in silence. He looked older and smaller than I had expected, and the crowd was thin. There were no breathless fans waiting with hoodies to sign outside the auditorium. He had none of the smooth jokes or polished media manner of the previous panels I had attended. There were tech issues getting his slides set up on the projector. I can't remember much about what Hank said — reminiscing about how the space had changed, replaying his old YouTube videos — but I can remember how strangely sad I felt, watching these shaky vintage clips and the softly spoken, bookish man before me; a vlogging veteran who represented a quaint cottage industry of content we had moved beyond.

In February 2018, VidCon was acquired by multinational media conglomerate Viacom for an undisclosed amount. The purchase was somewhat ironic given Viacom's history: nearly a decade earlier the company had sued YouTube for $1 billion over copyright infringement. 'I'm so happy that we found such a strong, successful, and progressive company to give our team the stability and resources needed,' Hank had said in an official PR statement at the time. 'We are building something truly unique by blending that with our team's deep care and passion for the community and culture of online video.'[2] The community, however, did not feel the same way.

Hundreds of comments under a four-minute 'VidCon Update' vlog uploaded to Hank's channel mourn the loss of VidCon's authenticity and independence: 'I'm personally worried that this means that Viacom will just pump it to be more about Shocktubers like Logan Paul now for all the free controversy (money)' said one. 'I'm … uncomfortable', said another. 'I remember Hank talking about how Youtube was totally different from cable and tv, and positing Big Media and youtube creators as entities that were practically opposed. Now, Youtube is just another platform for Big Media, and the people I thought were the most opposed to it are selling their companies out.'[3]

The conflict between grassroots creator culture and corporate interests is a complaint voiced not just about VidCon, but the influencer industry more broadly. Creators work hard to cultivate their authenticity, and commercial agendas are seen to pollute the purity of an influencer's output — obvious advertising is perceived as inauthentic, and 'selling out' or 'shilling' is a slur. Participants in creator fandom are protective of a community they view as niche and DIY. It's common for influencers and followers alike to invoke the 'good old days' before so many big brands got involved and sponsorship expanded it into the multi-billion-dollar industry it is today.

I've always found these criticisms counterintuitive. Without brands, influencers simply wouldn't exist. The more partnerships a creator takes on, the more legitimate their influence (why else would wannabe social media stars upload fake sponsored posts or pretend they have been #gifted items by a brand?). Far from being niche or DIY, the influencer ecosystem has always taken place on platforms owned by the largest corporations on the internet. Nostalgia for a pre-commercial creator community harks back to an imagined past that was never really there in the first place. What these misguided complaints do illuminate is influencing's central tension: it is a profit-driven activity engaged in the continuous obfuscation of its own identity and intentions.

In February 2020, for the first time in their history as a Google-owned platform, YouTube revealed how much revenue ads generated: nearly $5 billion in the previous quarter, contributing roughly 10 per cent of all of Google's income.[4] The true value of YouTube's creator engine had been quantified. In a blog post in early 2021, YouTube CEO Susan Wojcicki confirmed that YouTube's primary focus was 'growing the creator economy': 'Over the last three years, we've paid more than $30bn to creators, artists, and media companies,' her post stated. 'YouTube's creative ecosystem contributed approximately $16 billion to the US GDP in 2019, supporting the equivalent of 345,000 full-time jobs.'[5]

Once a self-initiated community event for a handful of hobbyists and online content enthusiasts, now a portfolio piece owned by an American mass media conglomerate with annual revenues of over $27 billion, VidCon is a perfect symbol of the influencer industry's evolution, embodying the balancing act between culture and commerce that underwrites the entire operation. As Hank pointed out in response to the commentators on his 'VidCon Update' vlog: 'Just to be totally clear, VidCon has, since like 2011, had a strong relationship with lots of corporations and advertisers. That's a really important part of how online video works. When YouTubers struggle with lack of monetisation and low ad rates, it's those advertisers that we need to have good relationships with to help creators sustain themselves.' And this intricate system of trading attention for revenue is one the 'shocktubers' invoked by VidCon's concerned fanbase have streamlined and perfected.

'This is 50,000 Orbeez,' declares a tracksuited 21-year-old, direct to camera. It's a grey afternoon and he's sitting outside on a garden bench in the backyard of a generic low-slung, red-brick bungalow that could be anywhere in America. His name is Jimmy Donaldson, but online, he goes by MrBeast. His face is pale, adorned with a patchy pubescent moustache; he's wearing a scruffy baseball cap and a hoodie emblazoned with his graffiti trademark. Looking at him, you'd never guess he was a multimillionaire. On the ground in front of him is a small box of colourful spherical gel beads usually given to children for craft projects or used as decorative filler in flower arrangements. There's a jump cut in the video, and several more boxes appear on the ground in front of his trainers. 'This is 200,000.' Another jump cut, the boxes double. 'This is 400,000.' Another jump cut, and suddenly the pile of boxes is waist-high. He's yelling now: 'That is 1 million Orbeez! And that is only 1 per cent of our Orbeez!' He pauses to reflect. 'That's a weird flex ...'

A gang of his identically dressed friends begin unloading industrial quantities of cardboard boxes from a truck, piling them higher and higher on the ground in front of him. 'We're gonna take these and we're gonna put them in the backyard and wait for it to rain,' shouts MrBeast exuberantly: 'Dude — these things get like 30 times bigger when you get them wet!' Epic metal music plays, and they throw the dehydrated Orbeez out into the yard. The boxes explode in a slow-mo kaleidoscope, spilling tiny candy-coloured beads in all directions; soon, they cover the entire garden in a rainbow carpet. Another jump cut later, and it has rained; the Orbeez have expanded overnight, enveloping the yard in a sea of gelatinous spheres that's now knee-deep.

MrBeast and his tracksuit-clad crew step up the frenzy: 'yeeting' (hurling) random objects into the pool, lighting firecrackers, and diving in fully clothed. Grunting and yelling, they wade around in the mess, skidding across the screen and taking turns to bury each other alive. Twelve minutes into the video and I'm not exactly clear what purpose any of this serves. Neither, apparently, are they. 'Idk what's going on at this point' flashes up a caption, as one of the entourage rolls around on the ground.

Welcome to the weird and wonderful world of MrBeast. This YouTube video, 'I Put 100 Million Orbeez In My Friend's Backyard', has been watched more than 96 million times and is the most-viewed video of its genre: junklord YouTube.

The term 'junklord YouTube' was first coined in 2019 by Anthony Padilla, founder of the legendary Smosh comedy channel and friend of many of the genre's most prominent figures. Padilla described junklords as 'YouTubers who use supersized quantities to get views,' a definition I would expand to include wacky and wasteful experiments, elaborate set-ups, and outrageous pranks. Junklord videos follow a standard format: a clickbait all-caps video title, expressive thumbnail, and improbable scenario; 'DESTROYING MY FRIEND'S CAR AND THEN SURPRISING HIM WITH A NEW ONE', 'ORDERING EVERY SINGLE THING ON THE WENDY'S MENU', or 'SPENDING 24 HOURS IN A HOT TUB FILLED WITH PEANUT BUTTER'. You think the videos are clickbait, but they're not: junklord YouTubers actually deliver on the crazy things they advertise. Yes, Collins Key really did order 10,000 pounds of candy and turn his house into a real-life Willy Wonka factory; Guava Juice really did put 10 million ball pit balls in the back of a moving truck; MrBeast really did build an entire inflatable city from hundreds of bouncy castles.

Junklord stunts are distinct from YouTube challenges or crazy science experiments in that the videos are never really about the possibility of pulling it off: failing to fill your swimming pool with Pot Noodles — and making a mess doing it — is worth just as much as completing the task successfully. The junklord agenda is more *Jackass* than Guinness World Records: the onscreen action inevitably goes wrong, something gets destroyed, and all the craziness is captured on camera. You click because the scale of the chaos caused is simply unquantifiable to the average viewer: *I can't even picture what 100,000,000 Lego bricks would look like! Is he really going to drive that Lamborghini into the pool? He spent how much in one hour?!*

Junklord videos perform incredibly well on YouTube. It's no surprise: the format was created specifically to hack YouTube's algorithm. Starting at 13, Jimmy had spent several years attempting to make it big — later dropping out of college to pursue a career as a creator — before becoming 'MrBeast'. His early efforts involved experimenting with a range of influencer identities: gaming (Minecraft walkthroughs, tips for playing Call of Duty), influencer tea (estimating how much top creators make, throwing shade at their video thumbnails), and growth hacking (education videos and subscriber tips for small channels). But it was his first viral hit in January 2017, a 23-hour video in which he counted up to 100,000 live on camera — that provided the formula for his later templates for success. Jimmy realised that the algorithm rewarded abundance. Soon he went viral again: spinning a fidget spinner continuously for 24 hours, saying the name 'Logan Paul' 100,000 times, watching Jake Paul's music video for ten hours straight. The MrBeast phenomenon was born.

His rapid rise to fame broke records: exploding from 100k to 25m subs in under two years, gaining over 10m views on every single video uploaded for over a year and adding, on average, 1.5 million new subscribers every month. Currently ranked the 20th most popular channel in the world with 50m subscribers, MrBeast's status within creator culture is mythical. The wannabe YouTubers I'd met on the Fire Tech training camp had been obsessed with him, and VidCon was littered with people sporting BEAST-emblazoned hoodies.

Other junklords boast similarly massive profiles: together Morgz (11.3m subscribers), Guava Juice (15.8m), Logan Paul (22.4m), the Funk Bros (6.11m), MindofRez (4.18m), Unspeakable (8.4m), Carter Sharer (7.13m) and Collins Key (22m) dominate YouTube's chaos entertainment ecosystem.

Before I stumbled into junklord YouTube I had written the genre off as mindless consumerist clickbait, an answer to the beauty guru's

'I spent $2k in Sephora mega haul' or the hypebeast's 'world's largest Supreme streetwear collection [must watch!]'. But junklord content offers more than just the spectacle of superfluity. It's the perfect demonstration of what internet academics and marketers refer to as 'the attention economy'.

A term first coined in 1971 by psychologist and economist Herbert A. Simon, the attention economy refers to a system in which information is abundant and human attention becomes a scarce commodity and thus a resource to be bought, sold, and brokered. 'A wealth of information creates a poverty of attention,' wrote Simon, 'and a need to allocate that attention efficiently among the overabundance of information sources that might consume it.' This system of allocation has today developed into an all-out war between brands, advertisers, influencers, publishers, and casual internet users, taking place on the battleground of social platforms. And just as speculators can strike it big in the traditional economy, this system makes millionaires of the junklords who have worked out how to profit off it: according to online estimates, MrBeast is worth around $16 million[6] and Logan Paul $19 million,[7] each with business empires of their own — apps, property portfolios, media companies, and merchandise brands worth six-figure sums. The fact that influencing is a digital American Dream is reflected in the kinds of activities that junklords choose for their videos — 'I BOUGHT EVERYTHING IN A STORE', 'I BUILT A MANSION USING ONLY CARDBOARD BOXES', 'EATING A $10,000 GOLDEN STEAK (24k)'.

In the attention economy, nothing succeeds like excess. The more stuff — items, minutes, ads, production value, shock factor — junklords cram into a video, the more views they get and subscribers they pull in, the more fame they accumulate, and the more money they — and YouTube — make. 'In a little bit there will be an orbee for every view' noted a commenter underneath MrBeast's video, as the view count ticked upwards towards 100m.

The video is itself also a commodity, and so this individual amplification process is mirrored in the wider social media marketplace: each video posted boosts the others in the junklord network as its creators are in constant discourse, competitively namechecking each other in their videos, which end up ranked against each other by the recommendation algorithm. Popular video formats are copied by wannabe junklords and referenced endlessly in other creator's reaction videos, ultimately driving more eyeballs to the platform as a whole.

Creators engage in attention arbitrage: trading money for products for videos for views, which in turn generates more money, whilst YouTube operates in reverse, selling this engagement to advertisers and converting it back to cash for creators via a 55 per cent cut of their AdSense revenue. By online estimations, the Orbeez video pulled in over $200,000 from ads alone; the branded MrBeast hoodies the crew wore — yours for £45 via Jimmy's Shopify store — netted an undisclosed additional sum. For scale, a later hoodie drop sold 68,337 units. However, it's the viral fame generated for the MrBeast brand which adds the most value.

But whilst attention is an intangible good, the props and products used in these stunts are very much material: in this sense the videos perfectly dramatise consumer capitalism and the machinery that underpins it. Junklord YouTube relies on the continuous circulations of cheap commodities and the outsourcing of the production of its materials to other countries, brokered via online commerce platforms such as Amazon and AliBaba. Someone must manufacture the bouncy castles, water balloons, leaf blowers, megaphones, paddling pools, slime, and spray paint cheap enough to be bulk bought and destroyed in the backyard of an LA McMansion.

The influencer industry is propelled by an exhaustive cycle of excess, impermanence and disposability, and junklords take this to extremes. The videos are either about attaining things on an exaggerated scale — 'I Adopted Every Dog at a Shelter', 'I Bought The World's Largest Firework ($600,000)', 'I Bought a Private Island' — or getting rid of them just as quickly; 'I Broke Into A House And Left $50,000', I Gave My 40,000,000th Subscriber 40 Cars', 'Anything You Can Carry, I'll Pay For Challenge'.

Each junklord video usually begins the same way: with a

timelapse clip of piles of bouncy balls or dry ice or merch or food or slime or Lego or Funko Pops stacking up in anticipation. By the end of the video, these piles will have disappeared: used up, given away, forgotten, or trashed. Acquisition is condensed to a few seconds at the start of a video and an item's utility is exhausted within mere minutes, flattening the consumer purchase cycle and making it seamless and intuitive. Visible wastefulness is an inherent part of the genre's appeal: the video 'World's Largest Bowl of Cereal', sees MrBeast float around in enough food to feed a street, 'I Filled My Brother's House With Slime & Bought Him A New One' delights in irreparably coating a home in viscous liquid — the crew fall about laughing as green gunge smashes through the windows and up the chimney.

But what happens after the camera wraps, the video ends, and the props have served their purpose? It's not something junklords ask their millions of viewers to consider. MrBeast occasionally posts videos tallying his wastage, such as scrapping ideas worth $800k that didn't work or he changed his mind about,[8] or writing off $70k on a single dog rescue stunt after running into US animal adoption regulations.[9] Junklord videos are pure consumerist pornography: a fantasy of endless 'stuff' in a world that's rapidly running out of resources.

Midway through MrBeast's Orbeez video, the mood turns sombre and the picture fades to black and white. 'Not enough of you guys are buying my merch, so I can't afford to feed my children,' Jimmy pleads to camera against a backing track of tiny violins. He's promoting his BEAST-branded merch line. Jimmy begins to hand out Orbeez-filled sandwiches as if they are foodbank rations, and a large animated link to 'shop MrBeast.com' unfurls across the bottom of the screen. Behind his fake poverty PSA (public service announcement), £16,000-worth of plastic balls are clogging up a swimming pool. Whilst 98m people watch MrBeast and his friends pretending to eat Orbeez because they don't have enough money to afford a proper meal, in the backyard of a house they can afford to trash, 23.5 million Americans live in food deserts and, worsened by the coronavirus crisis, the housing crisis continues to escalate. The top comment under the Orbeez video has over 100,000 likes: 'so this is how millionaires have fun'.

These obscene disparities of wealth should feel alienating — the Orbeez video is undoubtedly obnoxious — but somehow, MrBeast remains almost universally adored by the internet; though other junklords, such as Jake Paul, aren't held in such high esteem. Jimmy's personal popularity may be due to his cheerful nature, his notable rejection of the luxury influencer lifestyle, or well-documented internet philanthropy, such as his #TeamTrees environmental initiative. But his strategy appears to have something to do with it as well.

In YouTube comments and on Twitter, subscribers suggest what MrBeast should spend his cash on. 'You should play monopoly with real money,' commented one under a video. 2.6k people agreed, and so in February 2019 he invited several of his viewers to play on a gigantic board with actual cash, in a video that got 46 million views. 'Who wants MrBeast to rent a private island?' asked another, and in August 2020, MrBeast went one step further: purchasing, hosting a competition for, and subsequently giving away Golden Cay, a deserted atoll in the Bahamas.

By including his viewers in his videos themselves — bringing them into challenges and competitions, giving them cars, money, and anything they can carry — MrBeast gamifies inequality and allows viewers to participate in a shared fantasy of extreme wealth. MrBeast's viral instances of philanthropic individualism — videos in which he randomly selects a homeless man to gift a Lamborghini to, gives waitresses gold bars, or orders a pizza and gives the house as a tip to the delivery guy — make the audience feel like they could be next. This is the same philosophy of individual aspiration — the tantalising suggestion that 'anyone can make it' — that fuels the influencer industry as a whole.

After consuming countless hours of MrBeast's elaborate pranks, I begin to wonder if the joke is really on me for watching. I've probably just spent too much time online, but the videos feel almost deliberately parodic, a satire of YouTube's trash economy and junklords' rule over a kingdom of detritus. Junklords first achieve, and then systematically destroy, the fruits of influencer labour. MrBeast is one of the most successful creators on the planet, yet he appears to be acquiring money only to get rid of it. Purchasing a sports car to drive it into a pool, destroying a house, eating as many calories as possible in an hour, mindlessly sweeping items off the shelves as fast as they can: some of the most successful creators on the planet specialise in destruction. Having accumulated so many followers and so many material possessions, the destruction of those material possessions becomes a new kind of flex.

Videos like 'Spending $1,000,000 In 24 Hours', or 'I Ate A $70,000 Golden Pizza' feel like a send-up of materialism in general, and bougie YouTuber lifestyles in particular, the most extreme version of influencer culture reflected back to us. Junklords rule over an influencer economy in which value itself has been debased.

Just as events like VidCon have expanded to an international scale, and individual creators such as MrBeast have achieved unprecedented fame and fortune, the influencer economy has grown at a phenomenal rate: valued at $500 million in 2015, in 2020 it was worth $10 billion, according to Mediakix.[10] As the landscape has evolved, influencers' roles and revenue models have shifted, the type of work has changed, and the network of companies around them has developed through three economic phases — advertising, entrepreneurship, and — imminently — financialisation.

In the early days, influencers were mere advertisements for brands and businesses, #sponning products for them on social media in exchange for a fee. Either brands paid creators directly for their services, or creators made money from ads less directly via revenue sharing schemes like YouTube AdSense. This meant earnings were reliant on attaining brand partnerships or sustained levels of engagement. It fuelled an oversaturated market of Instagram sponcon, clickbait thumbnails, and elongated vlogs that crammed in as many ad-breaks as possible.

In 2018, it is estimated that 3.7 million brand-sponsored influencer posts were uploaded to Instagram; by 2020, this had almost doubled to 6.12 million.[11] As the market matured, the 'human billboard' model remained the basis of an influencer's income, but alternative partnership avenues were also opening up, fuelled by a new rhetoric of 'collaboration': longer-term brand-ambassador schemes, events and curatorships, influencers acting as consultants or participating as models in traditional advertising campaigns.

When I first started working, the wider influencer industry was still in its infancy: influencer marketing came second place to PR or advertising. The process was slow, laborious, and mostly manual, reliant on dogged influencer managers hired by brands to slide into creators' DMs and negotiate the value of a partnership through luck and guesswork. New tools soon sprang up though, to manage campaigns at scale and generate more sophisticated data than the platforms themselves offered.

Whilst old-school advertising agencies such as my former employer were slow to adapt to the shifting landscape, independent agencies like Gleam, influencer brokering platforms such as Whalar or Tribe, analytics tools such as Klear, and management or seeding software like Octoly sprung up quickly to capitalise on a growing niche. But traditional media agencies and advertising holding companies sensed there was money to be made and were increasingly keen to invest. In 2015, there were just 190 influencer platforms and agencies operating in the US, reported Influencer Marketing Hub; within a year this had doubled, and by 2018 the landscape had grown to 740 companies, many of them backed by larger operations.[12]

In their next evolutionary stage, influencers began to act as entrepreneurs, opening independent streams of revenue and establishing empires of their own. Many began to sell products — candles, make-up, gym kits, protein shakes, toys, snacks – that were in competition with the brands they had previously promoted. After collaborating with Nordstrom for a limited edition line in 2017 which drove over $1 million in sales in just 24 hours — and a repeat event just a year later that quadrupled this taking — Arielle Charnas went on to launch her own fashion label, Something Navy, in 2020, with a valuation of $45m. Beauty guru Huda Kattan — queen of explore page contouring clickbait — built her eponymous $1.2 billion cosmetics brand in just under five years.

At the top of the industry, influencers began to incorporate; by now the most successful social media stars were running businesses with teams of employees behind the scenes: production, promotion, admin, operations, finance. They had social media management teams of their own. The most successful influencer enterprises were landing billion-dollar valuations; founders were appearing on Rich Lists and starting to be taken seriously as CEOs. No longer just commodities, but corporations in their own right.

'A creator isn't someone who creates but an individual who scales without permission,' writes Hugo Amsellem, VP at Jellysmack, a creator accelerator, in his newsletter 'Arm The Creators': 'They are to the individual what startups are to the organisation. They are the future of scalable entrepreneurship. As a result, a new economy is growing up around — and through — them: the creator economy.' The industry around influencers was industrialising. In this phase of influencer entrepreneurship, creators 'need specific tools to meet their specific needs', explains Hugo.[13]

His extensive research into the creator economy includes mapping over 150 new companies that constitute the growing landscape: 'I've encountered various startups building tools that empower creators to run their business. Some are focused on specific verticals like project management, CRM [customer retention management], or lending; the others are building platforms to enable a specific type of creator to run their whole business all in one place.' A rush of supply-side startups aimed to help creators run their operations from end to end, with services and tools to aid every aspect of the creator's existence: from collaboration to monetisation, project management to finance.

As the influencer industry matured, influencers began to think long term. Critics and detractors were raising concerns around audience ownership, vulnerability to algorithm or platform updates, and income instability, triggering a shift in content and operation models. Backed by new tools and platforms, creators began a process of divestment: gaining independence from external brands and advertising for income, and from the restrictions of the social media platforms on which they are reliant.

Take Tana Mongeau, who began uploading videos to YouTube in 2015. Her 'storytime' vlog format, sharing wild anecdotes from her life, proved hugely popular, with her first video ('Hairdresser from

Hell?') viewed millions of times. As she grew, and her advertising revenue was threatened by not only algorithm updates but her own controversial antics, she began exploring new streams of revenue: selling merchandise bearing her name, starting a fragrance line, hosting a disastrous VidCon alternative called 'TanaCon', starring in an MTV reality show about her life, and announcing an influencer agency — Tana's Angels — of her own.

'As long as their audience is on the media networks, they're only renting it, not owning it,' Hugo writes, 'there's a whole class of startups whose main purpose is to help creators convert media network followers into owned community members. It usually means that they'll focus on creating new contextualised spaces where the audience can interact with the creators, like community platforms, interactive live-streaming experiences, an email-based newsletter, etc.' He highlights apps such as Clash (creator founded social media platform), Community (direct text messaging), and Circle (community platform for creators) which enable influencers to gain more ownership over their audiences and export them to a space that they control.

'Once creators have moved their interactions off mainstream media networks,' Hugo continues to explain, 'they can then work to extract direct financial value from them.' Other platforms and services help interact with and monetise audiences in new ways: Cameo allows fans to book influencer shout-out videos, Camelot enables audiences to pay creators to play chosen songs or make certain moves during video games. Tana is bookable on Cameo for $70 video shout-outs ('Annie, your best friend Amelia loves you so, so much,' she says to camera, bleary-eyed, whilst waiting in line in Starbucks), and she announced her use of Community with a Tweet: 'if u haven't texted the TANA MONGEAU hotline yet i'm bored and responding text me !!!!'

On 28 December 2019, mega-influencer Austin McBroom from The ACE Family — one of the top family YouTube channels that teen mumfluencer Mia Jeal had mentioned to me — vented his frustration at subscribers complaining he had failed to deliver on promised video uploads over the festive season: 'Some of y'all are ungrateful for free content,' he tweeted to his 1.72m Twitter followers. 'Some of y'all should be charged every time you watch someone's video. Idk why y'all think its just so easy to make videos everyday or every other day. If it was so easy everyone including yourself would be doing it...'[14]

Within minutes his tweet had been comprehensively ratioed: followers, tea channels, and fellow influencers flagged the financial entitlement of a 27-year-old who had recently purchased, and then renovated, a 10-million-dollar house in Los Angeles. Some pointed out that embedded AdSense breaks within their YouTube uploads meant the Ace Family were technically already profiting every time a user watched their videos, others that he'd got the creator-consumer dynamic wrong: 'You do realise you get paid because of us?' said one riled-up respondent. But Austin's comment was prescient: asking followers to pay to consume their posts would be the next development in the world of online influence.

Tired of relying on unstable advertising revenue and sensing the opportunity to monetise, creators began to move away from 'free content' models, ushering in a new model for influence. Subscription services for paid posts such as NSFW website OnlyFans, email newsletter platform Substack, and creative subscription service Patreon have surged in popularity. Even Tumblr, the platform that created space for OnlyFans' success by banning 'adult' material and thereby alienating a large swath of its user base in 2018, began testing an optional paywall feature.

In January 2020, a press deck from OnlyFans's PR had landed on my desk, in which the website introduced themselves as 'the social media platform that revolutionises influencer engagement'. They claimed to have 20 million registered users and 150,000 active influencers, though declined to mention that the overwhelming majority of the content hosted is explicit. Beauty guru Bretman Rock, controversy vlogger Trisha Paytas, and mukbang YouTuber Nikocado Avocado all signed up to share racy pictures, whilst Tana Mongeau 'broke the site' with a sudden influx of traffic when she announced the launch of her shared channel 'Tana Uncensored'.

Not everyone was selling nudes: Natalie Hanby of the comedy

YouTube channel The Hanby Family used OnlyFans to post new pranks and behind-the-scenes shots of her family's YouTube channel, whilst *Real Housewives Of New York* star Sonja Morgan shared fashion, travel, and behind the scenes posts. By December the same year, OnlyFans were adding as many as 500k users a day and had paid out more than $200m a month to its creators. The plaftorm was enabling increasingly granular ways to commodify identity, and increasingly intimate levels of audience access.

Octavia Outlaw, the outspoken fashion, beauty and lifestyle YouTuber behind the Glamazontay YouTube channel, offered another explanation, telling her 857,000 subscribers that she was planning on moving challenges, games, giveaways, and blog posts to her OnlyFans account. 'It just makes sense to do OnlyFans instead of YouTube,' she said in a chatty GRWM, gesticulating with an eyeshadow brush as she explained. 'I'm looking at it from a business aspect. YouTube as a platform is not what it was before, people are not making money on YouTube like there was before' — OnlyFans takes a 20 per cent cut of creators' earnings vs YouTube's 45 per cent — 'And it's not all about the money either … They're always flagging my shit, they're always flagging lesbian stuff … they discriminate against a lot of Black content creators. The top [YouTube] creators are that traditional apple pie white girl. I'm ratchet, I'm Black, and I'm getting to do what I want.' She shrugged her shoulders. 'I recommend any creator that's on YouTube to move over there.'[15]

For the first decade of the influencer industry, platforms had let creator culture develop almost organically, facilitating but rarely intervening. By 2020, this would change, as the explosive growth of TikTok forced platforms to compete harder, ramping up investment in their own influencer programmes, cultivating communities, and paying creators directly for their posts.

In 2020, TikTok launched their $2-billion-dollar global Creator Fund, eligible to anyone with at least 10k followers, 'to help support ambitious creators who are seeking opportunities to foster a livelihood through their innovative content'. Instagram followed suit by paying creators to use their TikTok competitor, the new 'Reels' format, whilst Snapchat launched Spotlight, a feature that shows users a stream of publicly submitted posts selected based on personalised algorithms, with a $1m daily payout competition for the most popular UGC (user generated content). Teenage users quickly began gaming the system by uploading over 200 posts every five minutes throughout the day to become 'Snapchat millionaires'.

'TikTok set that precedent of what kind of content people are looking for. Snapchat has done a really good job of recreating that in their own way, building that into their own app,' Joey Rogoff, 21, an influencer who made more than $1 million through Spotlight told *The New York Times*: 'They're the highest-paying platform right now. Hopefully other platforms see that and will follow their lead because ultimately that's what's going to make creators the happiest.'[16] Suddenly, the possibility of being paid by the platform directly became a plausible operating model. It was a development deeply satisfying to anyone familiar with influencer history: in 2015, 18 of the world's most famous Vine stars had met with company representatives to ask for direct payment from the platform. For $1.2 million each they would produce 12 original Vines monthly, they proposed, otherwise they would defect to other platforms. After Vine declined, the app died within a year.

Previously dismissive of the influencer industry, Silicon Valley entrepreneurs and venture capitalists now wanted in, and a digital goldrush began pumping huge sums of money into startups geared towards social media stars, rebranded as the slicker-sounding 'creator economy'. Li Jin, a rising star venture capitalist, is often regarded as personally responsible for the boom. Whilst a partner at Andreessen Horowitz venture capital, her work championing the creator economy in a series of blogposts went viral, triggering a landslide of investment around 2020: 'Pre- and post- me publishing [on the Andreessen blog], people told me there was a night and day difference in VC openness to their business,' she tells me over Skype, although she's too modest to take full responsibility for her impact: 'In my view, I was just describing something that was already happening: creators were already influencing purchases, they were already becoming businesses in their own right. I just got VCs to pay attention in a way that they hadn't before.' At the Summer 2020 cohort of Y Combinator, the Silicon Valley startup accelerator, Li remarked that 'almost one in three companies had some sort of creator focus, helping people monetise through fitness classes or audio courses or helping digital entrepreneurs in some way'.

When I point out that what Li has described is effectively acting as an influencer in the venture capitalist space — publishing content, building her name, and persuading an audience — she laughs, admitting that she 'considers herself a creator'. In the spirit of the space she invests in, Li has since struck out on her own, leaving Andreessen to establish boutique Atelier Ventures, one of a select few funds that invest exclusively in the influencer space: 'I'm living my thesis: platforms enabling people to pursue their passions, power shifting from institutions to individuals.' So far, she's invested in a roster of companies that support independent internet entrepreneurship, such as Patreon, Substack, Streamloots, and Stir, alongside first-generation YouTuber Casey Neistat, YouTube co-founder Chad Hurley, Cameo CEO Steven Galanis, and Patreon CEO Jack Conte. 'The fund is a secret way for me to fund the vision that I have for the future, which is that I want us all to live in a world in which people can do what they love for a living; can be rewarded for their creativity, and that it's viewed as a viable career path.'

On 1 December 2020, MrBeast tweeted: 'I wish there was a way to invest in social media influencers! Like when I see a channel that I think will blow up, I wish I could just like buy shares in it or something … Any small youtuber want to give me 10% of your channel for like $10k to $100k? Let's run an experiment and see how it works lol.' A hundred thousand Twitter users voiced their support.

The ask wasn't beyond stock market possibility. Back in February, the price of a barrel of oil had plunged briefly into the negative; in an economy this surreal, influencer futures didn't seem far-fetched. The influencer economy is already much like the stock market, it's premised on the accumulation of capital, it trades in reputation and return on investment as brands and businesses build. Social metrics function a bit like risk ratings provided by credit rating agencies: AAA or 100k followers both a solid indicator of market value.

Financialisation looks to be the creator economy's next life cycle, as gaps between social and economic capital converge: 'Everything that has happened in the business world to support the capitalist ecosystem, will also happen to creators,' confirms Li. The possibilities of financialised influence feel limitless: package together creators into an investment vehicle, sell the right to future posts, offer fans the opportunity to own shares in their favourite channels, and develop equity models for brand collaborations. When people invest in influencers, '[they] have dual motivations: they want to make money, and they want to support their favourite creators', Li says. 'So you'll have two overlapping segments: people who feel that there's a chance to profit — if creators are businesses, they can be invested in and traded like securities — and folks who like to patronise their favourite creators, who are invested in the social status element of "I found this creator first", just like how people post screenshots saying, "Look when I invested in bitcoin".'

The line between the world of venture capital and the creator economy is becoming increasingly blurry: 'Creators are becoming investors and investors are becoming creators. There's not that clear cut of a distinction,' Li tells me. 'More and more startups are interested in getting creators around the table as well as investors. More and more creators are interested in angel investing,' whilst on the flip slide, 'VCs are all trying to blog and podcast and create brand equity for themselves through content creation. Brand building is part of what they need to do to establish founder trust in a scalable way, which is the same playbook that influencers use.'

Creators are starting to ask brands for equity in lieu of fees; MrBeast's manager, Reed Duchscher of Night Media, discussed their early adoption of this model on his Creator Economics YouTube channel: 'We're not only taking equity in companies that we promote, we've made multiple investments in different game studios and things like that. We've been at the table at some of these very competitive deals, they've all been like: hold on, we'll make room for Night Media and "blank" influencer because we want them on the cap table.'[17]

His vision is a synergistic model in which, through equity sharing schemes, startups and influencers invest in each other at 'seed stage' in order to boost each other's bottom line: 'It'll start to be the norm where, not only are creators starting sustainable businesses, but they're also taking equity at early stages of successful companies that probably will exit in two to four years. The person that will be at the New York Stock Exchange if they go public, ringing in the bell with the founder, will be some massive YouTuber or TikTok artist that was like: "I invested at the seed level".

This reality is not far off: Sway House TikTok stars such as Griffin Johnson, Josh Richards, and Bryce Hall are now angel investors, and both MrBeast's Night Media and Jake Paul have launched VC funds of their own. In 2020, TikTok houses began to be publicly traded on the stock market, when the West of Hudson Group which operates the Clubhouse network in Los Angeles went public after being acquired by Tongji Healthcare Group in a reverse takeover. Influencers may not have floated themselves, but near enough: as no fixed rent is paid by the TikTokers in lieu of the WOH Group taking a percentage of their revenue, this model links the attention market with the financial market indirectly.

Experimental new startups are attempting to financialise influence in more direct ways: Karat, a new banking solution for creators, have launched a credit card specifically for influencers and developed an underwriting model that replaces credit scores with analysis of a creator's following and engagement rates; startup Rally has launched a cryptocurrency — dubbed Creator Coin — that will help influencers, creators, and streamers run their own next-generation virtual engagement economies, whilst fans can shop around at Clout Market, a digital marketplace where shoppers can invest in non-fungible tokens representing influencers whose worth rises and falls alongside their hype. Forget bitcoin: invest in $BEAST.

Midway through his Orbeez video, backyard transformed into a colourful candyland, MrBeast addresses the camera from the middle of the now-full swimming pool. He's nearly fully submerged, disembodied head bobbing above the colourful orbs. 'This took many days to film and was very expensive ...' he deadpans, 'like all our videos. so I'd appreciate it if you subscribe, because, like, that helps boost my self-esteem.' From off camera, a voice asks him if it also helps to boost his bank account. 'No ... the more subscribers I get the more I spend, so actually, the more subscribers I have the less money I have.' He starts to laugh. It is, admittedly, kind of funny: junklords become incredibly rich by making their videos, but they have to spend an incredible amount of money in order to do so.

Even compared with the most bougie luxury fashion hauls or exotic travel vlogs, junklording is an expensive business: MrBeast reportedly spends around $500k a month and infamously runs his YouTube channel at a loss. This is the economic paradox of Junklord YouTube: viewers flock to videos that demonstrate extreme spending, thus driving revenue for its creator, but the more successful the channel becomes, the more the audience expects in terms of outlay. Junklord YouTube must keep investing returns forward into the next piece of content, forever escalating. Start by clicking on something low-stakes — 'Going through the Same Drive Thru 1,000 Times' or 'I Ate the World's Largest Slice of Pizza' — and before long you progress to more elaborate and expensive stunts: 'I Ate $100,000 Golden Ice Cream', or 'Playing Battleship with Real Ships'. By the time you get to the top-rated stuff ('Spending $1,000,000 In 24 Hours'), the zeroes cease to mean anything at all.

The junklord economy is fundamentally unsustainable, subject to unchecked inflation: junklords must continuously one-up each other, and themselves, for views; each video must be bolder, bigger, and more expensive than the last. It's difficult to pinpoint exactly where the Orbeez trend originated, but it's easy to see how quickly the whole thing escalated; from a 2016 video of Mark Rober filling a pool with 25m Orbeez, to FaZe Rug's offering which used 50m, then MrBeast's eventual 100m. The original pool format spawned creative spin-offs, pouring Orbeez into increasingly bizarre locations in a bid for engagement: parents' backyard, a parents' bedroom, a car, a girlfriend's car, a moving truck.

As junklord stunts begin to push the boundaries of economic possibility, where will it end for creators and the influencer marketplace? The comments under MrBeast's Monopoly video have one suggestion:

'MrBeast in 2019: We played monopoly with real money

MrBeast in 2029: We created a real economic monopoly that crashed the whole economy then surprised the world with a new economy'

If the influencer economy is financialising — fast — then along with opportunity comes risk. A contact who has worked both as the influencer marketing lead at a major luxury label and as an influencer himself for over five years confessed to me he believes the industry is tainted by 'rampant influencer inflation', operating on shaky metrics and borrowed time. 'I've seen it from both sides,' he confided over drinks. 'Why is an influencer with 100k worth, say, £1k? There's no maths or logic behind the cost that we put on it. We don't really know what that worth is.'

He was once offered £10k for a post he would usually have charged £2k for: 'It takes one wrong brand or one wrong agency to overcharge, and that's your new rate.' He looked exasperated. 'My account has around 50 per cent inactive followers,' he continued, 'so technically, I don't have 290,000 followers, I have around 150,000, and I'm very open about that. Not all people are, and other [brands] aren't aware.' Plus, he reminded me, 'vanity metrics can be bought or skewed' — bots and hacking tactics can all artificially inflate an influencer's apparent status, as I had discovered when joining the engagement pod.

As a whole, the influencer industry's internal ecosystem embodies many of our pre-recession economy's flaws and failings: rapid expansionism in the pursuit of over-leveraged lifestyles, little to no regulatory checks and balances, industry bodies and watchdogs leagues behind the technology that had enabled its swift acceleration, funding being pumped into an unstable system that may be operating on borrowed time. Have we created a bubble? Will the influencer economy burst? Could we face a creator credit crisis?

To sound out the situation I turn to Tim Hwang, research fellow at the Center for Security and Emerging Technology at Georgetown University and author of *The Subprime Attention Crisis: advertising and the time bomb at the heart of the internet*, who thinks the attention economy as a whole is primed to pop, a situation he believes to be comparable to the previous financial crisis in 2008. It's an argument that can be extended to the influencer economy too, as both are the product of a platform-based, engagement-driven internet.

The bubble symptoms Tim lays out to me feel familiar. 'First, you need market opacity,' he explains.'It has to be difficult to understand what's going on. In programmatic advertising, we have a lot of data about how a given ad performs, but overall it's very difficult to get a sense of what's the average price of an ad, how effective it is, how much fraud is in the ecosystem.' The influencer industry — a decentralised network of individual actors with little infrastructure, industry bodies, or index — is similarly opaque.

There's little transparency around rates, fees, and figures, and no standardisation between brands, campaigns, and influencers. Obfuscated performance data is hidden behind individual accounts, and platforms withhold access to information about the aggregated size, shape, or distribution of creators, resulting in an ancillary industry of third-party sites and software that attempt to scrape data and gain visibility over the system. Regulators don't grasp the complexities of the influencer industry, and can't keep up with how fast the landscape is shifting. 'These systems tend to be really obscure, even to people working within the industry,' says Tim. 'It's similar in the influencer space as well.'

'Next, you need subprime asset value,' Tim continues. 'The thing you think is really valuable is actually decreasing in value over time,' To support this, he cites ad fraud, ad blocking, and the simple fact that 'people pay a lot less attention to ads than they used to'. Even though, as Tim points out, 'there's no ad block for influencers', reports of increasing consumer immunity abound: flipping past ads, ignoring sponsored content, muting influencer posts. In 2018, a survey of over 4k social media users in Europe commissioned by the marketing firm Bazaarvoice found that nearly half are 'fatigued' by the bombardment of ads on social networks.[18] In late 2019, a joint investigation by Grey and YouGov reported 96 per cent of people in the UK do not trust what influencers say.[19]

Plus, as Tim puts it, with online advertising: 'we have prioritised measuring what's measurable, rather than measuring what's valuable' — focus on so-called 'vanity metrics' obfuscates an influencer's worth. Occasionally, such as in the viral case of Miami-based lifestyle influencer @Arii, who failed to drive sales for 36 T-shirts from her 2m followers in 2019,[20] the projected worth is exposed as hollow. 'Finally,' says Tim, for a bubble 'you need an ecosystem of people who are committed to inflating that market'. Platforms themselves, agencies like mine, and the entire attention industry have a vested interest in upholding it.

I wonder how much time we might have left. 'The question of when a bubble pops is entirely dependent on how long it takes for a critical mass of people to see that the emperor has no clothes,' Tim continues. 'That's what we're debating over in influencer and programmatic advertising.' And what happens when it pops? 'First, it will create a crisis of faith, because so much financial capital but also cultural capital has been invested in it,' says Tim. Then, he hopes, it will trigger a shift in internet operation models that will reshape the attention economy.

'The argument is not "ads: yes or no?", it's whether we are happy with an internet that is built on a monoculture of advertising,' says Tim. 'All of the platforms that shape our experience are driven by a single business model: this is bad not just for choice but for the robustness of the internet economy. My dream is in a post-crash web, we have a neural net that features a larger diversity of business models, ads run alongside things like subscriptions. This leads to a healthier web.'

For now, at least, the creator economy's growth trajectory looks set to continue: *Business Insider* reports its value growing 50 per cent between 2020 and 2022,[21] and it is forecast to reach $23.52 billion by the end of 2025 according to research published by business consultancy Grand View Research.[22] But there's reason to believe that even this estimate is conservative, and that the influencer bubble will continue to scale; after all, compared with other sectors, it's still only in its infancy. Macro-level shifts in the way we produce and consume — the continuing progression towards platforms, a long trend towards self-employment, the rise of social shopping, the increasing commodification of previously uncapitalised areas of life — mean that the influencer economy feels set to increase in scope and valuation.

'Increasing automation means that in the future, the only types of work that exist are ones that require a uniquely human element of empathy, or creativity or imagination,' says Li. The influencer playbook is swiftly being introduced into other industries, integrating engagement metrics, platform mechanics and creator dynamics into new contexts. 'For existing businesses, creators are now viewed as this constituency that needs attention.' says Li: 'Creators are now recognised as the nexus of value for a lot of companies.'

Walmart are one of a number of retail giants training armies of influencer-employees to create TikToks on the job, rolling out a Spotlight programme that it aims to expand to its nearly 1.5 million US associates in the next few years. Amazon already operates an internal creator programme in which warehouse employees tweet corporate propaganda. New applications for influence are appearing in labour contexts every day. It's likely in the future that our concept of the influencer economy as an individual entity will disappear: everything will be influencer-driven, and 'the creator economy' will just be 'the economy' itself.

CHAPTER 6

SPILLING THE TEA

IS ALL ATTENTION GOOD ATTENTION?

It's a cold October evening in London, and I am about to break what every child of the 90s knows to be the cardinal rule of the internet: having told my mum I loved her and shared my live location with my flatmate on WhatsApp, I'm setting out alone to meet up with a group of total strangers from an online forum. I am going undercover as a troll.

I've accepted an invitation to attend a gathering of self-titled 'snarkers': participants of one of the many user-run gossip forums that exist to critique internet celebrities. Snarking is the flip side of the attention economy and the dark side of internet celebrity: though influencers build their brand on the cumulative support of millions of fans, for every fawning follower dropping fire emojis in the comments there exists an opposite, a jaded 'snarker' quick to pass judgement.

Given their public position and frequent displays of wealth and wastefulness, it's unsurprising that not all of the attention that influencers attract is positive. But even those who aren't notorious for driving Lamborghinis into pools or giving away private islands can find themselves subject to public scrutiny. Most of the influencers I have interviewed have pages upon pages of anonymous commentary dedicated to dissecting almost every aspect of their online presence: from the mundane — passing opinion on outfits or interior decor choices — to the invasive — speculating about medical history and digging up personal information about income or family members.

If you've got a grudge against a vlogger or want a second opinion on suspicious-looking #sponcon, the internet offers no end of outlets. Notoriously vicious blog *Get Off My Internets* (known informally as 'GOMI') has been running commentary on generations of web celebrities since 2009. Spiteful sites like Guru Gossip or Tattle Life host regular threads discussing famous creators that run millions of comments deep and update every day. Reddit, the forum that describes itself as the 'front page of the internet', is home to communities such as the scornful r/InstagramReality (903k members), the generally good-natured r/BeautyGuruChatter (230k members), and r/BlogSnark (65k members) as well as many smaller subreddits created to discuss specific individuals.

Snark Twitter is a loose nexus of accountability threads, parody accounts, and social media reporters posting viral scoops. Shade accounts on Instagram — dominated by the eponymous @theshaderoom (21.6m) — document whatever drama is currently animating the explore page, whilst call-out accounts such as @diet_prada (2.4m), @esteelaundry (180k) or @influencersinthewild (4m) share screenshots of misbehaving creators and misguided influencer campaigns with a tone that ranges from outrage to amusement. If sassy personalities and amateur theatrics are more your cup of tea, try 'tea channels': gossip vloggers on YouTube who dig for dirt, fuel rumours, and share 'receipts' for the drama *du jour* with their millions of subscribers. Commentary channels create hour-long video essays analysing influencer themes such as sustainability, authenticity, and accountability in vivid slideshow detail.

Together, this flourishing network is the influencer answer to showbiz columns, paparazzi, and TMZ. 'Celebrity drama has always been such a huge part of entertainment news. With influencers, there is so much more material than we ever got with traditional celebrities,' comments Kat Tenbarge, digital culture reporter for *Insider*, whose beat includes investigations of influencer scandals and malpractice.

'Their whole careers and their brands are built on sharing as much of their world as possible with their audience. So that just infinitely multiplies the ability for drama and tea.'

As the influencer landscape has developed, Kat has observed 'an explosion of drama and commentary' about the influencer space, not only the popularity of the accounts and channels involved, but the number of them out there. 'In terms of watch hours, viewership, and subscriber bases, it just keeps growing and growing and growing.'

On the internet, the line between fan and antifan is thinner than you'd think. Followers of famous YouTubers are just as likely to watch videos criticising them as by them, and gossip content can be both supportive and snide. The online landscape spans fans desperate for hidden details about their heroes right through to dedicated communities of anonymous commentators who spend hours each day posting lengthy, analytical criticism on anti-influencer forums. As I head out to a backstreet bar at close to midnight, it's the latter that I am about to become acquainted with IRL.

My journey really began half a decade ago, quite innocently, on Instagram. Snark sites lingered on my periphery, but I had never taken a serious interest in their activities, intimidated by their irascible inhabitants and a vague sense of moral murkiness about the whole thing.

In 2014, whilst I was a student, the landmark #Gamergate debacle drew the world's attention to the topic of online commentary and trolling. Several prominent women in the gaming industry, including a media critic whose YouTube videos analysing the representation of female characters I had enjoyed, were subject to harassment by anonymous trolls on an unprecedented scale. This included a campaign of doxxing — the deliberate leaking of personal information to the internet — hacker attacks and rape threats, organised by 'Gamergaters' on sites like 4chan, Reddit, and Twitter, and in Internet Relay chatrooms.

'It became possibly the biggest flame war in the history of the Internet,' wrote academic Angela Nagle in *Kill All Normies*, her study of the development of internet culture in the 2010s. Gamergate galvanised a new troll movement, refined the techniques of digital harassment and escalated the online culture wars. Against this backdrop, snarking on influencers felt shady and indecent, somehow mixed in with the 'strange vanguard of teenage gamers, pseudonymous swastika-posting anime lovers, ironic *South Park* conservatives, anti-feminist pranksters, nerdish harassers, and meme-making trolls' that lurked on internet forums and lawless chan sites, picking apart victims and instigating hate mobs against online figures they deemed worthy of their vitriol. For years I remained overwhelmed by Twitter, terrified of Reddit, and steered clear of GOMI's proprietary brand of insanity full stop. But eventually, something smaller and closer to home pushed me to overcome my inhibitions and drew me into the murky world of online snark. That something was controversial American influencer Caroline Calloway.

Caroline began to pick up widespread traction for her erratic antics around 2018 but our history predated this by several years. She had originally risen to prominence documenting her adventures as a student at Cambridge University whilst I was studying at Oxford, and we shared an overlapping social circle. Although we were both concurrent students, our experiences felt decidedly different; whilst Caroline frolicked through an Instagrammable arcadia of whimsical picnics, black-tie balls, and romantic moments in the deer park at dawn, I spent my time downing lurid drinks in bars with sticky carpets, biking late to lectures, and self-administering an uneven undercut.

With 300,000 followers, Caroline had become something of a student legend: she would immortalise the events she attended in Instagram captions that were liked tens of thousands of times, and had the ability to romanticise even the most mundane aspects of student life. You could be introduced to her and later find yourself appearing as a walk-on part in her extensive social media mythology, or accidentally papped in the background of a Snapchat picture that would end up reposted by one of her many devoted fan accounts. 'She was always on her phone at parties,' remembers a contemporary.

'Everybody knew who she was ... but nobody really understood what she was doing'.

These were the early days of influencing, and Caroline built her picturesque lifestyle brand with long, adjective-heavy captions whilst the rest of the world was, in her words, still "gramming latte art through a Valencia filter'. Her image proved popular with generations raised on tales of Hogwarts and the plucky heroines of YA Lit: 'American student's fairytale life enchants Instagram', gushed *The Daily Mail* in an interview with Caroline.[1] Student newspaper *The Tab*, which I wrote theatre reviews for at the time, countered somewhat less generously with the headline 'Cambridge, castles, and forcing people to be friends with you.'[2]

This period — pre Fyre Festival or Cambridge Analytica, before cancel culture had become a buzzword — feels quaint and antiquated today. My world was small, unsurveilled, and self-contained: though Facebook relationship statuses were religiously updated and grainy batch-uploaded archives of regrettable clubbing photos were a weekly feature of my student routine, we largely stumbled through our early years of adulthood unbranded, unoptimised, and unobserved.

Future generations of StudyTubers, who would film their essay crises in timelapse and pose with #sponsored pints, had yet to take their GCSEs. A popular YouTube series in which a student journalist interviewed inebriated clubbers on the street ('Austerity or stimulus growth?' 'Harold Pinter or pornography?') was the closest we got to social media celebrity; the willingness of Wahoo Bar and Grill's ejected patrons to engage in compromising conversations on camera was symptomatic of a particularly mid-2010s obliviousness to our internet footprint.

The university environment — the same context which had given birth to Facebook in the first place — operated as an analogue social network linked through colleges, hobbies, clubs, seminars, drinking societies, sports teams, tutorial partners, and one-night stands. Fortunes rose and fell, not via an algorithm, but library stack gossip, committee positions, and student council campaigns; circulated lists compiling microcosmic BNOCs: 'Big Names on Campus' earmarked for great things.

These were the rankings I was attuned to; I didn't see the digital shift taking place around me whilst I worked and slept and studied, nor did I grasp the scale of the reputation game that Caroline was playing. Whilst I was anxiously grappling with adulthood and experimenting with a cocktail of appropriated tastes, she appeared to be a fully formed commercial proposition with a coherent aesthetic, on the cusp of becoming a lucrative international lifestyle brand with a book deal worth nearly half a million dollars. Within a few years, Caroline Calloway would be a BNOC not just to us, but to the entire internet.

After graduation, the internet swallowed us up in different ways, her life unfolding in front of the screen, and mine behind it. Whilst I was churning out digital banners and brand campaigns as a graduate advertising trainee, Caroline continued to 'architect' her 'wild and precious life' on Instagram, posting pictures from glamorous New York parties and downtown bars, her follower count rising to nearly a million. She was one of the first of a new breed of Instagram success stories: it-girl outlet *Man Repeller* crowned her the 'original Instagram influencer' in a flattering portrait from her kooky East Village studio, books stacked wall-to-wall and mobiles hanging from the ceiling.[3]

As Caroline gained internet fame with Calloway-branded merchandise and fashion collaborations with trendy New York labels, she faded from my consciousness, slipping into the homogenous ranks of a sleek cohort of polished, interchangeable Instagram influencers that were populating my feed and eating into my marketing budgets.

I was too busy being immersed in its inverse: the old-school world of advertising egos and billboard placements and FMCG (fast moving consumer goods) brands demanding bigger logos; marketers who clung to the mythology of *Mad Men* and the sanctity of the 60-second TV spot. When we shot a Kit Kat campaign involving two members of The Sidemen, bewildered art directors raised their eyebrows and TV producers shrugged their shoulders. Influencers, the advertising industry implied, were the antithesis of craft and creativity. I eventually forgot about Caroline.

One day, years later, far enough into my career to have adjusted my attitude and abandoned the grad scheme, I unlocked my phone to find my one-time peer was trending fifth on Twitter. An explosive personal essay called 'I am Caroline Calloway' by her former friend and ghostwriter Natalie Beach had been published in *New York* magazine vertical *The Cut*. It lifted the lid on life as an influencer, detailing the pair's mercurial relationship and the hidden machinations behind the Instagram fantasy that was Caroline Calloway the brand.

The essay was studded with delicious, delirious details, such as Caroline bidding thousands of dollars on antique furniture on eBay and the pair's Adderall-fuelled overnight writing workshops Frankensteining her Instagram captions into a book proposal for celebrity literary agent Byrd Leavell. It came with staggering revelations that undermined my former admiration: Caroline had originally bought the Instagram followers that had made her name at university. Natalie had written her compelling captions. She had blown off her half-a-million-dollar book deal. Her Cambridge #adventuregrams had been faked.

The timing was right: it was 2019 and the internet had just endured the infamous 'summer of scam' with the exposure of gentrified grifter Anna Delvey, who had swindled New York's elite out of thousands of dollars, and YouTuber Olivia Jade's college admissions scandal in which her celebrity parents were discovered to have bought her place at USC for $500,000.[4] Frustrations with hollow influencers were peaking. 'I am Caroline Calloway' shot to public prominence overnight, becoming one of *The Cut*'s most-read pieces for the entire year.

As thinkpiece after thinkpiece appeared in the weeks after Natalie's essay, and Caroline-related conversation dominated discussion for far longer than the average viral life-cycle, it seemed that every hot take in existence had been taken, no possible angle been left uninterrogated. Yet, like the rest of the internet, I couldn't seem to let the story go. I was riveted by a combination of the compelling online drama and my tenuous connection to its subject.

I scrolled hashtags, clicked headlines, hunted for new hot takes. I messaged uni friends: *Did you see this? Do you remember her? Did you see what happened to her book deal?* They weren't that interested. But a *Sliding Doors* sense of serendipity meant I couldn't stop searching her name on Twitter. It was then that I fell down the rabbithole of influencer antifandom.

Twitter, it turned out, was just the tip of an iceberg. A viral thread about Caroline led me to a Reddit thread, until the volume of comments about her became too substantial for the moderators to handle and it split off into a dedicated Caroline Calloway subreddit group of nearly 8,000 users who discussed her life and history in investigative detail. The handle of a finsta — private Instagram — account which reposted her pictures and videos for the benefit of those she'd blocked or banned was passed around via private message. A Caroline Calloway-themed podcast hosted by a US-based woman named Shay Shades (a nickname rather than a spectacular act of nominative determinism) invited former CC fan accounts, journalists, and other snarkers on as guests.

It didn't matter that several years had elapsed since I'd last thought of Caroline: dedicated snarkers had been busy documenting her every move, filling in the gaps for a comprehensive 'primer' on her online life. It was all there, laid out in hyperlinks and screenshots: she had been ejected from a book group at 'feminist' co-working collective The Wing, she had posted about taking cocaine in a church, she had hosted a $165 creativity workshop in New York, for which she ordered far too many mason jars and far too little catering, arrived late, and asked attendees to sit on the floor whilst she taught them how to 'begin architecting a life that feels really full and genuine and rich and beautiful for you'[5] — in other words, an event which appeared to encapsulate everything that was wrong with influencer culture in early 2019.

There were threads critiquing her choice of footwear, comments debating her political views, memes created from screenshots of her Instagram Stories, nicknames, in-jokes, slang, poems. Anonymous members claiming to be exes and acquaintances offered anecdotes from their alleged shared past. The snarkers dug up real estate listings on Zillow, legal documents, a lien from her landlord, old newspaper articles: the *Tab* profile and *Daily Mail* coverage from all those years ago, an interview with her literary agent about the blown-off book deal. I scrolled through it all, astounded and enthralled. I had unwittingly stumbled across a thriving antifan community, a bizarre inverse universe where every like and comment on Caroline's Instagram account was matched by a hot take or screenshot on her personal snark forum.

In the ensuing weeks, I found myself checking back in to the subreddit almost daily. I was uncomfortable about my newfound appetite for snark, but increasingly transfixed: the community was somehow more compelling than their subject. The group had all the energy of an infatuated fandom, but in reverse. Hours of content, hundreds of accounts, and thousands of views were being generated daily, anonymous hobbyists logging in from around the world to participate in a shared pastime: criticising Caroline. Some began Calloway-inspired creative writing projects, others sold 'Adventurescams' merch — a parody of Caroline's own early #adventuregrams brand — on Etsy.

The forum left me with more questions than it answered: Who were these people? Why were they so invested in a random person they had never met? What made complaining about an influencer on the internet — or watching other people complain about an influencer on the internet — so addictive? When a snarker suggested a meet-up in London, I swallowed my nerves and volunteered to join, hoping that I would find some answers IRL.

The meet-up is a surreptitious affair, arranged by one of Caroline's most enthusiastic antifans at a private members' club in the backstreets behind King's Cross. I arrive from the Tube under a full moon, the flagstoned streets damp and shining in the lamplight, late-night punters stumbling out of pubs. Citymapper deposits me outside an anonymous entryway. After a few moments of equivocation on the pavement I enter the door code I had been texted, and am wordlessly ushered through a heavy set of velvet curtains. Come on, I think, even for my first clandestine internet gathering, this is a little heavy-handed.

Inside, the bar itself — low light, low ceilings, and even lower tables — is intimate, windowless, perfect for a secret meeting. Eyes adjusting to the gloom, the designer lamps and footstools that materialise are more trendy millennial get-together than dank troll basement. Knots of drinkers cluster in tight groups, oblivious to the insidious intentions of a small group of antifans hidden within their ranks.

Finding the snarker group is a bit like trying to find a Bumble date at a bar; I scan the room, neck craned, clutching my phone defensively, nerves bubbling in my stomach. I accidentally disturb a couple necking in a darkened corner before eventually locating the group with an awkward wave and sliding into a stylish mid-century sofa with my new companions.

The snarkers are not at all what I'd expected of a forum described by *The New York Times'* internet culture journalist Taylor Lorenz as 'scary' and 'unhinged'. They are well-dressed, gregarious women in their twenties and thirties. All clearly a few drinks in, from an outsider's perspective we could be a group of girlfriends or colleagues from a nearby WeWork, kicking off our weekend.

A giddy, conspiratorial energy — a frisson of excitement at all being strangers from the internet — is heightened by the arrival of another bottle of wine. Our waiter, pouring glasses of cheap white that glow in the half-light, is clearly confused: 'So you're telling me that none of you lot actually know each other?' I am late; they have already exchanged names and established their backstories, so we swap memes and complaints about London rents instead. The conversation is peppered with meta-jokes about one of us being an undercover reporter, or one of us being Caroline.

Eyes gleaming, we are self-conscious at first but emboldened as drinks are drained and the candles burn down. The group trash-talk reality TV and disclose increasingly personal intimacies — employment pressures, relationship strains, adolescent ambitions that remained unrealised. The meet-up is more like a millennial women's support group than the blistering bitchfest I had been led to believe it would be. Despite my best attempts to steer the conversation onto the topic of our mutual interest, it seems they actually want to talk about everything except Caroline.

The snarkers don't seem like trolls, stalkers, freaks, or internet obsessives. They live, not in dingy parental basements, but flats in Hackney and house shares in Hampstead. They have cats and boyfriends, and watch *Real Housewives* in their spare time. I'm not sure what I thought I would discover at the meet-up, but it's not what I've found: the snarkers are professional, fashionable, attractive, normal, fun. I am somewhat disappointed to find myself enjoying their company.

Months after the meet-up, I call Caroline to discuss her snark army — and admit to having briefly joined them. Killing time before the meeting, I realise I am suddenly nervous to be presented with the real person I've spent months reading mocking commentary about from behind a screen, in whose criticism I feel complicit. I am either afraid to face Caroline, or afraid to face myself, and have longer than anticipated to deliberate: she is ten minutes, then 20 minutes, then an hour late to our scheduled Zoom appointment. I stare blankly at the image of myself on screen as the minutes pass, wondering if I am experiencing an authentic Calloway scam first-hand. The snarkers, I think, would surely love this.

When Caroline does eventually turn up, she is prostrated in bed in her grandmother's apartment in Florida, effusively welcoming me and informing me we have only 20 minutes to speak, before launching, without warning, into tangential anecdotes without taking a breath. Her eyes are wide and earnest: she warns me that 'sometimes, I get really lost in my thoughts' and brushes off my concern for the potentially sensitive nature of our conversation with earnest praise for my 'really beautiful empathy' in a lilting, spellbound voice lifted straight out of her university fairytales. Even through the screen, I understand why she had appealed to her first fanbase all those years ago.

'I'll never forget the snarkers: they have made a huge impact on me,' says Caroline definitively. Discovering that her story had gone viral, and then that nearly 10,000 people were active in an anti-Caroline community on Reddit was 'a kind of trauma to the system'. 'In the first few weeks, I was really hurt, I took them so seriously,' she explains. 'It was really rough.' For a time, she emotionally shut down: 'I was so paranoid, so disoriented … I could no longer perceive social interactions with the same clarity that I can now.' Over time, 'once you make the transition from being not famous enough to have that level of scrutiny to being famous enough to *expect* that level of scrutiny', she shrugs, 'you learn to tolerate it. It's a lot easier to talk about it now that I'm out of the woods.'

I ask how she feels about it now. 'These people are not anyone I admire or would want to be friends with. What they think of me is not really relevant.' She pauses and reflects, then breaks into laughter, slipping into a whiny caricature of herself. 'Ask me again at 3 am when I'm blackout drunk and I'd be like "Why are they all so meeeaaaan?"' It's the first moment that Caroline indicates her online presence is anything other than invulnerable and deliberate. It's the only moment at which she feels relatable.

Though snarking is a largely anonymous, disembodied activity, it has tangible offline repercussions for those it targets, as British beauty guru and *Guardian* columnist Sali Hughes discovered when she became entangled with Tattle in September 2019 on a recurring thread several iterations and hundreds of comments deep.[6] Though she's not a traditional influencer, Sali's forays into sponsored content had brought her into snarkers' sights: 'So I guess that means she's now a bread and butter influencer,' says the first post on her first Tattle thread, 'what a shame.' From there, members of the forum began to dig up information about her family and friends, and speculate about everything from brand partnerships to house floorplans on threads titled 'Sali Hughes #22: pretty narcissistic' or 'Sali Hughes #17: So shady she doesn't need an SPF.' The comments would 'start at 5 am, and go on for 18 hours a day'.

'The impact on my personal life has been massive,' Sali tells me, as we sit in a sunlit Soho House between two London lockdowns. She remains perfectly composed, even as she recounts her gruelling, year-long experience: 'I will never be the same person again. When I walk down the street, I wonder who is watching me. I don't trust anybody. I'm in a heightened state of anxiety … It makes you incredibly self-conscious to know that every word you say, place you go, and thing you do that is identifiable as you is picked apart forensically.' In the wake of her discovery of Tattle, she felt afraid to be alone, and even now, she's cautious about giving interviews.

Sali reached out to other influencers in similar situations, to find she wasn't the only one: 'There are many people in our industry who are on medication because of Tattle Life. I know of one influencer who is agoraphobic, who goes outside, takes her pictures for Instagram, and goes back indoors … I feel utterly certain that someone will die by suicide at some point because of Tattle.' Sali has been investigating and campaigning against snark sites ever since, releasing a statement on IGTV, involving lawyers, writing columns, sharing petitions, and producing a BBC Radio 4 documentary about the topic, titled *Me and My Trolls*.

The word 'troll' invokes an image of anonymous aggressors spewing vitriol at helpless internet victims. The reality is not always as clear cut. Snarkers are caught in the middle of two competing definitions of their actions, in a context where nuance is easily lost and evidence can be deleted. Whilst influencers claim snark to be harassment worthy of legal action, snarkers defend their speculation as being protected by freedom of speech. In her Instagram captions, Caroline directly addresses the Reddit threads, Instagram pages, and Twitter accounts that discuss her as 'haters and trolls'. The Reddit threads, Instagram pages, and Twitter accounts, however, firmly disagree.

'There's a big difference between "hate following" and "snark following" — because of the attributes I would use to define those terms,' *Pardon My Snark* podcast host Shay Shades tells me over Skype. Trolls have 'no interest in creating intelligent discourse', whereas snarkers, she insists, are 'thoughtful and eloquent' internet critics, using influencers as a prompt for wider discussion.

This might sound more than a little grandiose, but during my time as a lurker I had seen for myself how Caroline had prompted nuanced discussions of the intersection between influencers and political polarisation, cultural appropriation, online activism, and wokewashing — conversations I had found stimulating, and which I had even, at points, joined in with. Of course, these came alongside more straightforward complaints about her claiming to be vegan whilst eating Sweetgreen salmon salads, failing to deliver on her promised creative projects, or the ultimate crime of simply wearing ugly headphones. I learned that the latter type of pettiness is known online as 'BEC' or 'Bitch Eating Crackers': when you find someone so annoying that even the innocuous act of snacking becomes a source of irritation.[7]

'It's not just a hate fest. It's about starting conversations about why this is problematic, how we can learn from it. There are things that she does that I would put the word hate on, but do I actually hate Caroline Calloway?' asks Shay. 'No, I don't.' Whilst trolling is attack, she clarifies, snarking is more like critique.

Sali is not so sure. 'What's interesting about trolls is that they always think the world troll describes other people,' she tells me. 'You need to afford yourself some degree of separation in order to justify it.' She outlines a distinction between traditional conceptions of trolling and modern influencer snark: 'Their vibe and MO is very different. A classic male troll will be mega-aggressive, nasty, the abuse will happen like that.' She snaps her fingers. 'Female trolls [most influencer snark comes from women] are complex, insidious, and emotionally cruel. They really like to dig deep, it's a subtle, systematic programme of abuse that goes on for months and months. It allows them to feel superior to the bloke that says, "I'm going to rape you", but actually the effect is much worse. It becomes a daily part of your life, it raises your anxiety levels on a permanent basis.'

'Trolls are not the same as snarkers', reads the title of one post on Reddit with 155 upvotes: 'The snarker community is, by and large, comprised of folks who just hang out HERE, don't directly interact with you at all, and just believe in holding you accountable. It's not our fault that you've pissed off so many corners of the internet. Thank you for listening to my TED Talk.'

On social media, there is little room for nuances such as these. 'The way that we understand how people interact with influencers and celebrities online is either you're a fan of this person or you're a hater of this person,' comments Kat Tenbarge. 'You're either a troll or a stan. There's a tendency for influencers to use 'troll' as a catch-all term to label anything from gossip forums right through to less-than-glowing Instagram comments, negating constructive feedback. '[They think that] if someone is commenting anything other than agreement [on an influencer's post], then that person is just jealous and sad, a lonely person with a pathetic life,' says Shay. 'It's such a cop-out response.'

The very architecture of the apps themselves — in which 'like' or 'block' are often your only public options — further flatten nuance and polarise roles. And it's understandable that influencers' frequent request for their audiences to 'be kind' can be received with cynicism on occasion, such as the time Instagram star Sheridan Mordew went on ITV's *This Morning* to defend a Dubai 'business trip' during the pandemic. The clip which went viral and quickly became a meme, perceived as a prime example of how 'kindness' and the rhetoric of mental health are weaponised by influencers to avoid accountability.

'There's a sliding scale,' agrees Caroline when I ask her if she agrees with the distinction between troll and snarker. 'People who click an article about me as a scammer, I don't think they should be lumped into the same group as people who spend 12 hours a day on Reddit threads.' However, she has no hesitancy about describing the latter as 'truly sick'. 'If you found out that one of the people in your life was anonymously sending hate messages to an influencer, or even had an account on Reddit where they were dragging people on the internet they didn't know, what would you think?' she challenges me. 'I would think that person was fucking nuts!'

In the comments of the Reddit post, another adds: 'CC snarkers are hardly saints, but we tend to try to call each other out for possibly going too far, and also that we (by and large) think it's gross and inappropriate to threaten Caro/make her feel unsafe.' Caroline, however, does feel unsafe. When I tell her that I went to a meet-up IRL, her eyebrows shoot upwards, and she cracks a joke that she's surprised I wasn't abducted. 'There is a part of me that locks the door at night because that Reddit exists,' she continues. Though she's not yet had any incidents: 'I have my assistant monitor it once a week, to check that there is nothing dangerous going on. All it takes is one crazy person to be extra crazy, and it goes too far.'

The Reddit snarkers dismiss Caroline's stalking concerns as

melodramatic, but she has cause to be concerned. In 2018, lifestyle and beauty influencer Andreea Cristina Bolbea described multiple harrowing experiences with online stalking and harassment to *VICE*, including one devoted follower who moved into a hotel room near her house and dropped off letters with her parents, eventually resulting in her hiring a private investigator. 'I am totally helpless against the people who are trying to make sure that I don't have an income, who are trying to destroy my marriage, and they can just pop up at any moment,' she told journalist Sirin Kale. 'It makes me feel terrible.'[8] In 2021, a 29-year-old man was arrested after being accused of stalking a San Antonio social media fitness influencer and threatening to kill her, harassment which started two years earlier when he first subscribed to her YouTube channel.[9]

The question of where things 'go too far' with online commentary is hotly contested. Unlike the laissez-faire approach of the troll forums that had freaked me out all those years ago — 4chan's /b/ notoriously operated with a 'no rules' policy — I was surprised to find the Reddit group governed by shared community standards and an ethical code of conduct. Fifteen rules prohibit the discussion of physical appearance, mental health, family members, minors, the sharing of private information, and ban contact — or even the mere mention of its initiation — with the influencer in question, as well as anyone connected to them.

This system of self-policing mostly appears to work: meticulous moderation and an active community means that disruptors are quickly banned or downvoted, and reading threads I am frequently confronted by the gaps, retractions, and deletions created by rulebreakers. However, Sali is quick to correct me. 'Every code of conduct rule they have is broken constantly,' she says. Firstly, 'it's not some small corner of the internet', Sali notes, 'it's on page one of Google.' Nor is commentary confined to voluntary information: Sali's snarkers dug up private information and targeted her assistant and the admin of her private Facebook group. 'The rule they have that they're only going after people in the public eye? Absolute bollocks!'

Even if the snarking starts out responsible and good natured, criticism can quickly escalate online, as George Resch — aka Tank Sinatra, the man behind the call-out account @influencersinthewild — found out. 'It seemed like everywhere you looked these days people are capturing content,' he explains to me via email when I asked him why he set it up. 'Usually, it's 90 per cent less glamorous before all the editing is done and all the filters are applied … The account was created to capture that feeling. It's more of a "laugh with", than a "laugh at" situation.' However, 'when the BLM protests were taking place [in June 2020] there were some people going to the demonstrations solely for the purpose of getting content, at least it appeared to be this way'. Followers were sending in videos that appeared to show staged protest pictures and faked attempts at rebuilding hoarding. 'I posted some of these videos, for the purpose of exposing the behavior, not the individual, and things went awry.'

@influencersinthewild's posts went viral and were picked up by international news organisations. Outraged internet users tracked down the influencers depicted, hounding them, sending death threats, and doxxing them.[10] George uploaded a statement to his Twitter page, pleading with these digital vigilantes to stop putting the subjects of his videos, despite their 'egregious' behaviour, in 'real physical danger': 'That is not why I started this page, I am not in the life-ruining business.'[11] 'I wish I never posted those videos,' he tells me over email. 'The mob mentality is out of control, and I assume it always has been, but the internet has probably just made it much more immediate and more intense.' @influencersinthewild has since reverted to more lighthearted posts: posing in bikinis in the snow, beach photo fails, and faked private jet pics. Other posts champion the efforts of the 'real influencers' — the crouching Instagram husbands toting iPhones who are also seen in shot.

Not all snarkers agree on a common code of conduct, resulting in friction and infighting within the various communities. Each site has different standards: Tattle is independently run and poorly moderated, resulting in harsh commentary and brutal opinions, whilst tea channels are subject to YouTube's community guidelines and are thus more family friendly. On Reddit, divergent philosophies have split the Caroline Calloway subreddit I first visited into two sub-groups, the former abandoning the rules in favour of an amoral anything-goes approach, and the latter more heavily moderated (but less heavily frequented) to create a 'kinder, gentler' space. Comments on the less-regulated forum are darker than previous iterations, users referring to each other as 'toads' and reclaiming the community as a 'swamp'. An 'unpopular opinions' thread criticises the need for a moral pretext as 'disingenuous social justice window dressing': 'I do like the interesting conversations on how various privileges intertwine to allow CC to do what she does,' says one user, 'but to act like all snark has to be based in that in order to be valid is so pretentious.' Better to give up the justification, they claim, and recognise that 'snarking is inherently hateful and petty and that's okay!'

Abby, an LA-based professional reality TV producer who has found her online niche in firing off critical opinions about celebrities, admits to trolling Caroline — though she'll use the adjective, she won't identify with the noun — deliberately 'baiting' her by tagging her in crudely drawn caricatures masquerading as fan art. Her preferred snark platform is Twitter, a 'fucking bird website' for '240-character shit talking', where her bio reads 'I just like drama ok'. She responds to Caroline's posts with real-time commentary: 'Caroline Calloway's essay that she released today only proves what a selfish, horrible, delusional, manipulative person Caroline is' (33 likes, three replies). 'Wring me to filth!' she challenges me about our interview: 'I love it.'

'People act like I'm some kind of evil genius,' Abby tells me over Skype: 'I just love stirring the pot.' She's not just after Caroline, but a whole cast of influencers she categorises as 'terrorists', and clearly thrives off the possibility of pissing people off: 'I'm drawn to train wrecks and drama and mess — that's just who I am … What can I say? Being a bitch is in my DNA.' There's something in her intonation that sounds vaguely theatrical; I wonder if, by agreeing to this interview, she could even be trolling me.

Over video chat, Abby's upbeat accent and energetic personality mean that when she casually mentions that 'when Caroline's dad died, I just found it a little too convenient', it takes me a few seconds to properly absorb what she is implying: that Caroline fabricated her father's suicide for internet clout. 'Months and months later the house is given away and there's actual proof,' she continues, unfazed. 'Lo and behold — he's actually dead! I was like, oh — my b guys!'

Reading Abby's tweets calling Caroline out for 'narcissistic ego masturbation' and being a 'fucking piece of shit human being,' it's easy to see why she's a controversial figure in the CC snark community. Many are quick to distance themselves from her, saying that it's the actions of a few bad actors like Abby that have led outsiders to brand the entire thing as bullying. None of this deters her: 'I love all these people that like talking shit about me. Whatever happens, I'm gonna keep writing dumb, mean, easy jokes about Caroline.'

Though much of influencer snark can be written off as 'dumb, mean, easy' entertainment, it is also more than just ephemeral gossip about undeclared partnerships or extravagant spending. It's part of a broader negotiation of the rights and rules of the social internet: the definition of public and private spaces, the role of platform moderation, and the argument around accountability vs anonymity online.

Snarkers, tea channels, and gossip forums often claim to hold influencers accountable: because the internet is fluid and inconsistent, they act as digital archivists — screenshotting and filing ephemeral social media posts, unpicking non-chronological timelines, and constructing exhaustive 'receipt threads' on their subjects. Because the influencer industry is so poorly regulated, they can position themselves as digital watchdogs, pointing to the many moments in which they have discovered illicit activity as proof that they are studiously uncovering untruths and exposing shady behaviour in the pursuit of public good and transparency.

It's techniques like these that have surfaced stories of top YouTubers grooming, gaslighting and engaging in unethical business practices. The online commentary community are behind the exposés of some of the biggest scandals in the influencer universe to date, from undisclosed partnerships and amateur Photoshop fails right through to faked marriages, racist tweets, stolen goods, tax avoidance, and domestic abuse. Receipts claiming beauty guru Jeffree

Starr had a history of sexual assault and physical violence had been circulated on the internet by gossip accounts for years before being corroborated in October 2020 by an investigation by Kat Tenbarge,[12] who has earned the title 'influencer watchdog' for her work.

Snarkers are also quick to point to a lack of investigative scrutiny towards internet culture, claiming that they fill a void of relevant reporting: as we have seen, influencers are comparatively absent from mainstream media sources. Followers and fans have developed their own internal media that serve the influencer space, a kind of crowdsourced news network. Tea channels boast ratings that compare favourably to many mainstream TV shows and magazines: top gossip channels #DramaAlert (5.54m) run by Keemstar, and Phil DeFranco (6.41m), each have a reach greater than *Good Morning America* or *BBC Breakfast*. Tea Spill (1.54m), Spill (1.31m), Here for the Tea (427k), Spill Sesh (409k), D'Angelo Wallace (1.4m), and Smokey Glow (364k) pump out new videos every few days, a self-made media empire to rival Rupert Murdoch's. 'There's an evolving conversation drawing the distinctions between [how] journalists and tea channels differ, or what makes them the same, what journalists do that a TV channel cannot and vice versa,' Kat says. 'And I think there's a healthy sense of competition.'

'A huge reason why I did this podcast was because I was so frustrated with the media representation Caroline was getting, it's a whole system that no one is reporting on. That's why we feel like we have to come in and be like, *this is what happened*,' agrees Shay. Even when mainstream outlets did pick the story up, 'there wasn't a single media platform that deep-dived fully and did their research'. Tea channels in particular stress the investigative nature of their work: they are full of tediously detailed hours-long videos and long-running sagas spanning several years, with hosts adopting the posture of detectives and forensic experts presenting evidence for the court of public opinion in highly theatrical video 'trials'.

'A lot of journalism is receipt-gathering, which is what tea channels do. Who does this person follow? Who did they unfollow? When? What did this person put on their Instagram story? Do we have a screenshot of it?' Kat tells me. 'A lot of journalists who cover the sphere rely on tea and drama channels who post everything that influencers do, because so much of what ends up becoming important in a story may not be a main post on someone's feed.'

But Sali warns against influencer gossip accounts aligning themselves with media platforms. In a disagreement with Instagram call-out account @esteelaundry, she recalls how the anonymous operators of the page had told her that 'If traditional media like you told the stories that needed to be told, then people like us wouldn't need to exist.' She grimaces. 'I said no, hang on, if I was publishing this, I would check the source, I would validate the story, I would not write a story that was completely unsubstantiated.' She laughs: 'If I published a story it would have my name on it!' When it comes to traditional journalism and its grassroots new media alternative, 'There are very key differences; one is regulated and subject to legal responsibility and the other is not.'

Kat agrees: 'It's not a monolith because different channels have such radically different approaches, but there definitely are channels who have done things, oftentimes in good faith, that would be major journalistic malpractices.' But unlike Sali, she doesn't see the relationship between snarking and journalism as necessarily opposed: 'Personally I think my work has been improved so much by like establishing relationships with people in the drama community.' She proposes a collaborative, rather than combative model of media old and new: tea channels feed Kat tips and leads they feel unqualified to investigate themselves.

'In order to do investigative work, you usually need a mainstream news institution behind you … you need lawyers,' explains Kat. 'Most channels don't have them so they can't put new information out there because — even if they say "allegedly" before it, as they so often do — that can land them in legal trouble.' With the backing of *Insider*, she uses the tea channel and Instagram gossip network to scoop stories, and regularly interviews those behind the accounts for their perspective on events unfolding in the YouTube space. 'It's the reporting process that separates us,' she says. 'At the end of the day, we're trying to cover the same narratives.'

Snarkers also point out that influencers are public figures, voluntarily uploading their lives to the internet for profit. Tattle Life takes pains to point out the voluntarily public nature of their source material, describing themselves as 'commentary and critiques of people that choose to monetise their personal life as a business and release it into the public domain'.

'There's no such thing as private space on the internet, it's a public space,' Shay asserts. 'You are in the public eye and you need to do better and I need you to do better.' Snarking, its proponents claim, is an inevitable part of being highly visible online: 'When reality TV first existed, people didn't know what they were getting into,' Shay continues. 'In this day and age, when you sign a contract, you know what's going to happen and you're saying you're okay with it.' Abby agrees: 'Every single time an influencer uploads a picture they are re-signing a contract with the internet.'

'A lot of people think of snarking on influencers as worse than snarking on celebrities,' says Shay. 'I don't see that. If you put yourself out there, you're giving up a piece of yourself and opening yourself up to criticism.' Influencer oversharing complicates the audience's understanding of where to draw the line. Unlike politicians and celebrities, influencers have built their profiles through the strategic revelation of highly intimate moments: uploading sobbing selfies, discussing their sex lives, bringing followers into births, marriages, divorces, and deaths blurs the boundaries for fans and antifans alike. To complicate things further, influencers' own oversharing doesn't always carry the consent of its participants. Whilst discussion of friends, family members and minors is technically banned from r/Blogsnark, as Mia Jeal noted within the mumfluencing space, many influencers continue to post pictures of their children without consent: a hypocrisy that's become snark circle cliché.

More broadly, snarking and influencer gossip animate the consequences of collapsing personal identity with professional profile: because the lines are blurred between influencers as people and commercial propositions, feedback on their work quickly blurs with personal attack. 'If your fame is based in personality, [then] in criticising your personality, they are criticising your job,' comments Sali, 'whereas for me, if someone disagrees with something I've written they are criticising my job.' Her Tattle threads now show up on the first page when you search her name in Google: a problem whether you're an influencer or a professional online columnist.

Though many of those who create content online — such as Sali — are desperate to distance themselves from online gossip networks, other influencers do the exact opposite. Negative attention can be a viable way to build your personal brand. Considerable profiles can be built by antagonising, rather than cultivating the admiration of their audiences: 'controversy vloggers' such as Tana Mongeau, Jake and Logan Paul, Trisha Paytas, and Jeffree Starr have accumulated many millions of YouTube subscribers for their outrageous behaviour, clickbait video titles, and public feuds picked with other influencers via TikTok and Twitter, which are in turn reported on by tea channels and gossip forums, boosting their audience and fuelling their relevance. They end up trolling the internet with staged relationships and manufactured drama, rather than the other way around.

'That whole ecosystem, it's like those fish that live on the backs of sharks, these much larger animals that are the top of the food chain,' Caroline says enthusiastically when I compare her career trajectory to theirs. Controversy influencers 'are apex predators, and yet they have these parasites that live off them and somehow benefit the animal in some way, cleaning them or attracting prey. The drama community is a really good example of that parasitic-symbiotic relationship within the economy of online fame.'

The tea ecosystem reverses the dynamics of being cancelled. Generating outrage usually doesn't ruin careers, but accelerates them instead, in an echo of the wider outrage grift: Logan Paul gained 80,000 subscribers after filming a dead body in Japan,[13] James Charles lost 2 million subscribers during a dispute with another influencer over sponsorship, but recovered them all within six months and had added 2 million more within the year. Leaning in to your criticism, and playing up to it, has been proven to be an effective way to cancel-proof oneself. The most controversial influencers are 'uncancellable', they merely bounce back stronger than before.

This outrage model of influence is also highly profitable. It's a technique that's most popular on YouTube, which awards advertising revenue based on views. Mongeau's most notorious act of trolling was a fake wedding to Jake Paul to which the couple sold $50 tickets to view the livestream to over 65k followers. *Insider* estimates that her eventual split from Paul was worth approximately $600 million in media value, whilst her personal worth increased 25 per cent during their staged marriage.[14] She now has an MTV documentary, *No Filter*, following her life.

'I love Tana and Trisha,' comments Caroline, 'they are such an inspiration to me. I follow them all, I watch the tea videos about them.' At the beginning, she recalls, 'I wasn't trying to play with the snark community, because I wasn't yet in the right space.' But once the dust had settled, she realised she could use it to her advantage. 'My fans are always my priority, but if the snark community is going to exist, I might as well manipulate it and use it for my interest and benefit.'

Caroline has since followed the example of her heroes and assimilated internet criticism into her personal brand; or, as she describes it: 'taking the imagery of what people use to rally a hate community around you — for me it's scamming — and consuming it, making it another part of your online kingdom.' She frequently tweets variations of the statement that 'chaos is my brand', promotes the Reddit snark forum on her YouTube channel and Instagram account, and says she will release a self-titled autobiography named 'Scammer', for which she's charging $25.

'You really defang an insult by calling yourself that,' she remarks. 'How is someone else going to hurt you?' After taking orders for *Scammer* back in 2019, she has yet to deliver on the project, leading many fans to wondering if they've been taken in: perhaps that's the point.

Of Caroline's nearly 1m followers, I wonder how many are friend or foe. I wonder if she wonders, too. 'Engagement is the only thing I want out of it. A retweet is still a retweet, it's still free exposure,' Caroline comments. Engagement doesn't discriminate, hate clicks show up the same in platform metrics: 'I don't really care who reads those news articles. I don't care where those views come from …' She shrugs. 'I just like being famous.'

Gossiping about influencers can be a viable way to build a brand for snarkers, too. Super-snarkers can become so stratospherically popular they evolve into meta-influencers themselves; tea channels in particular have a track record of creating internet celebrities. At 21, John Kuckian was the Louis Theroux of beauty YouTube, one of the original tea channel pioneers running the largest beauty-specific account on the platform.

A Glossier pink header once proclaimed him 'the original beauty investigator', declaring 'No beauty sponsorships. No ass kissing. Just the real tea', and promising 'exclusive investigations, statements, interviews and much more'. His oeuvre is a combination of 'shade' videos, in which 'beefs' between top creators are read into seemingly innocuous tweets, and 'series': documentary-style investigations into bigger influencer scandals.

In scoops entitled 'Jaclyn Hill Fired from Makeup Geek & Anastasia Collabs', 'NikkieTutorials Drunk Dumps Jeffree Starr', or 'James Charles Caught Faking Swatches For Morphe (Video Evidence)'[15] he shares hot takes, catty remarks, and 'receipts', weaving his narrative together with skilful storytelling, conspiratorial asides to his audience, and theatrical sips from a handy mug of tea. 'There have been some mind-blowing stories I've uncovered over the years,' John tells me, '… behind the scenes, business deals that went bad and so on.' Investigating these is a laborious process. 'Sometimes it's as simple as presenting a set of tweets and providing historic context. Other times, it's a few days of deep diving into business records, court documents, import data, and so on. Piecing things together is the final part. I usually just follow the rabbit hole and I get everything I need to present both sides of an argument.'

It wasn't long before John became famous himself: 'I just posted one freak beauty investigation which achieved a million views in a few days, then a second, then a third,' remembers John, recalling the

Tati beauty investigation that made his name: 'I gained over 100,000 subscribers in a single month.' As one of the original tea channel pioneers, John's celebrity came as a surprise: 'The niche didn't really exist in the way I did it before I started ... I was completely unprepared, I never wanted to be famous.' Even now his videos have over 73 million views, 'it still feels surreal that I get asked for photos in local restaurants'. In the years since, the tea channel community has exploded.

This provocation is highly profitable. 'People are seeing it as a job opportunity to make these types of videos, and create this type of content,' Kat confirms. 'People are recognising that [running a tea channel] is a way to have a stable income.' YouTube's Cost per Click advertising model remunerates views in volume (at 17m views, D'Angelo Wallace's viral exposé 'The Exact Moment Shane Dawson's Career Ended', the most-watched tea channel video of 2020, would have pulled in anywhere between $23k–$68k) though inconsistent policing of advertising on 'controversial content' means rewards can be erratic — but tea channels are also proving new territory for brands and advertisers more explicitly.

John claims to have been approached by 80 per cent of the brands he discusses in his videos, and has carried out a partnership with Fiji Water in the past. His observation is that brands also pander to tea channels who attack the influencers that have given their products bad reviews, in an effort to subtly discredit them: 'I feel like there's something very unethical about that, but that's the general nature for many of the transactions within the community.'

He also notes that the ultimate audience for this kind of advertising may not be the viewers, but the tea channel owners themselves: 'Whilst [public awareness] may be a side effect, the main reason one would publicly sponsor a drama channel is to inspire loyalty and bias from other drama channels, who hope they too may become sponsored in the future.'

Sponsorship of tea channels sparks other moral equivocation too. John says he has turned down partnerships, events, and sponsorship offers related to the beauty industry, 'as this would be seen as a compromise to my integrity ... I don't like the pretence of having to favour someone in my investigations because they've been kind to me.' This is, ironically, the very same issue tea channels snark on with influencers. John's response? Make like the mega-YouTubers he has built his career criticising, and launch a brand: the controversial (but of course!) Kuckian Cosmetics.

On YouTube, tea channels, fans, haters, and influencers are all tightly enmeshed in an incestous web. Snark videos are frequently the autoplay's 'next suggested' after the creator's own video is over, meaning you can shift seamlessly from watching Tana Mongeau to 'Everything wrong with Tana Mongeau' without lifting a finger. Creators often make direct videos in response, name-dropping tea channels, calling them out, and driving traffic in their direction. See Australian beauty guru Chloe Morello's 'John Kuckian Made A Video About Me: My React Video :'(Youtube Drama', which has 1,051,126 views.

Controversial beauty influencer Jaclyn Hill hosted a 'love me or hate me'-themed Halloween party in LA — to which she wore a dress emblazoned with the word 'CANCELLED' — following a disastrous product launch. She flew the tea channels who had cancelled her out to the event and added drama channels to her brand's PR list, ensuring her next product launch would be delivered straight into the hands of her detractors.

John's claims that YouTubers and tea channels collaborate more formally behind the scenes were corroborated in 2020 when drama channels Ashlye Kyle, Sanders Kennedy, and The Viewer's Voice (Nick Snider) each posted videos admitting that Jeffree Star sent them insider information that helped them rake in AdSense revenue.[16] 'I WAS ON JEFFREE STAR'S PAYROLL 💰' Ashlye's video is titled. Influencers view tea channels as a cynical 'opportunity to manage [their] propaganda' by strategically sharing tip-offs and gossip in a way that mimics the old-school PR machine. Instead of celebrity teams booking Getty to turn up for well-timed candid snaps of their B-list clients, influencers are DM-ing tea accounts to share scoops and attain favourable coverage. But eventually, as with Jeffree, this backfires.

'It's within influencers' best interests to increase their circulation and manage their image, but they're usually disappointed when they attempt to do this using drama channels,' says John. 'The ones without journalistic integrity — willing to collaborate on such projects — are also the ones who generally change their mind midway through and stab the influencers in the back.' Ultimately, it doesn't matter: even manufactured drama creates clicks and generates value, and everyone wins.

Inevitably, in a system geared for controversy and clickbait, the snarkers become the snarked upon. 'It's funny (and very meta) that the more snarkable an "influencer" is, the more likely it is that the larger blogsnark community will eventually turn on the users calling out the "influencer's" crazy snarkable behavior,' one Reddit commenter notes. John's personal philosophy — 'don't do to others what you would not like happening to yourself' — came back to bite him in 2018. After a series of incidents involving unfounded attacks on other YouTubers, including allegations of child molestation against a well-loved vlogger, and the backfiring of Kuckian Cosmetics as a 'whitelabeling scam', John Kuckian was cancelled in turn, signalled by a string of videos from newer, hungrier tea channels bearing his name: 'KUCKIAN COSMETICS IS OVER', 'How To Ruin Your YT Career: Featuring John Kuckian', and 'The Fall of John Kuckian'. He continues to upload irregularly, but snark sites and other tea channels regularly tear his videos to pieces, and they receive an average of 6k views.

The snarked-upon aren't above turning snarker, too. Sali tells me how she flipped the tables, becoming her own social media sleuth, hunting down and interacting with her aggressors: 'We uncovered about 25 of them. I would find their Instagram profile and I would like one picture — so that they would know I knew who they were — and then I would block them.' On Tattle, users claimed Sali had gone too far, stating that they were the real victims of her 'stalking' in reverse. 'The hypocrisy,' one commented on their thread, 'is absolutely outstanding.'

Sali's actions pale compared to mummy blogger Clemmie Hooper, public alias 'Mother of Daughters', Tattle alias 'AliceInWanderLust', who was discovered in late 2019 to have been snarking about her friends, husband — and herself — on the site. Using her pseudonym,

Hooper had called her own husband 'Father of Daughters' a 'class-A twat', and other influencer friends 'desperate'. In a *mea culpa* statement after Tattle users uncovered the conspiracy via an IP address, Clemmie's explanation for her behaviour was one with which by now I was familiar. She had succumbed to the alluring world of snark, participation had become 'all consuming': 'undoubtedly I got lost in this online world and the more I became engrossed in the negative commentary, the more the situation escalated'.

Sitting in that backstreet bar, sharing a table with total strangers from the internet, I can't quite work out why we are here. Beyond just plain novelty, what drives a group of individuals to leave their families, friends, and partners on a cold, dark Friday night to seek out other snarkers? We are bound together by Caroline, clearly, but also by something else: Jealousy? Frustration? Loneliness? It seems that snarking is a solo activity: nobody came with friends.

When I ask Caroline why she thinks people are drawn to snark, she goes quiet for so long that I think the Zoom connection has dropped out. 'When it comes to the larger cultural question of why we hate influencers, those macro answers are different from the micro answers …' she says slowly. 'Why does someone replace their life with obsessing over someone else's? I only understand them to a limit, and I tap out at the loneliness.'

Abby's answer echoes this, albeit more nihilistically: 'You have to understand, to me Twitter is just a void and I'm just screaming into the void,' she tells me. 'Every so often that void shouts back at me, and I'm like, it feels good to be heard in this void I've been yelling into for years and nobody's paying attention to me!' Though dramatic, this logic makes sense in an attention economy both for influencers and trolls alike, and aligns her with Caroline: prioritising engagement over the nature of the interaction. Abby's self-described isolation reminds me of Professor Rojek: snarking as the product of atomised audiences and professional influencers appearing to offer parasocial relationships as an alternative emotional infrastructure. Perhaps when everything is awful, snark becomes an outlet.

For Shay, snarking provides a distraction from the current state of the world, and the situation that she, and others of her generation, find themselves in: 'Snarking is something to think about instead of the fact we have Donald Trump as President!' she blurts out. At the meet-up, the snarkers seem to seek some misplaced sense of justice for what influencers, and influencer culture, represents. 'I need her to fail,' the snarker next to me at the table suddenly says, 'in order for the world to be just, I need to see Caroline punished.' There is a pause. 'Am I Caroline?' the snarker across from me asks, looking around the table at the now-still faces gleaming with wine and candlelight. 'No,' says the woman sitting on my right, 'We're all Caroline. She is literally every millennial woman.'

Perhaps, as Shay suggests, snark is catharsis; she is not really snarking on Caroline, but on something much larger: the structure that has allowed her, and other influencers such as Trump himself (with whom Caroline shared a literary agent) to flourish. It's something Caroline has hinted at herself, describing online hatred against influencers as 'collective bloodletting'.

'I wish I could live the life she leads and get away with it,' says one snarker. 'We're all striving, hustling, scraping by and desperately trying to make something of ourselves,' offers another, 'it's kind of fascinating to see someone just reject all of that, and flourish.' Shay agrees: 'People are 100 per cent projecting their feelings onto influencers,' she says, 'they are an epitome.' To her, following Caroline is 'almost like watching the worst parts of yourself play out — the parts of you that you don't indulge in. In that way,' she says, 'she really is the ultimate influencer.'

In February 2020, roughly a year after I had first become transfixed by the snarking universe, Caroline rejoined Twitter. She reclaimed her 27k latent followers from 2015 and replaced her header — a promo image of the original, blown-off book deal that had first set off the snarkers — with a picture of her upcoming self-published pamphlet about going viral at their hands. Next, she spent several hours name searching and retweeting thousands of her Twitter mentions, including months-old conversations between snarkers who had, until that very moment, been bitching about her in a supposedly self-contained section of the internet. Exposed by the very subject of their discussion, snarkers quickly found themselves in chaos. Her feed resembled a self-satire bot, with parodic self-criticisms lifted straight from her antifans: 'for exercise I prefer pilates, spin, and social climbing', she wrote. 'Nothing tastes as good as being elitist feels!'

Caroline began to refer to herself in the third person, dissociating entirely from her constructed internet identity: 'she's an irrelevant scammer who name searches on the reg', she tweeted about herself, before concentrically retweeting a retweet of her own tweet. Some people suggested that members of the snark community were secretly ghostwriting her tweets: 'Obviously my Twitter is being run by a ghostwriter,' responded Caroline. 'Do you think the REAL Caroline Calloway is this funny or smart or self-aware?'

Whether postmodern performance art or simply a prank, it felt like something had shifted. Snark had finally consumed itself, collapsing whatever tenuous distinction was left between influencer and troll, snarker and stan. Suddenly, Caroline made an announcement. 'Over the past 24 hours I've read a lot of snark about myself,' Caroline posted, 'and guess what? I've actually come to stan the trolls that tweet as CC satirically. And so! Henceforth my Twitter will be me, pretending to be a hater, pretending to be me. Welcome to the Golden Age of Internet trash.'

In many ways, my early trepidation about the murky world of online snarking forums has been realised in the discourse of today. The market for online gossip and the 'cancellation' of prominent internet figures is an evolution of the original culture war that I had observed all those years ago. Snarkers, tea channels, and gossip vloggers bear more than a passing similarity to the individuals who led a campaign of harassment as part of Gamergate: both are leaderless, allegedly truth-seeking armies of vigilantes engaging in trial by public opinion. The legacy of 4chan trolls is reflected, and commercialised, in controversy influencers, who use shock factor 'edgelord' humour and the defence of irony to hack the algorithm and accumulate large audiences online. The modern influencer gossip landscape has no ideological agenda, watching online reputations rise and fall has become pure entertainment: viewers can even log on to Social Blade to watch live follower counts rise and fall in real time.

I wonder what the end game is, both for influencer drama, and for Caroline. Influencers rise on controversy, to be taken down by vigilantes who are then taken down themselves. Drama breeds drama, scandal begets scandal, scams birth further scams, and the internet folds in upon itself in a never-ending culture war. Who wins? Where does it end? Where do we go from here?

I turn to Caroline for answers. 'I can tell you exactly what's going to happen,' she says. 'I'm going to finally release [my autobiography] *Scammer* and ride the "scammer" thing out for a while, then I'll reassess where my Google SEO is once I've fully reassigned the word to my brand. I had the fairytale chapter before this, now we're in the scammer chapter. After that, I'll definitely have new chapters. I plan to be a cultural icon, and stick around for a long time. I'm sure I'll reinvent myself a million times more.'

CHAPTER 7

PLATFORMS VS THE PEOPLE

WHO INFLUENCES THE INFLUENCERS?

A tanned man in black tie holds an oversized award shaped like a giant crystal hashtag above his head; beneath him, a well-coiffed crowd whistles and cheers. Against a panoramic view of the Riviera, a dark chopper descends onto a sun-bleached landing pad and deposits a gaggle of passengers bearing Louis Vuitton luggage and selfie sticks. Elegant guests sip cocktails on the uplit mezzanine of a sleek superyacht. A young woman in a frothy organza ballgown blows coy kisses to the camera, which suddenly pans out to an illuminated canopy of twinkling lights and streamers; beneath it, inebriated revellers sway to the sounds of a live band. 'Welcome to the world of influencers. Dreams become reality,' reads a caption, followed by a string of champagne flute emojis.

Instagram story by Instagram story, I'm reliving the 2019 Monaco Influencer Awards, informally referred to as the 'Oscars of Influence': an awards show soirée held at the iconic Salle des Etoiles, currently in its third iteration. Every year, a roster of top international influencers descend on the principality to party, take pictures, and compete for the prestigious title of Influencer of the Year. YouTube stars and Instagrammers arrive from Singapore, LA, and Bali, bound for suites at the Hermitage or the Hotel de Paris. Three days of shopping and sipping culminate in the ceremony itself: a lavish red-carpet event with performances from Algerian rappers and bikini-clad dancers writhing in giant cocktail glasses. Attendees include models, supercar collectors, fashion designers, minor French royalty, and an Instagram-famous shaman.

In 2019, the 300 influencers in attendance had over a billion cumulative views.[1] In 2020 — when my 500 followers and I were supposed to join them — the pandemic called off proceedings and I was left to piece together last year's snippets via social media instead. With political unrest, a plague, and the looming threat of recession lingering outside, I sat inside on my sofa and lost myself in luxury cars, tiaras, and champagne fountains sprayed by perfect-looking strangers.

In many ways, Monaco is the perfect place to celebrate Instagram-driven opulence. At just 2.1 square kilometres, the second smallest country in the world is a sundried concentration of status, luxury, and spectacle: every third person is apparently a millionaire.[2] It boasts the highest property prices and one of the densest populations in the world: if you can first find — and then afford — a flat, you'll be bumping up against heiresses, Formula 1 drivers, and a former James Bond enjoying his retirement. From the supercars parked conspicuously outside the casino to the overdressed crowds loitering on the promenade, Monaco oozes a particularly performative opulence. The notorious tax haven has been nicknamed 'a sunny place for shady people' — a description which dovetails well with the double lives of influencers.

The Mediterranean enclave has always had a complicated relationship with self-promotion, attracting celebrities and the eyes of the public since hosting Grace Kelly in the 50s, whilst simultaneously housing hidden billions in elusive offshore accounts. Scrolling the Monaco geotag in Instagram, it's clear it has since become a hotspot for Instagram opportunists: tight-trousered men in loafers lounging against sports cars, women snapping selfies in front of the casino.

In the past, Monaco was the place that the established elite retreated to for privacy and discretion; nowadays, it's a place the aspiring elite visit when they want to be sure they'll be seen. With the establishment of the Influencer Awards, the principality's historic frostiness towards paparazzi has been officially abandoned. The residents of Monaco may still be tax evasive, but they are certainly not camera shy.

The Influencer Awards were established by entrepreneur and St Tropez local Lolita Abraham, not only to 'promote and recognise the profession of influencers', according to the copy on their website, but apparently to #spon the principality itself, claims a 2019 BBC documentary. Monaco is currently facing the ultimate first-world problem: its population of ageing billionaires is beginning to die off.[3] As the global distribution of power and money shifts, Monaco has found itself competing with new luxury hotspots such as Dubai, Singapore, and Silicon Valley. The type of wealth in circulation is changing too, thanks to an influx of internet-related entrepreneurship: tech platforms, social media, and startups have created a new set of ultra-high-net worth individuals. Influencers are an attractive marketing opportunity to lure this next-generation elite to Monaco — the 2019 iteration of the influencer awards reached 500 million people and generated 30 million impressions.[4]

The awards are officially endorsed both by the Monaco administration and minor royalty themselves, with the Mairie de Monaco — the city hall — listed as an official partner on their website, and Princess Camilla of Bourbon Two Sicilies, friend of Albert, acting as President of the Jury and Ambassador in 2019. In the BBC documentary, Monaco royals express hope that influencers can be used to safeguard their survival. The ancient Monégasque establishment are leaning on their counterparts from the world of social media to reinforce their status.

The gap between traditional monarchy and its online equivalent has started to close in recent years — members of the British royal family in particular have begun to embrace their potential as online stars, abandoning dynastic power for its social media equivalent, such as the departure of Harry and Megan from the British monarchy to build 'brand Sussex' in April 2019. Their Instagram account @SussexRoyal broke records by reaching a million followers in under six hours.[5] Others are using it to reinforce their existing position: Kate and William began a family YouTube channel in 2021 — the world's least likely parenting vloggers.

'You have to try to anticipate the needs of the future, anticipate what the trends will be,' Monaco's Prince Albert told documentary director Michael Waldman.[6] The alliance with influencers also marks a significant shift in mindset; in a city awash with cash, online attention offers an untapped kind of currency. 'It's a different world, it's a different approach,' agreed Princess Camilla. 'Monaco — like everywhere else — has to move on. There is no choice. We just can't move back.' Perhaps, in the future, millions of followers will become a substitute for the millions of euros currently required to secure a place in Monégasque society.

Sifting through the social profiles of the nominees, I find fashion influencers toting Birkins outside the Burj Al Arab, supercar test drivers racing Bugattis up the autobahn, a collector of $500k diamond-encrusted watches with a bio reading 'Google me it's easier', and a travel influencer who seems to spend her time circulating the same four five-star resorts in the Maldives.

For an awards show attempting to crown the most influential influencer, #IAM appears to be over-indexing on luxury lifestyles and horology connoisseurs, with popular, but less glamorous, categories noticeably absent. Last year's contenders certainly don't reflect the diversity or variety seen on my newsfeed: no farmfluencers, family channels, or Instagram activists were spotted twirling under the chandeliers. The #IAM website states contestants are judged on numbers, as well as 'general look and feel, consistency, ability to generate emotions, inspire and empower their followers'. Its unspoken criteria appears to be being very rich, very chiselled, or both.

Though Monaco is undeniably an Insta-worthy backdrop for #IAM, the principality's adoption of influencers is not without its contradictions. If influencers represent a departure from traditional gatekeepers in favour of the popular elevation of the everyman, they are somewhat at odds with Monaco's historic constitutional monarchy, in which a single family line — the House of Grimaldi — has ruled since 1297 and appoints the country's government. The elite entry criteria of the second-smallest country in the world make it a strange place to celebrate the supposedly democratising opportunities of the internet.

Watching online as each winner receives their crystal hashtag statuette, I realise the concept of an influencer awards show is incongruous. If you want to know who's won 'best influencer' — who's truly broken the internet — all the numbers are out there already, quantified in fans and followers and brand deals. It's not up to a jury to crown the winners, especially not one composed of fashion designers, magazine editors, and minor royalty, representatives of the very institutions that influencers disrupt.

Why pay heed to the opinions of a hand-selected panel, when a million social media users have independently cast their votes — and likes — already? The awards show format feels somehow redundant. Of course, the selected winners of the Monaco influencer awards aren't necessarily intended to represent the most powerful influencers on the internet, but those that prop up a very particular kind of philosophy: the influencer evolution of an international jet-set elite. Unsurprisingly, a sovereign-supported celebration of the world's 'top influencers' is simply a reinforcement of the status quo.

The awards ceremony is less an attempt to crown the 'world's best influencer' than it is a skilful leverage of new avenues for advocacy for the Monégasque regime; recognising content creators' potential to influence not just a narrow range of lifestyle categories, but an entire social system. Though the influencers had arrived from all over the globe, ostensibly to collect awards for services to fashion, comedy, or cooking, they were all, in fact, there in the ultimate service of Monaco itself. And in that, the influencer awards aren't backwards at all.

Monaco isn't the first state to officially experiment with using influencers to extend their soft power. In 2019, Saudi Arabia invited social media stars to the launch of a music festival, MDL, held in the desert outside Riyadh. It was paid for by the country's $2.7 billion

Vision 2030 fund as part of a wider programme of geopolitical image rehabilitation,[7] dubbed 'a deliberate strategy to deflect from the country's image as a pervasive human rights violator' by Human Rights Watch.[8]

'Saudi Arabia isn't somewhere I would look at on the map and say, "I really want to go there,"' tech influencer GadgetsBoy, aka Tomi Adebayo, told me, '... they just said come along, see what you think.' Influencers were flown in from Europe and America on private jets and reportedly paid six figures for geotagged posts to turn the seventh least free country in the world into a hot new lifestyle destination.[9] Tomi wasn't paid or contracted to put up pictures, but his whole holiday — flights, tourist trips, and a luxury hotel — was provided *gratis* by the government. 'They invited a lot of people who probably shouldn't be there, in that they shouldn't have been supporting what Saudi is about.'

Tomi's decision to attend, he tells me, was motivated by a desire to see what the country was really like beyond his understanding from the media: 'The content I put up was nice, but with the caption there was a lot more of a thought process ... I didn't want to sound like Saudi Arabia was amazing, more "it was nice to be there to actually see it for myself". I didn't post anything about the festival.' MDL was a far cry from Coachella ('it was a festival with no alcohol — for four days, people were just on Red Bull and coffee') and Riyadh wasn't exactly set up to accommodate the influencer lifestyle: Tomi's attempt to capture pictures of a female fashion influencer friend in the street attracted stares and put his group of influencer friends 'on edge'.

The MDL experiment backfired: as stories and vlogs were posted, criticism spread quickly in comments sections and media headlines, condemning both the Saudi Arabian regime and the influencers who took up their invitation. 'What's worse than an all white @revolve influencer trip?' asked @dietprada on Instagram: 'Cashing big fat checks in exchange for #content creation (aka propaganda).'

In 2020, Russian government officials reached out to members of the country's booming influencer industry ahead of a constitutional referendum that would offer the opportunity to extend the Putin administration to 2036. Though Putin is, himself, perhaps Russia's most popular influencer — strategically releasing Insta-worthy topless shots shooting, fishing, and astride a horse — he was apparently not above collaborating with his counterparts. A handful of top Russian beauty gurus, vloggers, and automobile influencers were offered up to £100k to create posts advising their audience to vote in favour of the amendments, *The New York Times* reported, but many said no, citing damage to future partnership opportunities, authenticity, and brand image.[10]

In a 16-minute vlog uploaded to her 1.1m YouTube subscribers, outspoken Russian influencer Katya Konasova (Instagram bio Говорю то,о чём другие молчат — I say what others are silent about) detailed the brief. 'I had to explain to everyone, in accessible language, that the amendments are not evil, but a good deed. I immediately refused, because it was against my principles, to which I was told: "Well, that's a pity, but there are those who have already agreed."' Her video has been viewed over 700k times. 'Why didn't I agree to advertise the amendments?' she continued. 'Most importantly, the constitution, our country's fundamental law, should not be advertised by influencers and stars. It shouldn't be sold and bought, like some Instagram butt brush or some lotion. This is not a product or a service — this is the sale of our future.'

These political influencer experiments are merely a more advanced version of the system already operating in the West. After using bots, trolls, sock puppet accounts, and covert paid ads, governments employing content creators to advance their agendas is the logical next step in the convergence of digital and political influence. Politicians already behave like influencers, and platforms are increasingly politicised; presidential hopefuls run meme campaigns and Congresswoman Alexandria Ocasio-Cortez streams on Twitch. After all, influencers and politicians have much in common: churning out brand propaganda, amassing followers, swaying opinion, making and breaking alliances, working their way up a ruthless ranking in a bid to make it to the top.

Trump is possibly the ultimate example of a political influencer: he harnessed Twitter to cultivate his cult of personality and convert the cultural power of online influencer into its real-world equivalent during his election campaign. And once elected, he used this institutional power in reverse to continue amassing online influence: preferring to use his personal account (@realDonaldTrump) over the presidential handle (@POTUS), he acquired over 6 million new followers in his first year through prolific posting.

'He is an influencer who acts above and beyond party politics, applies corporate communication and marketing techniques, and has found in social networks an expeditious format and effective discourse that catches the attention of active communities,' stated a 2018 research paper in *Communication and Society*, which outlined 'the discourse of spectacle ... empowering new political strategists: influencers.'[11]

Not only are politicians influencers, but the platforms they exist upon have now amassed such influence they have become key political players themselves. Their banks of data, influence on the flow of information, and role as public infrastructure for millions of global citizens make Facebook, TikTok, YouTube, and Twitter a force for even the most skilful of political influencers to contend with. In August 2020, Trump issued a presidential executive order against TikTok, banning the app based on grounds of national cybersecurity unless its Chinese parent company could find an American partner within 45 days. Though the action was ostensibly a measure to protect the user data of American citizens, which officials worried would be passed back to the Chinese government, the statement was also symbolic of the battle for each state's claim to global platforms.

Claudia Conway, the daughter of Trump's Presidential Counselor Kellyanne Conway, who had created a separate political storm by posting anti-Republican TikToks to her 1.4m followers in previous weeks, tweeted in protest: 'yo @realDonaldTrump if you wanna just ban my tiktok account why didnt you just say so.' As major players on social platforms, influencers are caught up in a pervasive power system of colossal proportion.

But influencing is also a power system in its own right: a social media hierarchy that ranks and rewards all those who participate. The stratification of this digital class system bears some similarity to its offline equivalent. The ruling elite of any given platform — public figures, media outlets, and brands who import off-platform credibility, through to home-grown social media celebrities — boast millions of followers and have a tangible impact on trending topics and discussions. The fewer followers one has, the less visibility within the system and thus reduced ability to influence the flow of information. At the lowest ranks, those with the fewest followers largely post into a void.

The possible existence of a social media class system causes regular friction on Twitter, where users argue inconclusively about platform etiquette and 'dogpiling': small accounts claim larger accounts retweeting them critically constitutes 'punching down', larger accounts claim having fewer followers isn't exactly a protected characteristic.

Though it represents a hierarchy, the creator landscape is backed by a compelling promise: anyone can become an influencer, all you need is a mobile phone and the right mindset. Top creators are only there because the public have liked and subscribed, and they are free to follow and unfollow any time. The word 'platform' inherently implies equality; a flat organisational structure offering fair opportunity for digital class mobility. This industry — and my position in it — is predicated on the idea that the system opens doors, creates opportunities, makes life better for creators and audiences alike. Influencing is sold on a philosophy of freedom, flexibility, and individual empowerment — *living your best life, being your own boss, getting paid to do what you love, hashtag goals, hashtag good vibes only*. Influencers supposedly represent a power shift from institutions to individuals, a disruptive process of democratisation, and a revolution in information, culture, and technology.

Looking back, rather than forward, the history of technology suggests this may not be the case. 'I always baulk at the idea of terming something a revolution when it's not about power changing hands,' remarks technology historian Professor Mar Hicks on the tech-sceptic podcast *Tech Won't Save Us*, hosted by Paris Marx.[12] They describe a theory first put forward by computer scientist and 'father of AI' Joseph Weizenbaum in 1976: that the computer is fundamentally a conservative force, that technology works to preserve the status quo, and that its widespread adoption tends to hinder — not help — social progress, despite giving off the superficial appearance of advancement. Instead of transforming industries, technology allows broken institutions to become further entrenched, and enables them to scale and centralise in ways that that they wouldn't have otherwise been able to do.

Professor Hicks cites the introduction of the computer to society in the 80s and 90s: 'If there was a computing revolution, that should mean that the computerisation of the US and other nations changed who was in control,' they say. 'It really didn't. If anything, it just amped up the billionaire class and consolidated power in the hands of the people who already had it. And that's one of the reasons it has become so successful, honestly.' The same can be said of influencers. Trump dominating Twitter, the monolithic rise of social media platforms, and Monaco, Russia, and the UAE leveraging influencers to scaffold their authority are just another example of the ease with which supposedly democratising technology, claiming to put power in the hands of the people, can end up reinforcing power at the top. Who ultimately benefits from influencers' rise? And how meritocratic really is this system?

Although the influencer industry is theoretically open to everyone with an internet connection, in reality, becoming a creator isn't an equal-opportunity activity. At a basic level, it requires access to certain resources: an internet connection, digital literacy, equipment and software for editing, leisure time, energy, and money to invest. Aspiring influencers must be able to perform what social media academic Dr Brooke Erin Duffy terms 'aspirational labour' — unpaid work with little assurance of a future reward, work which naturally favours those with a safety net. 'As both a practice and a worker ideology, aspirational labor shifts content creators' focus from the present to the future, dangling the prospect of a career where labor and leisure coexist,' Duffy writes in *(Not) Getting Paid to Do What You Love*: 'aspirational laborers expect that they will *one day* be compensated for their productivity — be it through material rewards or social capital. But in the meantime, they remain suspended in the consumption and promotion of branded commodities.'[13]

People who work in the industry are aware of this: 'the idea that the internet presents the same level of accessibility for all often fails to consider lived experiences' notes talent manager Adesuwa Ajayi, who set up industry whistleblower @influencerpaygap in 2020. 'It has helped even the playing field but it in no way has it completely solved inequality and inequity'. There are various barriers and hurdles that aspiring influencers have to face. 'Racism for example, doesn't just exist offline,' Adesuwa continues. Fat, Black fashion influencers are subject to greater levels of trolling and harassment than their thin, white counterparts, notes Stephanie Yeboah. 'Influencing has really given minorities a voice where we didn't have one before,' she says, citing social media's role in creating space for queer, plus-sized, neurodivergent, disabled, and Black communities, but 'attractive, cisgendered, able-bodied people are still the formula'. A glance at the 'top 10' tables on industry aggregator sites such as Social Blade or Famous Birthdays confirms that, on the whole, the most successful social media stars are those that fit that mould.

'As time goes on, more barriers to entry present themselves, especially when money is involved,' Adesuwa continued. 'Those with privilege are able to monetise in ways others may not have the ability to do, the commodification of particular aspects of the space naturally presents increased barriers to entry when controlled by those with privilege.' White influencers received 61 per cent of sponsorship opportunities in 2019 (down from 73 per cent five years before) according to research by digital agency Magnetic North.[14]

Creators of colour regularly earn far less than their white counterparts, even when deliverables and metrics are identical and they are booked on the same campaigns, something that Adesuwa's @ influencerpaygap project seeks to call out by aggregating anonymous tip-offs and rates from creators, arming influencers with a greater understanding of their value. Stephanie has called out all-white influencer brand trips on her Instagram page, which she attributes in part to a lack of diversity on behalf of those behind them: 'Marketing and PR is still overwhelmingly white and able-bodied,' she says, 'I worked in PR for three years, I was the only Black person there, the only fat person there.'

Influencers with minority characteristics can find themselves locked into certain niches, whilst those who meet the norm find themselves able to flexibly shift between categories, develop new interests, and open up new sources of revenue. 'There is definitely pigeonholing going on,' Stephanie says. 'I have been referred to as a plus-sized beauty blogger before, I'm just like no — it doesn't exist. I just like beauty. It's ridiculous.'

In their 2019 Influencer Marketing Rate Report, Klear reported that female influencers were paid 33 per cent less than male influencers, a pay gap of $108 per post on average. By 2020, this gap had widened to $128. 'Rates are often set by the influencers and then negotiated,' Klear offered as explanation in a blog post. 'A process that typically favors men, who often set high rates and are more assertive in negotiations.'[15] Fans complain about the 'glass elevator' for male influencers, a phenomenon in which men enter traditionally feminine careers and advance higher and more quickly: the top two most-viewed beauty influencers on YouTube are teen 'Coverboy' James Charles and controversial glam guru Jeffree Starr.

In a post on r/BeautyGuruChatter entitled 'frustrated at men in makeup', a Reddit user complained: 'i feel like female beauty people are criticised a lot more harshly than any male beauty people. for example, i fully believe that if J* [Jeffree Starr] were a woman, he'd be cancelled so quickly.' (Starr has a history of racist outbursts, and several allegations of sexual assault, physical violence and hush-money offers, as *Insider* has reported.[16]) 'Mentrification :(' replied a sympathetic commenter.

Inequalities are often hardwired into platforms. Social media networks operate what Dr Safiya Noble, professor at the University of California's Department of Information Studies has termed 'algorithms of oppression', automated decision-making that reflects and amplifies the biases of its human operators and often limited datasets, leading to 'racial and gender profiling, misrepresentation, and even economic redlining'. Material perceived to be 'adult' or 'sexual' often ends up impairing queer influencers, even when it doesn't specifically address adult themes.

In 2019, a group of LGBTQ YouTubers in California sued

YouTube for discrimination: the class-action censorship lawsuit claimed that the platform featured 'unlawful content regulation, distribution, and monetisation practices that stigmatise, restrict, block, demonetise, and financially harm the LGBT Plaintiffs and the greater LGBT Community'. The suit claimed innocuous videos by LGBTQ creators had been demonetised or restricted whilst others by non-LGBTQ creators had not[17] — organising claimant Sal Bardo had seen his revenue drop 75 per cent and views decline from 60,000 to 5,000 each day.[18]

Other restrictions are less visible. Accent — and thus gender, class, and regional demographic — can hinder a creator's visibility within the YouTube index. In 2017, a study of dialect bias within YouTube's closed captions system from the University of Washington Linguistics Department demonstrated that the platform's automatic speech recognition software, or ASR — the technology used to generate transcripts and closed captions for every video upload — was less accurate when interpreting 'regional' or non-Received Pronunciation accents, as well as struggling with female pitch. Scottish women were the worst affected cohort, a significantly higher 'word error rate' frequently rendering their dialogue incomprehensible gibberish.[19]

Unreliable ASR stops videos by non-RP creators attaining the same level of visibility as their RP-speaking peers, as YouTube uses transcripts and closed captions to determine a video's ranking in their search results. It also excludes a hard-of-hearing audience who need these captions. 'If … ASR systems consistently perform worse for users from disadvantaged groups than they do for users from privileged groups, this exacerbates existing inequalities,' the report concluded.[20]

Stephanie has come up against Instagram's restrictions herself. 'When it comes to fat acceptance/BoPo [body positivity] posts, we're getting banned and blocked all the time for showing our bodies in swimwear,' she tells me. 'We often find that after a couple of days they get removed, or we get shadowbanned. For some reason bigger bodies are seen as explicit.' She has confronted the platform about these inequalities on multiple occasions, and even succeeded at persuading Instagram to review their semi-nudity policy in 2020.

The uneven application of community standards is sometimes a byproduct of a broader system of inequity: outsourced subcontractors working in different time zones often have mere seconds to assess each post backing up in the so-called 'terror queue' of flagged posts, interpreting and applying moderation guidelines that can be ambiguous and culturally specific. In 2019, investigative reporting from *The Verge* into Instagram parent company Facebook's content moderation sites likened conditions to sweatshops: workers were underpaid, undertrained, and overburdened with the brutal task of sifting through child pornography and animal abuse videos alongside making split-second decisions about whether influencer content contained 'male' or 'female' presenting nipples.[21]

Other platform policing is more explicit. In 2019, TikTok admitted that their moderation team had intentionally flagged and suppressed videos featuring disabled, ginger, and overweight users, claiming the policy was an anti-bullying measure for the purposes of their own protection.[22] Hacking the 'formula' to succeed on the #ForYou page is a game on TikTok in itself. Towards the end of 2019, a wave of algorithm-baiting videos began to go viral under the hashtag #algorithmexperiment, in which creators conducted their own investigations by uploading two videos of similar content (dance, song, meme), with visual differences (smile, outfit, make-up, filter, background, wheelchair) to test which 'version' of themselves the platform deemed most popular.

In 2020, *The Intercept* published two internal moderation documents that took this revelation several steps further. The first document detailed the censorship of videos ByteDance deemed unattractive, instructing moderators to restrict videos containing a list of flaws including 'abnormal body shape', 'ugly facial looks', 'obvious beer belly', 'too many wrinkles', 'eye disorders', and many other 'low quality' traits, videos in which 'the shooting environment is shabby and dilapidated', such as 'slums, rural fields' and 'dilapidated housing'. The second detailed restrictions to livestreams on ideological grounds: classifying certain kinds of political speech — such as that against the Chinese government, military, or police — as dangerous or defamatory.[23]

'These documents contain no mention of any anti-bullying

rationale,' *The Intercept* noted, 'instead explicitly citing an entirely different justification: The need to retain new users and grow the app.'[24] Though these revelations caused ripples in the news, and TikTok claimed the policies were either no longer in use or ever used,[25] for creators, it merely confirmed something they had long suspected: the system was rigged, not through oversight, but through profit-seeking motives and deliberate product design.

'This is my story,' begins a 5,000-word confession post that's been upvoted hundreds of times on a leftist group on Reddit. 'In June of 2015, Donald Trump announced his campaign for president of the United States. I voted for him on November 8, 2016. Almost three years later, my position on him flipped from seemingly unending enthusiasm to deep regret. What the hell happened?'

In the long, descriptive paragraphs that follow, poster u/FmrTrumpistThrowaway recalls his teenage journey down the alt-right pipeline: first conservative parents peddling conspiracy theories, then a youthful enthusiasm for memes and gaming, later feeling self-conscious and out of place IRL and subsequently spending more and more time unsupervised online. Then came Gamergate, the event that scared teenage me off internet forums.

'A huge, divisive scandal happening all around the gaming community was something I couldn't get my eyes off of,' he recalls. 'I would lurk on 8chan day after day getting the latest news on what pink-haired feminist was getting harassed this time, and the inevitable conclusion from all of this was that gaming journalism was not to be trusted even a little, and as an extension of that, mainstream media shouldn't either … What I was not skeptical of, however, was the opinions of the figures on YouTube and elsewhere who actually live in this world like most of us do.'

What he is referring to is the emergence of a new kind of online influencer that would later come to be known as the alt-right. Throughout the 2010s, a landscape of increasingly extremist individuals began to gain traction through social media. Peddling a mixture of 'bloodsport' debates, homophobic and anti-feminist talking points, and thinly veiled arguments for scientific racism, its proponents included self-styled 'Intellectual Dark Web' authorities Dave Rubin, Jordan Peterson, and Ben Shapiro, internet talk show host Stefan Molyneux, *InfoWars* conspiracy theorist Paul Joseph Watson, antifeminist trans vlogger Blaire White who denounced LGBTQ activism, and tradwife lifestyle influencer Ayla Stewart, aka 'Wife with A Purpose', who shared skincare routines, parenting tips, and white genocide conspiracy theories with her subscribers.

This Who's Who of unsavory YouTubers was officially outlined as the 'Alternative Influence Network' by researcher Rebecca Lewis for Data & Society in 2018. She described them as 65 'scholars, media pundits, and internet celebrities' from 81 channels that 'leverage YouTube to promote a range of reactionary political positions, from mainstream versions of libertarianism and conservatism, all the way to overt white nationalism'.[26] And they were fuelling the rise of America's new right. 'I occasionally watched Steven Crowder and Stefan Molyneux and Internet Aristocrat (aka Mister Metokur),' recalled u/FmrTrumpistThrowaway. 'There were a bunch of miscellaneous channels that I'd go to laugh at the stupid SJWs [Social Justice Warriors].'

Whilst the ideology of the alt-right was appealing, 'the cherry on top of all of that was that it was honestly fun', u/FmrTrumpistThrowaway says. 'There were memes, jokes, shitposts, and hilarious videos ... the alt-right didn't just give me hope, it gave me a home.' Over time, 'immersing in these spaces without interruption continually perpetuates these same ideas over and over again to the point of feeling true'. Rejecting mainstream media and established narratives and spending more and more time in front of the screen, he had — in internet terminology — 'taken the red pill'. 'I was a pawn who thought I was a spirited free-thinker,' he recalls, 'but in reality, my anxieties as a person were being exploited for political gain and crafted into an objectively wrong worldview that neo-Nazis have created to put me through the alt-right pipeline.' Trump's eventual election in 2016 'felt like a legitimate victory ... I owned the libs! I cucked the SJWs!' For a time, u/FmrTrumpistThrowaway was fulfilled. 'Then I discovered ContraPoints,' he says. 'Everything changed.'

———

Late one evening, so do I.

Hunched over my laptop, several hours deep into YouTube drama videos and QAnon conspiracy vlogs — a self-flagellating content spiral that characterises many nights under coronavirus lockdown — I am auto-played a video that jolts me from smooth-brained stupor. Against lurid lighting and set to a backing track of medieval choral music, a glamorous young blonde woman in a shimmering ball gown beckons to me from a velvet chaise lounge, costume jewellery dripping from her ears and throat. As the music soars to a crescendo she addresses her audience in a theatrical manner, one part proselytising, one part performance art: *'Comrades, losers, and haters!'* The scene cut and suddenly she is lying nude — save for a wig and spiked dog collar — in a gold bath filled to the brim with glittering trinkets, sipping from a champagne flute clasped between acrylic talons. She smiles seductively. *'The plotline of our central cultural myth is the story of rags to riches ...'*

From her position in the bathtub, she begins to weave a narrative that unites a dizzying series of disparate touchpoints: McMansions, Kant, Nicki Minaj, trickle-up linguistics, leopard print, Nietzsche, ballroom, and Bed Bath & Beyond. *'For the wealthy and powerful, opulence is a flex, a demonstration of their wealth and power,'* she continues, *'but for the marginalised and impoverished, opulence is a simulacrum of the wealth and power they've been denied ...'* The visuals cut fluidly through music videos, screenshotted tweets, and a photoshopped Statue of Liberty with the face of Donatella Versace clutching a bottle of Cristal, inserting clips from beauty guru Gigi Gorgeous's 2017 vlog 'I Wear Walmart For A Week' and Jeffree Starr's 'Private Jet Burger King Mukbang' to illustrate how class and status interplay with aspiration and aesthetics.

The disembodied voices of other prominent YouTubers interrupt her monologue to quote passages from Susan Sontag, John Waters, and Oscar Wilde. She pauses to ask pressing questions, such as *'Why does Donald Trump's apartment look like Liberace married a Turkmenistani dictator and moved into a Cheesecake Factory?'* and to wonder where YouTubers fit within a Marxist class struggle, slipping into the empty commercial upspeak of a beauty vlogger to make her point: *'Like, Bourgeoisie & Proletariat — Whomst? Who is she? Where's her summer collection?'*

The YouTube rabbit hole has led me to a video essay entitled 'Opulence: The Aesthetic of Owning Everything' by vlogger Natalie Wynn, known to her 1.3m devotees as ContraPoints. It is 49 minutes and six seconds long, has 1.5 million views, and is a potent mix of visuals and critical theory translated into social media slang. Natalie's channel hosts parodic vlogs that eloquently blend pop-cultural analysis, kaleidoscopic stage sets, internet in-jokes, and capitalist critique — Nicolas Winding Refn meets Adam Curtis meets the algorithm. Much later, eyes burning, electrified and unaware of the time, I've devoured *What's Wrong With Capitalism* (Parts One and Two), *Canceling, The West, Incels, The Aesthetic, The Apocalypse, Men,* and *Gender Critical*.

I soon discovered a network of creators making work along similar lines, many of whom collaborate and feature in cameos with Wynn: Abigail Thorn's 1m-strong channel Philosophy Tube which hosts a series of surreal dark-comedy sketches that dramatise the works of Camus, Burke, and Kant; Harry Brewis, aka hbomberguy, who boasts 800k subscribers to his film reviews, gaming streams, and video essays covering everything from *Ghostbusters* to global warming.

It seems that the deeper the videos delve into issues that impact lived experience, the more decoupled from reality they become: Wynn cosplaying as a K-Pop stan to chat about fandoms, then a drag queen and a beauty guru to explore aesthetics and trans identity, and a cat girl, a fascist, and both dominant and submissive participants of a BDSM relationship simultaneously to animate a conversation about boundaries and consent. Thorn riding around on a horse whilst expounding on the British monarchy, donning a space suit to discuss suicide and mental health, lying stretched out on a sequinned chaise longue to ruminate on artistry and fandoms. I am hooked. By the time I manage to break free I've been transported through swathes of political ideology and internet lore: I've been 'breadpilled'.

BreadTube (referred to as 'YouTube but good' by its insiders), is a term used to refer to a loose collective of left-leaning influencers who use their platforms to interrogate capitalism, neoliberalism, consumerism, identity politics, pop culture, and philosophy. A user-run aggregator website, BreadTube.tv, is cheerfully blunt in describing the genre as 'left-wing propaganda' or 'quality content going against the prevailing winds of the internet'. 'We wish to educate people on how their world operates, the alternative possible visions for our future, and how we organise ourselves to get there.' Looking at the videos listed on their index, this often takes the form of colourful and dramatic video essays, such as the ones that I'd watched, but gaming streams, vlogs, movie reviews, comedy sketches, beauty tutorials, tea videos, and other popular YouTube formats are also used as vehicles for political conversation.

The term 'BreadTube' is inspired by an 1892 political polemic called *The Conquest of Bread* by anarco-communist Peter Kropotkin, in which he laid out his vision for the organisation of post-revolutionary Russia. On Reddit where the term 'BreadTube' was first coined in 2018, its creator noted that its obscurity proved useful, avoiding the potentially off-putting nature of a more overtly political name, like LeftTube, whilst acting as a dog whistle to rally the politically pre-aligned.[27] Over on the community Discord server — an off-platform refuge where BreadTube fans chat away from the chaos of the YouTube comment section — self-identified 'an-com/lib-socs' debate 'progressive soc dems', and 'anarcho-syndicalists' exchange reaction GIFs with run-of-the-mill Marxists.

It's important to note that not everyone associates with the BreadTube label or its community: it's something that tends to be externally applied by viewers, rather than identified with by creators. 'Ugh, I *loathe* the term "breadtube!"', Abigail tells me over email. 'I know that some people claim it for themselves but I prefer to keep it at a distance … even "Leftube" grates a bit now.' The YouTube group it refers to is an informal, decentralised network of creators with no official allegiances to any political party, or to each other, and they are often in conversation about competing definitions of its identity, debates about its goals, or complaints about the name. Still, viewers continue to use 'BreadTube' and 'LeftTube' as helpful shorthand to find left-learning content — and each other — amongst the maze of sponsored vlogs and consumeristic prank videos that is YouTube.

Whether you prefer a particular term, or none at all, there is a clear network of popular vloggers and streamers of which Philosophy Tube, hbomberguy, and ContraPoints are just the tip of an iceberg: my YouTube recommendations bar suggests 'armchair anarchist' and gaming streamer Vaush, self-titled 'cringe advocate/left video pervert' Peter Coffin, intellectual pop culture critics Big Joel and Lindsay Ellis, 'leftist princess' Jordan Theresa, comedian and movie reviewer Maggie Mae Fish, and Kat Blaque, a mermaid-haired opinion vlogger, illustrator and activist I discovered via her analysis video 'Why Is LeftTube So White?' (405k views). There are many more still with smaller followings or a more specific focus.

What the BreadTube community are aligned on is a common opposition: the right-leaning ideologies that have become synonymous with YouTube creators in recent years. Many of the community's key protagonists were galvanised by particular moments of conflict, either against other online creators or the political system. Peter Coffin had been creating anti-establishment comedy videos on YouTube since early 2007, but it was various brushes with the emerging 'corporate class' of creators, who were angry with their criticism of the growth of brand sponsorship on the platform, that pushed them into investigating power structures, 'which led me to leftist politics, which led me to Marx, which puts us where we are now', Peter recaps for me when I interview them over Skype.

Abigail began her channel following the UK's Conservative-led coalition government's decision to triple tuition fees in 2012, 'because I wanted to give away my philosophy degree for free', she remembers. 'That's not an apolitical genesis.' Though she recognises she has acquired an online reputation for spreading anti-capitalist ideas, she's also keen to point out that her work is as much about philosophy, art, and learning as it is leftism, though 'that does inevitably inform the show, as any artist's political ideology informs their work.' Other creators began as a more direct reaction to the rise of the YouTube alt-right, to offer an alternative point of view and act as a tool for political deradicalisation: Natalie Wynn began her ContraPoints channel in 2016, citing Gamergate and its fallout as her direct inspiration.

'It's honestly because of [Natalie Wynn] that I strayed away from the alt-right,' says u/FmrTrumpistThrowaway. 'She was completely unlike anyone else I had ever seen, in that her videos are not antagonistic. She was a voice of reason that rose above the chaotic sea of noise. All the right had was pseudo-intellectual dogma and memes whose sole purpose is to be loud, offensive, and most importantly, pander to the people that believe … ContraPoints succeeded where the mainstream media failed in conveying the actual reasoning behind why these racist, bigoted people online were really racist and really bigoted.'

Now deradicalised, the Reddit user credits BreadTube as a key tool for undoing years of brainwashing. 'When I'm watching ContraPoints, Philosophy Tube, and hbomberguy, I'm engaging in an environment in which dissenting opinions and thoughts are allowed, and dialogue and critical thinking are encouraged. None of these things are true of the alt-right.' This is a fascinating story, but it's not the reason that I find BreadTube so intriguing.

At first glance, BreadTubers resemble any other successful creators. They vlog, stream, and collaborate, posting weekly videos for their many millions of devoted fans. They sell branded merch. They feature at VidCon. They're verified on Twitter. They post memes and complain about algorithm updates. They open videos with an apology for not having uploaded in a while, and close with a reminder to like, comment, and subscribe. They cultivate exactly the same parasocial relationships with their viewers as any other influencer. And yet, where mainstream influencers leverage this relationship to flog us fitness routines or yet more skincare we don't need, BreadTubers are selling us on its subversion: BreadTube isn't just taking on the right, it's tackling influence itself.

Young, fresh-faced, and gregarious, sporting a pixie cut and bold, neon-pink eyeshadow worthy of a beauty influencer, Maggie Mae Fish sits, vlogger-style, in front of her camera in her room for a tea video digging into drama surrounding beauty guru Jaclyn Hill's disastrous launch of contaminated lipsticks. 'Like every other warm-blooded person who needs a distraction from our reproductive rights being ripped away from us, recently I've been fascinated by Jaclyn Hill and #LipstickGate,' announces Maggie. 'Here's just a quick look at what's been going on with Jaclyn Hill, and what's led up to this latest catastrophe.'

Her video draws you in like any other drama channel, with a gleeful recap of the story details and customary screengrabs of shrieking recipients unboxing their dodgy lipsticks: so far, so drama YouTube. But Maggie offers more than just the usual gossip, unpacking the manipulative relationship between Jaclyn and her fans ('Jaclyn is the perfect example of a social media capitalist,' she informs her audience) before introducing viewers to some startling new information that's been missed by the rest of the influencer tea community: Jaclyn's father is linked to a Christian non-profit that exploits tax loopholes, and now, she theorises, Jaclyn's doing exactly the same.

'Shameless rich people use lobbyists to influence state and federal politicians, specifically so that these laws are written in a way that they can exploit. It's a feature of capitalism, not a bug,' says Maggie: 'This kind of tax avoidance is one of the key ways Donald Trump has been able to cheat the American public and evade paying taxes for decades.' The screen recordings of Jaclyn's hysterical apology videos and designer handbag collection give way to inserts of the IRS website's policy on 501(c)(3) tax exemption and the dissolution of the Trump Foundation. Eighteen minutes in, and Maggie's connecting #lipstickgate to broader patterns of capitalist exploitation. 'Jaclyn is just one example, just one symptom of a much much larger problem,' she enthuses to her listeners.

The swing from specific to systemic is so smooth, so slick, it feels organic. 'Celebrities, corporations, and shady nonprofits do these kinds of things all the time. There are metaphorical shards of plastic in lipsticks everywhere.' Maggie draws her audience through to her political conclusion: 'Do we want to give these uber capitalists of the world, the Jeff Bezos, the Jack from Twitter, more influence so they can keep taking advantage of the system?' By the end of the video, Maggie has called for a radical revisioning of the political system and status quo as we know it, along with 22,000 upvoters who have gone from gossip mongers to change advocates in 25 short minutes. The comments section is full of viewers being visibly 'breadpilled': 'I can't believe I get to watch makeup drama and learn about tax avoidance at the same time,' says one commenter. 'Holy shit. Besides this being some HOT tea, this is also very educational,' writes another. 'Talking about beauty industry drama AND educating people about the exploitative nature of capitalism is such a winning move. I love this video so much!'

In a Philosophy Tube video that's been viewed nearly 200,000 times, Abigail sits in the middle of the screen, eyes closed and legs folded. A wash of coloured lighting casts two symmetrical shadows behind her. The scene is calm. 'Find a place where you can sit comfortably, perhaps resting your hands on your knees. You may wish to sit on the floor with your legs crossed. Or, if you're not too tired, you may like to lie down on your back,' she intones hypnotically, in the intimate whisper typical of online guided meditation. I can feel my eyelids growing heavy. 'As you sink deeper and deeper into this relaxed state of awareness you may begin to notice the position of your body,' she continues. 'You may also notice your body's position in the system of global capitalism.'

We begin breathing exercises: 'Breathing in … political revolution … and out.' After 24 minutes of relaxation and education delivered in the style of ASMR, Abigail gently guides us to 'return to the present moment: to breath … and the desire to abolish the class system'. It may be tongue in cheek, but this Philosophy Tube video — 'Reform or Revolution? An ASMR Guided Meditation'— like Maggie's video before it, is a classic example of algorithm hacking: embedding leftist teachings into one of YouTube's most popular video genres in a sly game of social media bait and switch. 'I came here for some good ASMR,' jokes a commenter, 'and I came out a communist.'

Many BreadTubers produce videos that fit with popular YouTube genres: Lindsay Ellis incorporates left-wing talking points to movie reviews, Angie Speaks to history videos, hbomberguy to video game reviews, Kat Blaque to sex ed Q&As, Jordan Theresa chats through class theory whilst applying make-up. Slipping in invisibly amongst their commercial influencer contemporaries, they leverage profit-driven algorithms to organise against them, and in hacking the information infrastructure of YouTube to spread leftist beliefs, BreadTube weaponises capitalism against itself. BreadTubers are perhaps the ultimate anti-influencers; the only content creators I'm aware of who are actively engaged in undermining the structures enabling their own existence.

'I very intentionally moved into a role where I'm persuading people of something,' Peter Coffin tells me. 'I am very cognisant of the dynamics of the platform and I do try to take advantage of them.' Their goals are 'persuasion, awareness, hopefully getting people to take action: organise, find others locally, work together in some way'. Through video essays and the chatty vlog series 'Very Important Documentaries' ('if materialist criticism of ideology and laughing about farts had a baby'), Peter tackles everything from personal branding to Logan Paul, Marvel's cinematic universe, and Zoom fatigue, questioning how social systems are set up, dissecting the tools and techniques of influencing, and discussing the hidden dynamics between creators and platforms along the way.

'My channel is all about getting the audience to think,' says Abigail, or as she puts it, in typically eloquent and theatrical fashion: 'Does this serve the interests of the many? Does this serve the true democracy where people control their own lives and governance is by the consent of the governed, or the illusion of democracy where we choose what colour tie the slavedriver wears?' Philosophy Tube often uses dramatic monologues, theatrical sketch shows, and acerbic one-liners to question the YouTuber-fan dynamic and draw attention to creator labour conditions, sometimes spoofing influencer culture in the process.

Regarding one popular upload, a 30-minute video about toxic masculinity and trauma that has over a million views, Abigail tells me how she deliberately appropriated YouTube tropes of vlogger authenticity. 'For research I watched a lot of YouTube videos where people discuss similar experiences,' she says: influencer apology videos, 'story time' vlogs, and serious life updates 'all have a common visual language: the speaker sits centre-screen, usually on a grotty couch next to a plain wall, the colours are desaturated, they don't use a lot of cuts, they always leave in their pauses … it's a style that instantly says, "I'm super sincere, you guys!"' For her own version, 'I carried that visual language to the extreme, parodied it almost: a plain white background, no music, one very simple costume change, and I didn't even edit it — the whole thing was one 30-minute take.'

Other videos satirise individual influencers more directly. One of Abigail's recurring characters, Ian N. Drivel is 'a bombastic and politically incorrect Australian YouTuber, a shock-jock whose role on my show is to be factually correct but ideologically wrong'. Ian N. Drivel pops up to make tea-channel style melodramatic call-outs, not against other YouTubers but 'philosophers who are already long dead'. 'He was inspired by a real vlogger who I won't name,' she teases.

These techniques — repeatedly breaking the fourth wall, drawing attention to their own artificiality and the commodification of their operations, combining expressive visuals with artistic skill and metatextual humour — are typical of BreadTube's anti-influence toolkit. 'It's very easy to watch a YouTube video passively and just let the pretty costumes and lights wash over you, but I don't want my audience to do that,' Abigail tells me: 'Reminding them that they are watching a show, that it's all a construction, is a great way to ensure that the rational bit of the brain doesn't switch off.' It's also a way of highlighting the highly staged nature of digital influence.

Peter takes a more straightforward approach. '[Influencer strategies and techniques] are snuck into everything — it's so invisible to the audience — a lot of it is used to manipulate people,' they say. 'Deconstructing that stuff and putting it in terms that someone who is not initiated can understand is really important.' Coffin's videos critically dissect the influencer playbook — parasocial relationships, self-branding, revenue models, audience maintenance, cultivated identity, algorithms, self-optimisation, and the relationship between influencers and the platforms they are on — in their straight-talking, stereotypically vlogger style, eschewing visual trickery for punchy dialogue and self-referential jokes: 'Hey you!', they open a vlog about self-branding and optimised identity with a tongue-in-cheek glance at the camera, 'I'm a personally branded Peter!'

Playing the system from within means BreadTubers can quickly run into contradictions and conflict, the most prominent of which is a complicated relationship towards getting paid. 'I did an ad criticism show for three years — I was like why is nobody doing this?' Peter tells me. 'Well,' they shrug, 'it's because no advertiser wants their ads on a video that's saying all adverts are trying to manipulate you.' A struggle against self-branding and advertising agendas is common amongst BreadTube anti-influencers: in an effort to divest themselves of YouTube's profit-driven model, many eschew brand deals and in-video advertising in favour of subscription plans or merchandise.

In the links in the YouTube drop-down bar, I can see Peter has an e-book, T-shirts, and socks reading 'Liberalism Sucks' for sale, and a link to book them for Cameo videos. 'I don't particularly love the idea of being a commodity. It's a dehumanising concept, that's partly why I resist it,' Peter tells me, but they have bills to pay: 'I have to try to make money in a way I feel comfortable with.' Their followers are supportive. 'The way I see it, donating directly to creators has a lot more socialist energy than passively sitting back and allowing a corporation like YouTube, and its hyper-secret algorithm, to decide who gets what share of profits from other corporations,' says one comment under Peter's 'Leftist vs Funding' video, which addresses the topic. 'FUNDING CREATORS YOU LOVE IS GOOD PRAXIS' reads another.

Philosophy Tube is similarly crowdfunded through monthly donations via the community subscription platform Patreon. However, Abigail notes that even this is still 'a private company and very much beholden to the venture capital firms that have invested in it'. Abigail does work with brands, but only if they align with her artistic and ethical vision, and says that she approaches sponsorship 'very carefully'. For BreadTubers, brand deals can be used to redirect revenue towards activist causes. 'During the height of the George Floyd uprising I took a sponsorship deal and said in the video, "I'm taking this so I can donate the money to a Black LGBT organisation,"' remembers Abigail.

Brand deals can also be an opportunity to draw audiences' attention to the techniques and strategies of sponsorship: hbomberguy's video 'WOKE BRANDS', a breakdown of faux-progressive marketing and the growth of sponsored content that has been viewed nearly 2 million times, is itself sponsored. 'Thanks, CuriosityStream, for the sponsorship,' Harris says in the perky timbre of a vlogger selling his audience on protein powders or discount codes, before bursting out laughing. 'I'm screwed.' The video ends with a pointed reminder: 'Um, yeah, take care of yourselves, and have a good night, brands are not your friends ...' As the video fades, Harris accidentally on purpose cuts off his own advertisement: 'Oh, I also have a Patre—!'.

For the bravest BreadTubers, brand deals can even be an opportunity to subvert the sponsor themselves. Abigail recalls a past partnership with a UK university: 'I talked about what a fine institution they are and plugged some courses and so on. I published that video, then published a follow-up in which I said, "Everything I said in that video is true, but here's what I wasn't allowed to tell you — their cleaners are on strike because their contracts are being outsourced, their teaching staff are on strike because they aren't being paid enough ..." I highlighted how inappropriate it was that they were spending money on influencer marketing when there were better things they could be doing, and I publicly donated my fee to the Student Union. Needless to say the brand and the agency were not happy!' She believes the stunt resulted in her being blacklisted by marketing agencies, but by then she'd achieved her aim: educating hundreds of thousands of her advertiser's target audience on their unethical business practices. These digital adbusting techniques allow BreadTubers to hijack sponsorship mechanics with messaging of their own.

Individual revenue models are just one of the tensions created by anti-influencing; BreadTubers are more broadly grappling against the agenda of their host platforms. 'I make content that is critical of advertising, content that is critical of centralising power, basically a lot of antithetical ideas to what Google actually is,' comments Peter. 'I feel like an outsider.' In order to get their message out there, BreadTubers have to comply with the demands of the YouTube system, which Peter describes as 'borderline invincible incentives to an outside onlooker', from building a personal brand and optimising your output towards YouTube's specified requirements, to avoiding any number of perceived offences, such as criticising advertisers or even swearing, that risk demotion within the algorithmic ranking system or even being banned.

'The mechanics of the platform push you to prioritise the demands of the platform, over what you actually want to do,' Peter notes. 'You have to engage in these dynamics in order to get out there.' In being an anti-influencer, Peter says, 'you're putting yourself into a hazardous place where your work or your message may actually end up being what becomes subverted, rather than you subverting the platform ... It's really hard to maintain an actual critical viewpoint.'

BreadTubers have to work harder to gain popularity on a platform that's designed to work against their views. Right-leaning content tends to affirm an audience's worldview, and keep them feeling comfortable, Peter observes, aligning neatly with YouTube's measurability index for a video's worth, which is based on metrics such as upvotes and watch rate. 'System critical content isn't validating [for audiences], it's content that makes you feel unsettled.' Peter says: 'The response I often get to videos is "thanks for ruining my fun" ... It gets less engagement, it gets less repeat viewers, it's harder to create that fanbase.' Though there's no evidence that the YouTube algorithm might, like TikTok, deliberately suppress subversive views and anti-capitalist ideologies, Peter believes there's a risk of creators censoring themselves due to the pressures of the system, and over time, their message being subsumed into the platform's paradigm. 'The algorithm really doesn't want marginalised stories, class struggle,' Peter says in their 'State of Leftist YouTube' video, 'it wants lifestyle content.'

In 2020, a widely shared report from influencer marketing platform inzpire.me declared that influencers needed just 42,575 followers to earn the equivalent of the average UK salary.[28] But influencers themselves often tell a different story. YouTuber Gaby Dunn was one of the first to call attention to the chasm between internet fame and income back in 2015, in a viral blog post entitled 'Get Rich or Die Vlogging: the sad economics of internet fame'. She laid out a common paradox: 'Many famous social media stars are too visible to have "real" jobs, but too broke not to,' she explained. Her sketch channel, 'Just Between Us', had half a million subscribers, but 'despite this success', she said, 'we're just barely scraping by'.

Her income was 'not enough to live, and its influx is unpredictable. Our channel exists in that YouTube no-man's-land: brands think we're too small to sponsor, but fans think we're too big for donations. I've never had more than a couple thousand dollars in my bank account at once.' A classic case of Instagram vs reality: 'My Instagram account has 340,000 followers, but I've never made $340,000 in my life collectively. One week, I was stopped for photos six times while perusing comic books in downtown LA. The next week, I sat faceless in a room of 40 people vying for a menial courier job,' she admitted. 'I've walked a red carpet with $80 in my bank account.'[29] On YouTube, the top three per cent of creators receive 90 per cent of the views.[30] On Patreon, only 2 per cent of creators made the federal minimum wage of $1,160 per month in 2017.[31]

In a 2020 essay for the *Harvard Business Review* entitled 'The Creator Economy Needs a Middle Class', Li Jin observed that, despite its claims about a democratising revolution, the current creator landscape more closely resembles a system in which wealth is concentrated at the top. Li sees this as a problem to be fixed by platforms. It is their job to work harder to cultivate a self-sustaining 'middle class' of creators, she argues, in order to protect their business model, viewing wealth redistribution and the rebalancing of the creator class system as a method for de-escalating platform risk. 'Creator platforms flourish when they provide opportunity for anyone to grow and succeed,' she writes. 'When the American Dream is just a dream, the fate of platforms becomes precarious.' Though Li herself admits, when it came down to individual creators: 'some inequality is inherent in the nature of the passion economy'.[32]

But rather than seeking to iron out inconsistencies within its system, perhaps it is the concept of the passion economy itself that is flawed. Rob Horning, editor at *Real Life Mag*, an online technology journal funded by Snapchat, is critical of the entire concept, which sees creators pitted against each other to survive whilst the platforms that claim to 'support' their passions ('i.e. "owning the means of production and distribution that creators depend on for their livelihood"', he reminds us) parasitically profit from this army of labourers to grow ever more powerful. 'Don't forget: it's not exploitation if you are passionate about it!' he writes in his newsletter 'Internal exile.' In the so-called 'passion economy', 'economic self-exploitation is represented as an artistic pursuit, and the value is there to harvest as long as people believe that'.

Peter agrees with this analysis of creators' positions, pointing to the double standard between the way influencers are perceived, and how they operate in practice. Influencers are not 'some amazing independent business owner, who's elevating themselves and using this platform to empower their voice,' they say. 'Instead of being an employee, we're a contractor.' YouTube is 'entertainment Uber.' Influencers work in the service of the platforms, but have none of the workers' rights or protections formal employment would afford. Unlike other, more concrete, career paths influencing isn't a stable occupation; it's a subjective and contested identity embodied by a constant quest for relevance: the next like, the next post, the next brand deal.

'At the entry level, you're really fighting,' confirms Peter. 'You're not established, you have no resources, you're not plugged into any audience unless you've managed to catch some other creator's eye and they are willing to promote you.' Even mid-tier channels with a few hundred thousand subscribers — channels such as Peter's — aren't secure. 'Those creators are still disposable,' Peter says, 'if one of them goes away, there are hundreds of thousands [more of them].'

The creator economy is an endless marketplace: influencers are pitted against each other, every job is contested, every brand deal or advertising revenue tenuous. 'It's a brilliant exertion of power via the idea that you're always in danger: there's a huge reserve army of labour — if I don't do it, someone else will.' Not only are influencers pitted against each other, they are pitted against the platform itself. 'It's not a group of individuals doing exactly what they want,' continues Peter. 'There's incentives, there's metrics, there's rewards, there are consequences.'

In order to combat inequalities and fight for a more equal employment system, influencers have begun to form a labour movement. Hollywood's biggest union, SAG-AFTRA, approved a new 'influencer agreement' in 2020, covering creators from TikTok, Instagram, Facebook, Twitch, and other platforms. Two independent union bodies — The Creator Union in the UK and the American Influencer Council, not-for-profit membership trade association — were set up in 2020, aiming for proper labour recognition, lobbying power, and to 'usher in a new era of legitimacy for career influencers, who are ... small business owners and media innovators', according to AIC founder Qianna Smith Bruneteau.[33]

It wasn't the first time influencers had attempted to unionise. Vlogbrother and VidCon founder Hank Green both founded and funded an early labour organisation designed to protect and support influencers, known as the Internet Creators Guild, in 2016. It shut down just three years later: 'the amount of support has declined to the point where we cannot maintain our work actively and has impacted our ability to recruit new members', a memo announcing the closure read. 'Creators with big audiences often don't feel the need for support from a collective voice.'[34]

No labour movement will ever combat the inherent asymmetry of the influencer-platform set-up. Influencers are trapped in a permanent state of precarious codependency with their hosts: they don't own their audience but merely rent it off a platform, and they exist at the whims of a constantly changing creator landscape — platform updates, the boosting of certain formats, changes to platform programming interfaces which disrupt the use of third-party tools and applications.

Platforms exert power over influencers in the form of an invisible system of rewards and reprimand. They retain the power to penalise, delisting or demonetising videos en masse (recurrent events known to creators as the 'adpocalypse' — blocking, banning, and suspending accounts without warning), reducing revenue randomly[35] or even, as YouTube announced in November 2020, updating their terms of service to include the 'right to monetise' all content on its platform without paying its creators. The influencer system exerts power on its subjects, muses Peter; creators are 'co-opted by platforms'. Every anti-influencer BreadTube video uploaded, every million views accrued, ultimately feeds the YouTube beast, in keeping with BreadTube's key critique of late-stage capitalism — that it commodifies any form of resistance to it, undermining any threat to its supremacy by making resistance ultimately serve its purpose.

The ultimate influencer is the algorithm: platforms deliberately hide information about their ranking systems, keeping influencers beholden to its updates. The power dynamics at play in this relationship are coded into the way influencers relate to the algorithm. It's not uncommon for them to invoke the algorithm using the language of coercion and surveillance. 'It's so insidious,' says Stephanie, when I ask her how she feels about making her living by navigating a piece of technology she can never hope to fully understand. 'Part of it is about control — they're so popular, they feel they can get away with making us do all these things. Hiding our content is definitely a way to punish us for using their platform to create careers, so that in the end brands and individuals then have to pay or put spend behind specific posts so that it can be seen ... We've all been sucked into this machine. We're trapped in this weird cycle of having to meet Instagram's demands. I don't like it at all.'

Within creator culture, the algorithm is viewed as a powerful, god-like entity that's omniscient, omnipotent and opaque, ruling over its subjects. Algorithmic mythology has developed into a genre of its own. Influencers spend a lot of time attempting to understand it, entire cottage industries of growth hackers claim to have 'reverse engineered' it and dispense advice to creators via YouTube videos. 'There's a part of me that thinks the platforms love it,' says Stephanie. 'They love that there are so many influencers and bloggers that are creating content about the algorithms and how to beat it. All that's doing is making all of us engage with Instagram more.' Exactly how the algorithm operates doesn't really matter. Creators condition their posts, self, and performance based around what they think it wants anyway.

Algorithms supposedly work in the service of social media users: every time you like, pause, mute, skip, or save a post on a social media site, the algorithm theoretically 'learns' what you like and what you don't, in order to serve future posts more in line with your indicated taste. The stated aim of this tailoring is to curate, create, and eliminate content on the basis of its 'relevance' to our perceived desires, in short — to redesign the platform around the tastes of its own users. But in actuality the inverse is also true: we allow algorithms to dictate our taste, to condition us into certain behaviours and opinions which users then adopt as their own.

'Algorithms don't reflect existing needs or wants; they are a system for instilling new ones,' Rob Horning writes in *Real Life*. They 'serve the capitalist process of producing consumers in its image and instilling in them the desire for the kinds of standardised culture it can reproduce profitably'. Algorithms ultimately only serve the motives of the platforms they occur on. 'The only real goal the algorithm has is to keep people on the website for as long as possible,' says Peter: the only thing the algorithm can ever be relied on to recommend is more of itself.[36]

Reframed this way, it's difficult for me to reconcile my role, however small, within the industry. Until I spoke to creators and discovered BreadTube videos, I hadn't fully considered the implications of its set-up or the asymmetry between its participants. It's hardly surprising that most influencer audiences are unaware or unengaged with conversations about the power struggle between platforms and creators, the invisible conditioning of the algorithm, and the precarious positions influencers find themselves in. Part of the reason influencing is so successful is because of its ability to sell us on itself, using sleights of self-branding and its own ability to aestheticise, to distract, and to entertain. It promotes heroic narratives of individual achievement and entrepreneurial success, whilst obfuscating the conditions of a much broader base of labourers, who won't ever reach the six-figure pay cheques or astronomic subscriber counts of those most visible within the industry. With every sponsored post and vlog uploaded, influencers are selling us not only fitness shakes or eyeshadow palettes, but the influencer system as a whole.

If BreadTubers believe the current system is broken, what would an alternative social media system look like? Will BreadTube help them get there? How successful can an anti-capitalist movement fuelled by influencers really be? 'We haven't created a movement, we've created a market,' Peter says in a 30-minute video that critiques the state of BreadTube: 'Leftist content itself is not going to bring the revolution.' I ask them to explain. Some BreadTubers have managed to amass large audiences by creating what they call 'lifestyle content with an anti-capitalist flair … stuff that perpetuates the status quo, with a radical aesthetic', they tell me. 'You may be changing things that are more symbolic than material.' The work BreadTubers do may appear to be actively undermining influence, they say, but ultimately, its impact is limited. 'You have to abandon the core conceit of an anti-capitalist message in order to do particularly well [on YouTube].' They continue: 'I'm not seeing someone getting millions of views by saying, "You shouldn't be spending time on YouTube".'

'I can be true to my mission whilst navigating the contradictions,' offers Abigail. Influencing may be an imperfect way for leftist creators and educators to operate, but it can have tangible benefits too: reaching new audiences, organising protests or relief efforts, amplifying other causes and voices, offering a form of collective solidarity, or simply providing a space for 'weirdos and gadflies like me', as Abigail puts it. Though YouTube has prevented her from participating in what she describes as 'some of my spicier activist work', as getting recognised became a security risk, she's since moved her efforts online, donating $130k to the Samaritans from a five-day livestream in which she performed Shakespeare plays for her audience on Twitch. 'That's the kind of "influence" I don't mind having.'

Whether through dismantling the platforms and the system they rely on, or modifying the influencer industry's internal structure, both BreadTubers — and influencers of all genres and sizes — are clearly calling for a change. They want better working conditions, more equitable payment systems, fairer and more transparent platforms, and an environment in which everyone, no matter how small, can not just survive but thrive. The industry, which had so long been seen as a tool for democratisation and disruption, itself needed democratising. Though we didn't know it yet, we wouldn't need our imagination to envisage a world beyond influence, nor to rely on BreadTubers to bring about a revolution. With 2020, and the arrival of the coronavirus, my industry — so used to being disruptors — suddenly found itself disrupted. The institution of influence was about to be challenged and dismantled: a systemic reckoning was on its way.

CHAPTER 8

LOGGING OFF

IS THIS THE END OF INFLUENCE?

At first, Covid-19 was a 'world news' story on the BBC, then a meme, then viral images of empty shelves, Instagram Stories of incarcerated Italians blasting disco from their balconies, forwarded WhatsApp voice notes claiming that a government-funded lasagne was being constructed in Wembley Stadium, political posturing on Twitter, and then — eventually — lockdown.

It was the first truly internet pandemic: spread and shared through social media. The way the virus operated was not unlike the same virality I had been studying, a signal spreading fast and fluidly through global information veins, spiralling outwards to an exponential network of interconnected receivers and transmitters. It's hard to pinpoint the exact moment at which coronavirus eclipsed everything else — somewhere in between Twitter telling Kim Kardashian to shut up when she posted nine times in a row about the ongoing feud between her husband Kanye West and Taylor Swift ('Kim, there's people that are dying'), and a grim FaceTime with my parents about a friend hooked up to a ventilator — because time itself had collapsed.

Though my family caught the virus early, in the days when it was still a novelty, I don't think it ever occurred to me that I might actually get it, or if it did, I didn't entertain the concept very seriously. As a young, solo marketing professional with the ability to work from home (WFH) I was, statistically speaking, buffered from an experience which, despite celebrities telling us we were 'all in this together', was not an equal-opportunities illness. My apartment block, located in a low-roofed residential area of east London between the lonely monoliths of Canary Wharf and the City, quickly began to fill up with home workers, as infection rates began to spike upwards to some of the highest in the capital.

I could not ignore the 'red thread', to use the flabby ad-speak I had spent five years perfecting, that connected vital workers wheezing on Dyson-branded emergency ventilators to a wider crisis of capitalism, of which my own small corner — consumerism, brands, advertising — played a small but still significant part. Swift and slippery, my industry had done the only thing it could ever be relied upon to do: it had rebranded the pandemic as not a crisis but a catalyst, not an apocalypse but an awakening. My job — volleying increasingly ornate versions of 'unprecedented times' in and out of my inbox, responding to a barrage of Slack messages with smiley-faced reaction GIFs, attempting to muster enthusiasm for brand positioning in a pandemic — began to feel increasingly performative, like a child playing a grown-up playing an office job.

I didn't contract coronavirus, but I did experience a different malaise. Whether from the isolating effects of months spent living alone, a news cycle that appeared increasingly detached from reality, or the fact that, despite it all, many seemed determined to continue 'business as usual', at some point in 2020 I started to feel like I was living in a kind of simulation. Nothing was real. I wasn't going mad: the facts were there to back me up. 250k Americans dead and Disneyland still open. An infection rate that had flattened along the wrong axis. Lockdown joyrides to Barnard Castle. A tech billionaire and a popstar naming their baby X Æ A-Xii. Kim Jong-un's staged death rumours. Presidentially approved Clorox cocktails. A swarm of murder hornets. Megxit. Quibi. QAnon. 5G conspiracies. Four Seasons Total Landscaping.

During lockdown, a pet dog named Bunny had been given a speech therapy mat by his owner in an effort to teach him to communicate with humans, accumulating 5m followers and the title 'Talking TikTok Dog' in the process. But mere weeks later, Bunny began using it to question his own consciousness, pressing his paw against a single button — 'why' — repeatedly. I didn't blame him; I kept tapping away at my own keyboard, wondering the same.

By December, I had become blasé: a deepfake Queen doing TikTok dances on TV? 17 million Covid-infested minks rising to the surface of mass graves in Denmark? A series of mysterious mirrored monoliths appearing in the wilderness around the world? Sure! Why not! Over time, holed up in my apartment with just my phone and laptop, I began to periodically dissociate: my physical distance from family and friends, my theoretical distance from the status of vital worker, and my alienation from any kind of functional reality were culminating in complete neurosis. YouTube wasn't even going to release its annual Rewind video. It was official: 2020 was a glitch.

Confined to home and glued to the news, my world had shrunk down to the dimensions of a screen. Living through a significant period in global history turned out to be a strangely passive experience, trapped in a paralysing purgatory of doomscrolling. Across the world, social media usage was soaring: internet access spiked 40 per cent between February and April with YouTube as the single largest traffic source.[1] Houseparty — a previously low-profile video app for virtual teenage hangouts — became an overnight sensation, downloaded 28m times within four weeks before a hacking scare killed it almost as instantly as it had caught on. Instagram Lives increased by over 300 per cent.

Twitch's unique monthly streamers more than doubled to 6.2 million, users consuming 5 billion hours of content between April and June. I began to log on periodically, flipping listlessly between livestreams of videogames I didn't play and Spanish podcasts I couldn't understand, just to hear another human's voice in the background as I shuffled between my bathroom, fridge, and kitchen table, caulking the silence that otherwise filled with my anxious internal narrative. TikTok added over 12 million unique US-based visitors in March

2020 alone,[2] crossing the 2 billion install mark in April to become the fastest growing social media platform in the world,[3] crowned the 'download of lockdown': a provider of ephemeral filler for the endless ad break that was life in quarantine. My screen-time reports were up to ten, 11, then 15 hours a day. I went to sleep each evening with my hand frozen in a phantom iPhone-clutching claw, only to wake up with it still in this shape when I regained consciousness each morning.

In this state, it was impossible not to be sucked into the coronavirus content vortex. A carousel of think pieces and webinars and newspaper columns and branded social posts rehashed the same repetitive uncertainties into escalating hysteria: desperate GoFundMe pleas, nihilistic memes, opportunistic targeted ads, mental health infographics, and branded platitudes urging me to embrace this state of perpetual strangeness as 'the new normal'.

A *New Yorker* writer I followed on Twitter hosted a periodic 'pandemic Instagram splurges' thread, where followers lucky enough to still count on an income shared the randomest things they'd purchased online in a fit of end-of-days extravagance: vintage beaded flapper dresses they couldn't wear anywhere, expensive make-up that would be barely visible through a webcam, books they would never get round to reading, 20 neon wigs, two inflatable kayaks, rubber flip flops shaped like fish, platform glitter heels, a $100 dice set, a lemon tree, a live axolotl.

'Who is buying boob tubes during a pandemic?' wondered a Leicester factory worker, paid £3.50 an hour to fulfil Boohoo orders in a warehouse described by a *Guardian* modern slavery investigation as a 'breeding ground' for the virus.[4] Many people, apparently, as Boohoo's sales surged by 45 per cent in the quarter to the end of May. ASOS added 3 million new customers and reported pandemic sales increases of 19 per cent.[5] At the end of the second quarter of 2020, Amazon reported it had doubled its year-on-year net profit to $5.2 billion, and the value of its stock had increased by 97 per cent.

The world had turned online, scrolling and swiping and shopping so feverishly that YouTube were forced to temporarily reduce their video quality to avoid *actually breaking the internet*. Though it put a halt to my research — interviews cancelled, industry events called off, and research trips postponed in perpetuity — the pandemic had unwittingly created the perfect conditions for a particular type of person to thrive. Instagrammers, YouTubers, TikTokers, and Twitch streamers — the four horsemen of the virological apocalypse — suddenly found themselves at the centre of our newly online existence.

Creators were quick to capitalise on an influx of attention: lockdown vlogs and at-home hair routines and easy banana bread recipes and WFH outfit edits and living-room workouts began populating my recommendations bar on YouTube. Engagement with influencer content across all platforms surged by an average of 51 per cent — with a 67 per cent increase in likes from the moment the pandemic was declared in March through to June — according to research from digital agency A&E.[6] Whilst travel, lifestyle, and restaurant influencers were the hardest hit — sponsored content for travel and tourism brands slumped to record lows in April — other verticals such as interiors, fitness, food, gaming, and family did particularly well.[7] Trends platform Talking Influence claimed parenting micro-influencers' engagement rates jumped by an average of 130 per cent between March and May, and YouTube channels grew at an average of 304 per cent month-on-month, as families adapted to new living arrangements under a single roof.[8]

A crop of 'lockdown influencers' — commodifying a new cosy domesticity and promoting stay-at-home accoutrements adapted to the pandemic lifestyle — exploded within weeks: fitness influencer Chloe Ting went viral for her home workouts, growing her YouTube channel by 4.73 million subscribers from March to May and becoming the US' sixth most popular YouTuber creator. NYC-based plantfluencer Christopher Griffin — aka @PlantKween — added 150,000 new botanical enthusiasts to their Instagram account from March to September. Breakout TikTok stars included 41-year-old Tabitha Brown, who gained 2 million TikTok followers in four weeks by sharing comforting POV videos encouraging followers to 'relax' and 'sleep well' in her buttery Southern accent, earning her the accolade 'the world's favourite mom', and retired petrol tanker driver

Joe Allington, 87, known to his 2.5m fans as @grandadjoe1933, who went viral for comedy sketches filmed by his granddaughter in their garden.

I realised just how distended the influencer industry had become when, one afternoon in the summer months, sometime between our first and second lockdown I left my flat for a weekend of self-imposed resocialisation and walked in on my own mother hunched over her laptop watching YouTube: a tutorial by post-menopausal beauty vlogger 'Hot and Flashy' entitled 'How To Look Good on a Zoom Call'. 'Look,' she said, gesturing towards her screen, 'she's just a normal person who shows you how to put your make-up on. She's got 3 million views!' By the end of 2020, the video would be among YouTube's most-viewed beauty tutorials uploaded that year.[9]

The pandemic offered influencers more than just the chance for clicks, as the marketing industry newsletters crowding my inbox were eager to point out: the crisis was an opportunity to transcend their role as lifestyle gurus and redirect their sway to social good. Many used their platforms to spread the message to #StayHome, wear masks, and socially distance, or posted in support of key workers. There were influencer charity campaigns, where creators leveraged their public popularity to plug the gaps of an overburdened state system: fashion influencer Chiara Ferragni raised $3m to set up a new ICU unit for Milanese hospitals, British YouTuber Fleur De Force rallied beauty gurus for a #Bloggers4NHS auction to provide mental health services to frontline medical workers, and 3,938,325 viewers tuned in to lifestyle creator Saffron Barker's #YouTubers4NHSHeroes campaign which encouraged creators to sacrifice their YouTube AdSense revenue.

As politicians flailed and guidance wavered, influencers stepped into roles usually reserved for more traditional forms of leadership. UK schools closed for everyone except children of vital workers, so Joe Wicks, aka @thebodycoach, (3.3m) pronounced himself 'the nation's PE teacher' on a mission to keep kids fit and healthy by running morning gym classes via YouTube — his subscribers doubled in a week. As the US government announced a single $1,500 stimulus relief check, beauty YouTuber Carli Bybel ran a competition to cover her followers' mortgages, and Jeffree Starr hosted a spontaneous $30k CashApp giveaway on Twitter which garnered over a million retweets.

The line between political leadership and its commercial alternative continued to blur as official bodies began to leverage digital influence: the UK government paid *Love Island* stars an undisclosed amount to #spon the NHS Test and Trace system on Instagram, reaching an audience of over 7m people, and the Department for International Development pledged half a million pounds to a vlogger fund to help stop the spread of misinformation about the virus in Asia and Africa. Increasingly, institutions became influencers themselves: the World Health Organization partnered with CGI influencer @KnoxFrost (930k) for a series of sponsored posts, and then joined TikTok, quickly amassing over 1m followers and earning the accolade 'the planet's most important social media influencer' from *Forbes*.[10] To those within the industry — including brands and agencies like mine — all this activity appeared to legitimise digital influence, amplifying creators' status and realising their leadership potential.

To others, the marriage between social media stars and public services was disaster capitalism in action, a crisis cannily exploited by opportunistic brands and individuals; online — in comments sections, messaging forums, tea channels and gossip accounts — the tide was turning against creators. Many followers found influencers' leveraging of the crisis and continued insistence on generating pandemic lifestyle content to be distasteful. As an occupation, content creation felt trite compared with the commitments of key workers, and influencers' labour of leisure hit a nerve with followers who were furloughed or suddenly unemployed. There was no shortage of comments-section-schadenfreude as lockdown dismantled highly visible influencer lifestyles: no trips, no parties, no restaurants to share or sell.

As news outlets scrambled for low-hanging hot takes and clickbait to punctuate their daily Covid bulletins, creators were first criticised for making masks into fashion statements. Next in the firing line were travel influencers with the gall to complain about cancelled trips, or who were 'sheltering in place' from tropical beaches in Bali. Then wellness influencers suggested the virus could be avoided by eliminating any number of imaginary pathogens or purchasing prophylactic diet supplements using their exclusive discount code (swipe up!). Australian mumfluencers began spreading anti-mask propaganda with the hashtag #NoMaskSelfie. YouTubers entertained 5G conspiracy theories or spread vaccine misinformation. Jake Paul joined in looting at the Los Angeles BLM protests; YouTubers Nikita Dragun, Tana Mongeau and James Charles vlogged through 'pandemic parties' hosted in the TikTok mansions of Beverly Hills; and a 21-year-old TikTok star licked a private jet toilet seat for a 'coronavirus challenge'. By the time we made it to December to observe an industry-wide exodus to Dubai — now informally referred to as the 'London Borough of UAE' — the flight of the social media elite from a plague-ridden city in pursuit of bottle service and Salt Bae steak had become a cliché of the worst pandemic misbehaviour.

Some time in the future, historians of 2020 will look back at Arielle Charnas, an NYC influencer with a wardrobe of designer dungarees, founder of $45 million fashion empire Something Navy and purveyor of $630 rainbow friendship bracelets, as the apotheosis of outrageous pandemic posturing. On 16 March, a fortnight after the first confirmed case of coronavirus in New York, Arielle hopped onto Instagram to inform her 1.3 million followers that she was feeling funny: 'fever, chills, started with a very sore/dry throat, headache' she reeled off in the typical stream-of-consciousness oversharing style her audience was used to. Her DMs were quickly inundated by followers and fans voicing their concern. Governor Cuomo had just that day announced restrictions for New York restaurants, bars, and gyms, and the city — along with the rest of the country — was awaiting the oncoming spike in fraught anticipation.

Though tests were not yet widely available for 'ordinary' Americans, Arielle managed to snag one via a personal connection and brought her followers along, documenting the process of being swabbed through the window of her Volvo. As she would with any other brand collab, she tagged the Instagram account of the doctor friend who had provided the test: '@drjakedeutsch @cureurgentcare tested for both 😷😷 thank you so much.' Whilst her followers waited breathlessly for her results, Arielle passed time by unboxing a Louis Vuitton bag she'd received in the mail.

Two days later, she posted a series of screenshotted iPhone Notes in the obligatory format of an authentic influencer announcement. Over the course of several lengthy paragraphs, Arielle revealed she'd tested positive and shared the details of the treatment plan provided by her doctors: 'get lots of rest and drink fluids … continue to quarantine'. She was, she wrote, committed to 'protect[ing] the healthy [sic] and safety of my family and … those around me.' But less than ten days after posting, Arielle tagged a picture of herself in the Hamptons.

'Fresh air 🙏', read the Instagram caption, as a beaming Charnas stretched out in a designer rainbow tracksuit in the sun. Another picture showed her strolling down the street hand in hand with her daughter, deadly virus presumably still coursing through her system. In the time that elapsed between her concerned Notes post and the outdoor pics, Arielle had relocated against government guidance and joined NYC's wealthy elite in fleeing to an area whose residents were begging them to stay away. As eagle-eyed followers spotted in the background of an Instagram Live, she had even brought their daughter's nanny along with them — she promptly tested positive too.

'SHAME ON THEM AND SHAME ON ALL OF YOU,' read one of thousands of angry comments, '#thisisacrisis #StaytheFhome'. 'People are big mad,' explained journalist Sophie Ross, in a viral Twitter thread that brought the Arielle situation to the attention of the wider media, 'Not only is she literally putting people's lives at risk, but she's setting a horrible example for her 1.3 mill followers (even if they're mostly bots).'[11] But instead of an apology, or even an acknowledgement, Arielle posted swipe-up links on her stories to shop her tie-dye tracksuits. 'Arielle's now back to posting (in Chanel ofc!) as if nothing happened,' Sophie continued. 'No apology. No acknowledgement of the 1000s of former fans asking for answers. No accountability.'

Though the Charnas saga had all the hallmarks of a classic piece of juicy internet drama (a self-styled girlboss! A dramatic fall from grace! The Hamptons!), it also hit on something more fundamental: a failure of influence itself. Creators were supposed to be just like us — or at least pretend to be — to navigate the space between the everyman and the elite, maintaining a calculated balance between the aspirational and the authentic.

But in an atmosphere of growing tension and class consciousness, with privilege dictating very different pandemic experiences, influencers stood on increasingly contested ground. With a doctor on speed dial, hired help, and a house in the Hamptons to retreat to, Arielle's position had become clear. She was one of them, not one of us, a fact confirmed weeks later when it came to light that she had received up to \$350,000 from the US government's coronavirus paycheck protection programme for her brand Something Navy.[12] (Other high-profile influencer recipients included MrBeast, Jeffree Starr, and FaZe Clan.) The relatability illusion that sustains influence had collapsed.

Arielle's story spiralled out from social media to make headlines everywhere from US broadcast television to French news networks and tabloids as far as Australia. Everyone was saying the same thing. 'Influencing? In This Economy?' remarked *The New York Times*. 'Could the Coronavirus Kill Influencer Culture?' wondered *WIRED*. 'Is This The End Of The Influencer?' asked *Marie Claire*. The infinite months of 2020 wore on, marked by blood-red skies, wildfires, and police brutality. The race towards humanity's extinction appeared to be narrowing between the prospect of a Kanye presidency and an impending meteorite. As the cracks continued to appear, I kept returning to the same question.

'Around April 2020, I must have had five different editors approach me asking me to write something like "influencers are going to die out", influencer culture journalist Amelia Tait tells me over the phone. 'I didn't say yes to any of them. I just didn't buy it.' An influencer backlash doesn't signal the end of influence, she explains, 'it feeds the beast. Attention is where influencers' power comes from ... it's not going away.' Far from ending, influence was accelerating, becoming normalised: 'everybody's life has gone online. Being at home, creating content, and putting it out there has become a more everyday thing,' says Amelia. 'A lot of people might not think, "I bought a ring light, I'm part of this wider cultural phenomenon," but of course you are.' The rituals of influencing were now ubiquitous.

Given that our current wave of influencers had emerged in the aftermath of the 2008 crisis — from the contraction of the creative industries, the creation of the gig economy, and the subsequent atomisation of workers and audiences — it seemed more likely that the 2020 crisis would only amplify their existence. I thought back to Chris Rojek, and his description of the ideal conditions for influence. Creators suit an atomised and fragmented state of being in which human interaction is mediated through a screen. They excel in an atmosphere of fear and uncertainty, in which mistrust of institutional figures is displaced by alternative sources of authority. While labouring at home, detached from friends, families, and communities, there is more need for alternative emotional support systems now than ever. 'Whether through loneliness or just having nothing else to do, people are more and more willing to just front-face camera talk for a few minutes about their day, what they've been up to, what they bought,' agrees Amelia ... 'all that stuff that we usually associate with influencer culture.'

Their flexibility and adaptability make creators the ideal labour scavengers of a crashing economy and troubled state, skilful at pivoting to shifting needs, at hacking and hustling and finding opportunities. They are well suited to a decimated jobs market, in which opening up new sources of revenue from previously un-commoditised spaces becomes both attractive and necessary. 'With a lot of job losses, people will have been looking into it as an economic solution,' Amelia notes, comparing an increased interest in influencing to the surge of sign-ups to multi-level marketing schemes during periods of financial contraction. 'MLM ambassadors are influencers — that commodification of self and seeking out alternative sources of income is only going to increase.' Influencers were perfectly placed to emerge in a new decade in which we all find ourselves labouring individually on the internet; a world in which everyone has become an influencer. 2020 wouldn't dismantle the institution of influence, it would catalyse and crystallise it.

Influencer culture may not have been ending, but it was going through a period of flux, taking away opportunities from some and gifting them to others. The chaos arising from the crisis enveloped the influencer system along with the rest of the internet, disrupting its hierarchies and dismantling the patterns upon which it was reliant. I — along with the rest of the friends, family, followers, politicians, public figures, co-workers, and creators who populated my news feeds and cycled through my fevered brain at night — had entered an elastic period in which it felt as though anything could happen. It may not have been the end times, exactly, but it was to be the end of influence as I understood it.

The most immediate impact on influencing was an abrupt reshuffle of the social media status quo. First, social media stars first faced threats from above, as out-of-work Hollywood actors turned their hand to social media. When Dame Judi Dench appeared on my TikTok #ForYou page bumping to lyrics by Yung Gravy — 'ice, wrist, little bit of flexing', 1.1m views — the extent to which social media platforms had become gentrified by institutional celebrity became clear.

Then influencers faced a challenge from below, as members of the public usually occupied from nine to five now found themselves with time — and an iPhone — on their hands. The bizarre and banal were proving more appealing than curated lifestyle content: our new influencers were an Australian man uploading daily updates of his attempt to kick a fizzy drink addiction (246k followers), a part-time paint store worker mixing cans of emulsion with deadpan commentary (1.4m followers), or a teenage girl raising 37,000 tadpoles in a backyard paddling pool in Derry (1.6m followers). The year 2020 was not only dismantling the parameters of influence, but who could constitute the influential.

Fuelled by the energy of BLM and the soaring temperatures of a sweltering summer spent indoors, the internet was calling out individuals and institutions that had fallen short of their promised principles: girlboss empires like The Wing and *Man Repeller* who had failed to include non-white women in their empowering agenda; trendy Instagram brands like Glossier, Reformation, and Away, whose aesthetic surface hid a toxic workplace culture; and exclusive media institutions like Refinery29 and Condé Nast, who failed to hire, promote, or pay Black employees their worth. All were brands with close ties to influencer culture and the industry of aspirational lifestyle content. This new spirit of online accountability soon carried over to the adjacent creator industry, resulting in an hour of reckoning as quotidian influencer gossip ramped up to unprecedented levels of hysteria and long-held grudges bubbled up to breaking point.

Dramageddon 3 — a continuation of long-held controversies between beauty gurus James Charles and Tati Westbrook — broke out anew, and a top cohort of social media stars — including Shane Dawson, Gabi DeMartino, and the previously 'uncancellable' beauty guru Jeffree Starr — were ousted by a new clique of commentary vloggers embodied by 21-year-old 'King of Commentary' D'Angelo Wallace, who offered a more nuanced critique than any generation of tea channel before them.[13] D'Angelo — a deadpan intellectual Texan with a BA in Mass Communication who only uploaded his first video to YouTube in January 2020 — gained 17m views for his video 'The exact moment Shane Dawson's career ended', and added 400k subscribers to his channel in seven days.

Cancel culture reached inflection point when first-generation YouTube legend Jenna Marbles preemptively cancelled herself; in a tearful apology video on 25 June, titled 'A Message', Marbles explained she was 'privating' all her problematic content — internet hits such as 'What Girls Think About During Sex' — and abandoning her channel altogether.[14] 'I think there was a time when having all of my old content exist on the internet showed how much I have grown up as a person, which I'm very proud of,' she said, 'however, I think now it's hard for that content to exist at all.'

The summer of 2020 was an influencer limbo: fortunes could rise and fall, creators topple, and the support of the internet shift in the space of minutes. A YouTube video in which TikTok queen Charli

D'Amelio jokingly complained to James Charles about not reaching 100m followers in a year went viral with calls to cancel the 'bratty' and 'ungrateful' 16-year-old. Charli lost half a million followers in just 48 hours — a TikTok record — but the tide of public opinion more than reversed after she released an apology video. Mere weeks later, Charli had surpassed her original milestone, hit 102m followers and triumphantly announced 'The D'Amelio Show' airing on Hulu.

Underlying online cancel culture and the actions of specific individuals, a broader reckoning was taking place. Followers were beginning to question the fundamental principles upon which celebrity and influencer culture had been based. Within the space of weeks, *The New York Times* declared 'Capitalism Is Broken' and The World Economic Forum called for a 'Great Reset'. Political galvanisation around the BLM protests brought key activist concepts, such as anti-racism or defunding the police, to the front of public discourse, questioning institutions of authority and the status quo. Pandemic inequalities were leading to political unrest and simmering class consciousness. As key workers were denied pay rises, government relief checks were delayed, and millions lost their jobs, billionaires increased their collective wealth by more than a quarter at the height of the crisis.[15] As visible expressions of consumerism and social media 'upper class', influencers were implicated in these conversations.

This sentiment was reflected on social media: 'No more celebrities', ran a viral Twitter meme, 'society has progressed past the need for celebrities'. Guillotine memes began trending. Marxism explainers began filling my #ForYou page on TikTok. A commune in Tennessee went viral. The cottagecore aesthetic trend — with an emphasis on crafting and growing your own vegetables — rose to meet new interest in living off-grid, low-impact lifestyles removed from technology and consumerism. If celebrity culture had met its match in a global pandemic, influencers — now unsure of where they stood — were left on uncertain ground.

While celebrity culture's court of public opinion was in session, the platforms were officially on trial themselves. In July 2020, a historic Congressional anti-trust hearing put tech CEOs on the spot together to determine their companies' ethics and compliance with monopoly regulation. Though the hearing turned out to be mostly inconclusive — it turns out giving Congress members two minutes each to ask anything of the four most powerful figures in the tech industry means they end up demanding to know why their campaign emails file into their dad's spam folder[16] — outside, the verdict was being made for them. Social media was beyond repair. Tensions between platforms and their communities had been stoked by several unwelcome platform updates, mismanagement of disinformation around QAnon and the pandemic, debates about apoliticality and moderation, and their perceived ineffectuality for serving their community.

As the role of social media was shifting in response to global crisis, and platforms were co-opted for community organising, activist campaigning, and mutual aid, these flaws became amplified. To overcome the limitations and restrictions of social media platforms, new formats and features had to be hacked: open-access Google Docs circulated and updated, link lists forwarded on WhatsApp, encrypted messaging apps superseding public feeds and Zoom rooms bombed for virtual protest.

The widespread rise of link-in-bio tools like LinkTree or Carrd — originally marketing features enabling brands and publishers to link to sites and product pages, appropriated to share anti-racist resources, charity donations, and protestor bail funds — enabled normal users to circumvent Instagram's restriction granting swipe-up functionality only to users with more than 10k followers. '@instagram release the link in stories feature to everyone, not just influencers', read a Tweet liked 20,000 times. 'You already know how your users work and how difficult it is to get them to leave the platform if it involves more than one step (the point, I get it). Make helping right now more effective.' 'Social media giants support racial justice,' reported *The New York Times*, 'their products undermine it.'[17]

For a moment, it felt like social media was becoming a space that truly served its community. Attention shifted away from mainstream commercial influencers and towards online educators: activists, authors, campaigners, race scholars, and medical professionals.

Non-Black influencers collectively participated in a mass muting, or in hashtags like #AmplifyMelanatedVoices, and influencers #SharedTheMic, handing over the passwords to their social media profiles for 24 hours to spotlight communities and causes who had been working tirelessly to provide support services through the pandemic. Calls to decolonise our feeds meant shareable guides collating 'alternative influencers' to follow circulated widely online,[18] boosting the social profiles of creators and educators such as data visualiser Mona Chalabi, author Layla F. Saad, and race scholar Ibram X. Kendi, who shot from 30k followers in May to 1m followers by September.

It was the year of the Instagram infographic. Endless graphic micro-guides broke down our most pressing political issues into actionable chunks optimised for the algorithm: a ten-page guide to defunding the police, a bullet-point breakdown of the impact of the Beirut blast, a Helvetica-lettered carousel illustrating voter suppression, an ideological explainer about non-optical allyship rendered in soothing beige tones that garnered over a million engagements. Instagram account @soyouwanttotalkabout was born on 11 Feb 2020 and by October had 2 million followers, indicative of a new breed of 2020 influencer: one that eschewed fall outfit edits or home decorating guides for posts like 'So You Want to Talk About: Preparing for a Coup.'

Lucy is one of three New Zealand-based millennials behind the @shityoushouldcareabout Instagram infographic account, which provides 'daily, no-bullshit updates on the world' in an attempt to create 'a level playing field of accessible info', she tells me over email. The account was originally set up in 2018 to counteract 'a flood of people trying to sell us detox tea and teeth whitening products' with global news, culture, and mental health perspectives, but 2020 saw a rush of new followers and engagement as there was so much information that their followers needed to know and wanted to understand. During the BLM movement, they lent their platform to US-based activists: 'We gained 800,000 followers in one month.' Following 2020, Lucy thinks 'people with "influence" are now more inclined to use their platform to speak up about injustices', however, they are personally keen to distance themselves from the term.

But 2020 just proved that social media platforms aren't engineered for action, but for advertising, promoting call-out culture over community and individualism over solidarity. The Instagram infographic industrial complex aestheticised social issues and inevitably fed the very optical activism it claimed to be against. A surge in new follows for Black creators began to damage their engagement rates and jeopardise commercial opportunities. 'Blackout Tuesday' — a synchronised day in which allies posted black squares to social media in solidarity with protestors — ended up clogging up the algorithm and obstructing access to valuable BLM resources. Just as social media's potential for community organising was becoming apparent, key platforms leaned into deeper forms of monetisation, and tensions spiked as a result. Instagram sneakily replaced the notification button with a shop feature, YouTube quietly updated their Terms to include the 'right to monetise' on every creator's video without providing them with a cut.

I felt like I had arrived at a breaking point. Twitter was too fraught and caustic. Facebook — long the hunting ground of MLM huns, QAnon conspiracists, and an ageing demographic communicating via blurry Minion memes — had completed its transformation into a cultural wasteland. YouTube was bloated by commercial clickbait and promoting algorithm-induced radicalisation. Instagram — now no longer masquerading as anything other than a glorified mall — could only offer an anaesthetic blanket of self-care, brand pandering, and performative wokeness. The introduction of a stories function across LinkedIn and Twitter meant every major social media app now offered nearly identical features. The internet — once a spectrum of unique experiences — was now dominated by a handful of monolithic platforms that were increasingly indistinguishable, patrolled by brands and policed by algorithms.

Perhaps the platforms had just run their course. 'I like looking for signs that social networks are dying or atrophying,' tech reporter Ryan Broderick wrote in his 'Garbage Day' newsletter in December

2020, listing symptoms including: 'power users aggressively dominate discussion on the site ... no longer any internal cultural memory ... Users have become so obsessed with the minutiae of the community that the site now functions as a meta discussion of itself instead of whatever its intended purpose was.' Twitter's increasingly introspective discourse — the majority of the trending discussions were now about the platform itself — was, he claimed, a symptom of its imminent demise: 'It's a dying website. Even if it sometimes grows in users, even if it still drives culture, even if it lasts for another ten years, without a serious intervention and changes to its core structure, it will only become increasingly difficult to understand what is happening on the site.'

In June, a series of emojis — 🥀🔁🥀 — began to crop up in tech insider's bios and mysterious tweets. Overnight, hype began to spiral around the phrase 'it is what it is', with rumours that an elite new invite-only social media platform was imminent. The phrase became a top search term on Product Hunt, and a sign-up form on the otherwise-blank 'it is what it is' website claimed waiting list places could be bumped up by donating to BLM. After days of frenetic speculation, the anonymous account — now followed by thousands — released a statement. 'It is what it is' simply wasn't: the mysterious new platform was a hoax. A 'ragtag group of young technologists tired of the status quo within the tech industry' had ridden the Silicon Valley hype cycle to spotlight the superfluity of social media and raise money for activist causes. Not only did this stunt expose collective desperation for the 'next big thing', it proved Broderick's point: social media had begun to eat itself.

Even new platforms that weren't performance art were quickly descending into infighting and toxicity, every bit as fractious as the apps they challenged: as Twitter began to roll out misinformation tags for the first time — over a third of Trump's tweets were flagged for disinformation following election day — Parler, an alternative 'free speech' social network known as the platform of the deplatformed, exploded to the top of Apple's App Store with downloads increasing by 2,000 per cent in the two days after 7 November. Clubhouse, an audio-based startup social network valued at $100m in only beta mode, had promised to foster intellectual debate and cultural exchange, but quickly became mired with claims of anti-Semitism, misogyny, and bullying only months after launching. Nextdoor, a community network originally designed to strengthen ties in urban neighbourhoods, descended into a system of local self-surveillance and self-righteous curtain twitching. The app was overrun with snoopers, scammers, and vigilante militants calling for the institution of curfews — along with multiple reports of UFOs.

Being Extremely Online in 2020 was also extremely exhausting: the year's events highlighted the deficiencies of our existing arenas for any sane, sustained conversation. Netflix's documentary *The Social Dilemma* — released in September 2020 and watched by 38 million viewers in four weeks — only confirmed what we knew already. Our platforms were broken, and so were we.

It's difficult to see TikTok as anything other than the perfect product of this period, a space every bit as absurd and chaotic as the world it offered escape from. This is your brain on TikTok: *Patagonia finance bros, queues for Tesco, medieval WAP, cottagecore, beanz* 🌱🫘🌱*, dancing Purell bottles, Sims characters but IRL, creating my own fonts, coming of age, top secret things to do in London part 7, confronting the stalker who climbed into my window (3.2m views). Choose your character: e-girl 🐱, simp 😳, softboy 😌, lost millennial (anyone else here over 30? Help!) A giant percy pig caught sleeping on Zoom, cats singing to Mr Sandman, private school check, y2k outfits suitable to meet your grandad, nobody asks you questions when you say you're an* accountant 😌*, six things in my NYC apartment that just make sense* ✨*. Bicep glue and it's 6 am and you're talking to a lamp, rainbow strobe effect, POV: you're Draco Malfoy and I'm late for Potions!!! Check out these instagram story hacks, perks of dating a ginger, British people sound like 'chewsday', innit? Nobody's gonna know — they're gonna know — how would they know? Rare aesthetic: early 2000s SeaWorld Orlando or Sixth Grade Spanish Class* 🎵🎵*, Gossip Girl spoilers, name a more iconic duo: Dreams by Fleetwood Mac and Ocean Spray cranberry juice — no thoughts, just vibes* 😌*.*

Powerpoint night celebs we should date; why Glee's Matthew Morrison deserves to be sent to Guantanamo Bay and Marx is Zaddy, Zara haul part two, uwu 😊 ⌐■. *I'm using TikTok to catch my sister's killer — I used TikTok to catch my sister's killer! You've got to start romanticising your life: I don't dress so guys will like me, I dress cool so younger girls will look at me in the street and think I'm cool, I'm the main character* 😊. *Oh my god what is thaaaaaa-?* 👀

Open the app for the very first time, and without explanation, you'll be plunged into an autoplaying video selected by the celebrated TikTok algorithm: bright colours, flashing lights, and energetic footage edited with in-app filters, text, stickers, and backed with sound effects, voiceovers, or rips of music tracks. You almost certainly won't understand what you've just watched, but it will already be too late — the app will have moved on — because TikTok is never still: a vertical conveyor belt drops clip after clip from the top of your screen in a waterfall of looping videos anywhere between 15 and 60 seconds.

Navigating TikTok is disorienting. It's an app that takes its name from the steady progress of a clock yet offers no stable sense of time or place and is devoid of grounding signifiers: it's difficult to tell when a post was uploaded or an account created, and impossible to trace where trends originate. Forget attempting to construct any sort of continuous narrative between posts, content circulates in an endless loop and videos are abrupt, self-contained units of information with no continuity or context. It's not chronological and old content can go viral weeks after posting. Nobody on TikTok cares about maintaining a personal brand — they churn out decontextualised pieces of content that circulate as free-floating signifiers within the algorithm.

TikTok does not make sense: even Charli D'Amelio (the most famous TikTok teen on the planet) and Holly H (the UK's largest TikTok star) have admitted they don't know why they're so popular or how the algorithm works. 'I still have no clue what I'm doing,' confessed creator Connor Darlington (4.5m fans) at VidCon, 'There's no difference [in understanding] between someone new to the platform vs us, who have been on there for ages.' Alienation is an intrinsic feature of the app's architecture. There is an overwhelming sense of restlessness about the TikTok experience: users never settle for long on anything, the platform has no centre, the screen is in constant motion — even video thumbnails are rendered as a glitching boomerang.

Although captions announce your arrival at a certain section of the app ('if you're reading this, you've reached finance TikTok') it's never really there in any real or tangible sense. The whole experience is imbued with instability, content feels equally repetitive and fleeting. It is an app perfectly suited to an existence that seems to repeat itself every day, trapped in a perpetual present with no prospect of progression. What better way to demonstrate the lockdown experience?

Sascha Morgan-Evans is Talent Development Director at Bytesized Talent, the UK's first TikTok talent management agency, representing 39 of the biggest platform stars. She brokers brand partnerships as well as developing commercial and talent strategy with the figures she represents, giving her unique insight into the currents and conditions of the creator marketplace. TikTok has transformed the landscape, she tells me, resetting expectations about how creators should behave and reshaping the cadence of commercial deals: 'TikTok is offering a new type of influencer and a new wave of influence,' she confirms, one defined by 'more content, more competition, and more churn'.

The platform's architecture is simultaneously reinforcing and undermining influence: users have no need to subscribe to a creator to be entertained when they have the ultimate influencer — the algorithm — and the #ForYou page; but its addictive qualities and widespread uptake mean that it has reinforced the institution of influencing as a whole. Its arrival drove an increase in mainstream attention for the influencer industry, with a spate of gushing headlines and glossy profiles, something internet culture journalist Amelia confirms: 'A lot of editors seem to sort of be overcompensating for the fact that they didn't pay attention to the internet before. There's a real renewed interest in the fame that people find there and what it means to be an influencer.'

TikTok is faster and more demanding than any of its predecessors:

accelerated trend cycles are harder than ever to keep up with, and can keep influencers locked in for even longer than before. Going viral isn't enough any more, Sascha explains. 'Back in the day you could have one video go viral, and that's it, that's your career sorted for the next few years at least,' she tells me, citing Rebecca Black, an early viral star whose single 'Friday' blew up in 2011, from which she's established a career as an Instagram influencer with a million followers a decade later: 'it's not that easy any more. You have to be a viral person, more so than just [producing] viral content, which is mad.' TikTok's easy virality has broadened competition, making anyone a potential influencer. Though getting views may be easier, converting these to followers, growing a profile and sustaining a trajectory are much harder. Traction is more random and inconsistent. 'There's not a long-term graph, they're just sort of thrust into it,' says Sascha, and 'because they're thrust into it, they're very inexperienced and they don't necessarily have a deep understanding of how the industry works'.

The ease of going viral is devaluing virality itself, debasing the influencer economy. Three million subscribers on TikTok are 'worth less' than the equivalent on other platforms, reflected in a lower payout. Already, TikTok is undercutting the influencer economy: top creators, and those that came up through it, make less money per post than on any other platform. 'On TikTok the opportunities are a lot more abundant, but they're lower value,' says Sascha, corroborated by influencer platform Followchain, who claim: 'TikTok's CPM [cost per 1,000 impressions/views] is much lower as compared to other social media platforms ... some TikTokers with over a million views get less than $1,000 per sponsored post.'

And TikTok fame is less stable than on previous platforms. 'TikTok is creating more churn. You see creators rise and fall more quickly,' remarked Sascha. 'When YouTubers come up they last a few years. TikTokers pop up and disappear [into] the ether.' Nor is TikTok a place where creators want to stay long term: 'Not a lot of them are very interested in remaining just within the silo of TikTok,' Sascha says. 'A lot of them see TikTok as a springboard to the rest of their career.' I thought back to Abby and her off-platform ambitions.

The idea that you can go viral for doing anything on TikTok makes anything and everything a potential source of content, collapsing previously defined lifestyle influencer categories into a feed of life itself. There is something about TikTok as a platform that makes users feel like they need to commodify aspects of the human experience which wouldn't usually be packaged up, I notice, as my #ForYou page serves me an escalating series of confession videos plumbing unseen emotional depths for viral content: a front-facing video in which a girl sobs that she had just been made homeless, a harrowing montage of developing domestic abuse, a skin-crawling competition for the most embarrassing intimate anecdote shared with 6 million strangers.

It seems there is no topic, theme, or experience that can't be subjected to the influencer effect. TikTok is a turning point; past which nothing is off limits. TikTok has fundamentally changed the conditions of influencing, not by offering release from the algorithm, but by intensifying it, and along with it the conditions of creator culture, rendering it more precarious, more accelerated, and more extreme.

On 6 January 2021, mere days after the end of the year we had pretended was the problem all along, the revolution is livestreamed on Twitch. Along with 225,000 other viewers, I tune in to coverage of the US Capitol coup attempt from @HasanAbi, aka Hasan Piker, a creator who grew his political commentary channel to over a million followers on a platform more traditionally used for streaming video games. During 2020, Hasan had found mainstream fame playing Among Us with Congresswoman Alexandria Ocasio-Cortez, breaking Twitch viewership records and attracting the attention of media outlets in the process.

For the presidential election itself, he streamed over 80 hours of commentary in ten-hour shifts, reading and reacting to each state declaration in real time, his luxuriant beard, 'Bernie 2020' sweatshirt, and expletive-laden analysis offering an alternative to the manicured, shiny-suited anchors of traditional TV news. 'Can Hasan Piker's stream of consciousness save America?' *Highsnobiety* had wondered in a September 2020 profile, in which the broad-shouldered streamer posed in Nike high tops and a leather bomber jacket. By January 2021, it felt too late to save.

As the Capitol protestors smash windows and push into private offices, Hasan — now hunched over his podcast mic in a black sweatshirt, computer set-up reflecting in his wire-framed glasses — narrates through his shared computer screen in real time, flipping restlessly between right-wing livestreams, official news networks, viral tweets, and updates from the official @POTUS account, while the chatbox hums with memes, political hot takes, news links, PogChamp emotes, and professions of adoration for our influencer pundit.

'Dude!' Hasan exclaims, 'the hogs have reached the senate!' By the time the protest has become a riot, it is dark outside in London, and from my position slumped on the sofa my laptop screen glows red and blue as my internet connection struggles to buffer a sudden influx of online horror. Audio clashes and video glitches; updates come through in 15-second iPhone clips and 'BREAKING' tweets; government computers have been abandoned with programmes still up and running; guns have been drawn, someone has been shot.

Hasan's multimedia remix of the internet mirrors my own, by now over-tabulated brain, dipping between Discord servers, Twitter feeds, BBC Reality Check explainers, and bewildered WhatsApp group chats with my friends and colleagues. Like a gamer running voiceover commentary over Minecraft, Hasan responds to politicians, tweets, and talking heads with his own characteristically acerbic analysis: 'Really dude, is it un-American dude?' he retorts to house minority leader Kevin McCarthy being interviewed on CBS, furrowing his eyebrows in mock empathy. 'What the fuck did you guys think was going to happen? Y'all did this shit!' His voice rises to a static crackle as the Twitch chat notifications bristle and McCarthy appears strained under CBS's studio lighting. 'Oh no, I can't believe all our racial agitation ultimately ended with those sick hogs acting out on the desires we placed there for them!'

As the rioters leave notes for Nancy Pelosi and adorn bronze statues with MAGA caps, Hasan's quarter of a million viewers gather information in real time: collecting memes, sharing links, offering comments and hot takes. News anchors from MSNBC and CNN — embedding the same social media clips we have, by now, already seen a hundred times — express amazement that the protestors willingly show their faces, that they are bold enough to livestream an uprising or share selfies with their feet up in politicians' offices.

'It seems like the crowd is getting bigger out there,' Hasan warns, as the supposed coup begins to take on the appearance of a perverse revolutionary pantomime. What is the end game, the political pundits of cable TV wonder: surely a ragtag group of protestors and aggressors know they can't occupy the Capitol for long? Why does it feel like, as they pull up image after image of rioters waving for Getty photojournalists and sporting Viking costumes ('cultural appropriation!' someone in the chatroom joked), the so-called revolutionaries are playing the whole thing for entertainment? For those watching Hasan on Twitch, the answer is obvious: digital influence.

The coup is a right-wing influencer meet-up. Amongst the crowd are banned YouTubers Nick Fuentes, streamer Tim Gionet, known as Baked Alaska, and Jake Angeli, a popular QAnon figure known as the 'Q Shaman' — clad in fur and skulls as if the task is to siege Valhalla, not the US Senate — along with smaller streamers hoping to establish themselves and attract views to their budding channels. Many have turned up in branded merch: hoodies with their social media handles declaring '6th Jan 2021: CIVIL WAR', Pepe meme paraphernalia, body rigs, and selfie sticks to document the chaos as it unfolds. Rioters take selfies with police and live-stream from inside the speakers' offices, uploading directly to YouTube, Twitch, and blockchain streaming site DLive, reminding viewers 'Don't forget to like and subscribe!' Some streams are even monetised.

The rioters are using the coup as a collaboration opportunity, networking with and promoting others' channels: DLive streamer Zykotic — declaring himself 'the real news media' as he stands in front of the battered remains of a professional crew's destroyed recording equipment — invites shoutouts from those filming near him. 'Everybody go follow him!' Zykotic shouts, after one YouTuber identifies himself by name and handle, 'I've got 3,000 people [watching], go follow!' Rioters make off with 'hauls' — clutching letters, wooden nameplates, a five-foot wooden podium stolen from the Senate — and pose for pictures. The coup is a collective content creation activity, a fascist Fyre Festival, a social media stunt engineered to generate engagement and impressions.

Surfing YouTube's recommendations bar afterwards, I click on YouTuber Stephen Ignoramus's Capitol coup video, simply titled 'DC': an eight-hour marathon that was streamed to a total of 331,493 viewers. 'What's up everybody, Stephen Ignoramus here!' Stephen announces as he starts his stream on the long walk through the landscaped grounds towards the building, streaming camera strapped to his chest like a travel vlogger documenting a brand trip. 'We're going to the Capitol to do some Minecraft shit.'

As he and his companion trudge in the direction of the protest, the sound of Survivor's 'Eye of the Tiger' blares from a speaker somewhere in the background. 'I wonder if they'll give me a strike,' Stephen asks aloud, referring to YouTube's automatic identification of unlicensed music playing in uploaded videos, apparently more concerned about a copyright strike than the seditious activity he is about to broadcast live under an identifiable handle. 'No, they'll give you a demonetisation,' his friend off-camera chips in. 'They're all homos over there at YouTube, man,' Stephen complains.

I drag the timestamp forward: Stephen and his friend approach the Capitol building in double time, glitchy figures milling about in the crowd, home-made banners jerking and jittering at accelerated pace. Three and a half hours — several seconds — later, I drop my cursor and hit play, and suddenly the camera surges forwards; the crowd is rushing up the Capitol steps, whooping and yelling. Steven pans to show the crush of bodies, waving flags, a screaming sea of red, white, and blue. In the background, shouts of, 'We're taking back our country' and 'We want Trump' flatten into a static roar. 'Share this out, link my shit, love you guys!' Stephen yells. A few seconds later, a shot is fired. I close the tab.

Whilst I was curled up on my sofa stabbing my laptop keyboard, rewinding and replaying Capitol coverage in an endless loop, social media platforms had been thrown into a state of emergency, scrambling to restrict coup content and deal with Trump's incendiary video urging 'very special' protestors to 'go home'. YouTube hadn't removed Stephen's video, but they did add content warnings in front of many DC livestreams, taking down videos that featured weapons and included incitement of violence. Twitter swiftly announced new platform restrictions, limiting interaction with Trump's posts, whilst Facebook declared a state of emergency, locked @POTUS accounts, and began to remove videos and photos relating to the protest.

I had been searching for an ending, and this felt like it. If the coup was the result of four years of progressive political escalation, it was also the culmination of ten years of social media and influencer culture as well; a decade that had begun with the first YouTuber to make the *Forbes* internet rich list in 2010 and ended with a social media president and influencer insurgents in the halls of power. The intertwining threads of political, economic, digital, and cultural influence had all converged in one place for a spectacle of unprecedented proportions. Influencing had reached its point of singularity, not just for social media stars, but for everyone else as well. I, along with my colleagues and contemporaries in the sanitised environment of Instagram stars, were now unable to ignore the truth: that polished commercial influencers and fascist streaming hogs were two sides of the same algorithm.

Hasty headlines had been quick to proclaim the coup a 'failed attempt', but I was not so sure. It was never really about votes, it was about views. The true site of power was not within the Senate walls: it was online, in the audience, in the engagement, in the algorithms. The coup was pure performativity, an event without a centre, familiar enough to any influencer accustomed to staging life via an iPhone. I remember standing at the Babe event in central London all those months ago, staring at my own repeated reflection in the infinity mirror, and wondering where the party really was: the dissociative sense of spectacle and projection had felt disconcerting then, but it is so much more disturbing now.

For the first time in months, I powered down my laptop, watching as my 37 open tabs slid laterally shut and my browser windows inhaled themselves, disappearing into infinity. The notification pops stopped, the posts vanished, and I was left to stare at the blurred reflection of myself, looking back through the now-dark computer screen.

ACKNOWLEDGEMENTS

Thanks go first and foremost to my agent Max Edwards at Aevitas Creative Management for his encouragement, enthusiasm, and advice through the whole process, from coffee in Hackney to panicked mid-pandemic phone calls. Your support has been invaluable.

I have eternal appreciation for my incredible editors Molly Slight and Sarah Braybrooke for taking a chance on a book about digital influence from an author with fewer than 100 followers on Twitter, and for shaping it so thoughtfully. Working with you has been a delight, as has discussing everything from mumfluencers to BreadTubers. Thanks to the whole team at Scribe — I am so grateful that my first publishing experience has been in your expert hands.

I am indebted to entrepreneur and industry expert Eve Lee and the incredible team at marketing agency The Digital Fairy for their support during the research and writing of this book, and for permission to reproduce material from their trend report, 'Influencers 2025'. I would wholeheartedly recommend anyone seeking influencer services to head in their direction.

Many thanks to the creator community and everyone who gave their time, insight, and advice to this book, some of whom are directly quoted, and many of whom are not. They have all contributed to the finished product, whether through conversation, introduction, or simply lending a willing ear.

The influencer industry is so complex and fast-paced, I wouldn't have been able to write this book without relying on the vital work of those who are already out there reporting in this field. I'm thankful for the fantastic internet culture teams at *Business Insider*, *The New York Times*, *Tubefilter*, *Mashable*, *The Verge*, *BuzzFeed*, *No Filter*, *Wired*, *Real Life*, and many more.

Specific journalists I would love to highlight include Taylor Lorenz, Chris Stokel-Walker, Morgan Sung, Terry Nguyen, Tanya Chen and Stephanie McNeal, Amelia Tait, Sarah Manavis, Kat Tenbarge, Ryan Broderick, Lauren O'Neill, Kate Lindsay, and Sophie Ross, but this list is by no means comprehensive! I would encourage anyone interested in the space to seek out their work.

I've also benefited from reading the work of social media researchers and academics such as Dr Brooke Erin Duffy, Dr Crystal Abidin, Dr Sophie Bishop, Dr Alice E. Marwick, Becca Lewis, and Zoe Glatt. From a business perspective, I'd love to highlight the ongoing creator economy research and writing of individuals such as Zoe Scaman, Rex Woodbury, Li Jin, Peter Yang, and High Tea's Alice and Faye.

Many thanks to all the managers, agents, and behind-the-scenes teams I liaised with, and who represent the unsung heroes of the influencer industry, including Tracy Willis of WHE Agency, Giorgia Aubrey at Kyra Media, Martha Atack at InterTalent Group, Bambi Haines at The Booking Project, the Vault House team and Six Degrees of Influence, Freddie Strange at Komodo, and Hannah Henshall at If Not Now Digital. Thank you to Fire Tech and their team for hosting me at influencer camp, and Michaela Efford for shielding my dignity as I stripped down behind a van for our photoshoot.

Closer to home, I'd like to thank friends and family who have put up with me during the creation of this book; and specifically Jane Macfarlane, Hannibal Knowles, and Eleanor Metcalf for their direct contributions to the text. And lastly I'd like to thank Zander Sharp, without whom *Break the Internet* would still be a series of bullet points in my iPhone Notes.

GLOSSARY

ASMR – Autonomous sensory meridian response, a calming, tingling sensation felt on the scalp and upper back, triggered by soft sounds like whispers, crackles, and taps. Videos designed to trigger this response have become a popular genre on YouTube and Twitch.

BOOMER — Slang for someone in the baby boomer generation, born from 1946 to 1964. 'Ok boomer' became a meme used by younger generations to mock reactionary attitudes associated with the baby boomer generation.

BOOMERANGS — A function on Instagram that allows you to film mini videos that loop backwards and forwards continuously.

RED PILL, BLUE PILL — From a scene in *The Matrix* (1999), this refers to a choice between the willingness to learn a truth that may be unsettling or life-changing (taking the red pill) or remaining ignorant (taking the blue pill). The concept has been co-opted by alt-right internet users to refer to the process of online radicalisation.

BREADTUBE — Refers to a collective of left-wing influencers on YouTube. The name was inspired *The Conquest of Bread* (1982) by anarco-communist Peter Kropotkin.

BREADPILL — A pun on the right-wing 'red pill', the 'breadpill' refers to the conversion of individuals to left-wing ideology.

CAP TABLE — The breakdown of a start-up or early-stage venture company's ownership and the distribution of equity amongst founders and investors listed in a spreadsheet. Also used informally to refer to parties who have a stake in the business, as in being 'at' or 'around' the cap table.

CHAN SITES — Loosely moderated, interest-based, anonymous internet sub-forums or 'bulletin boards'. Sites like 4chan, 8chan, 8kun, and endchan have become synonymous with trolling, racism, and abuse.

4CHAN'S /B/ — The first board created on 4chan in 2003.

DEEPFAKE — Deepfakes use artificial intelligence and machine learning to convincingly generate or manipulate image and video.

DEMONETISATION — The process through which content creators are denied revenue that would be gained from viewers watching their YouTube videos. YouTube may choose to deny a creator monetisation for various reasons including using inappropriate language or profanity in their videos, or uploading adult, violent, or graphic content. However, many have complained that YouTube demonetises videos for things that fall outside of these guidelines.

DM — A direct message sent privately via a social media platform.

DOOMSCROLLING — Spending an excessive amount of time endlessly scrolling through negative online news to the detriment of one's mental health.

DRAMA COMMUNITY/CHANNEL — Creators who make videos breaking/commenting on internet news.

DROPSHIPPING — An order fulfillment method wherein a shop sells a product, then passes on the order to a third-party supplier who ships the order to the customer. It is a method that allows a business to sell products without ever stocking any items themselves.

EDGELORD — Someone who maintains a provocative or extreme online persona with the intent of shocking others.

ENGAGEMENT — Users interacting with a post on social media, for example, liking or commenting on a video. Used by marketers to measure the popularity of a post or campaign.

FAN CAMS — A celebratory video montage of clips or pictures of a celebrity, edited together by a fan of that person, often set to music.

FANDOM — A community or subculture of fans of something in particular, be that a person, fictional series, band, sports team etc.

FLATLAY — A popular style of social media post, particularly on Instagram. A still life image shot directly from above composed of carefully arranged objects, for example clothes, accessories, food, or beauty products.

FINSTA — A second, private Instagram account users create to share things with their friends and family that they wouldn't share on their public Instagram account.

FURRIES — People who are a part of a subculture that are interested in anthropomorphic animals. They may also dress up in anthropomorphic animal costumes or create a specific furry character/avatar called a 'fursona' that they identify with.

GEN Z — The generation born from the mid-to-late 90s to the early 2010s.

GONGBANG — A 'study with me' video wherein someone films themselves studying to motivate others and provide them with companionship as they study. The name originates from South Korea.

'GRAMMING — Instagramming, sharing something on Instagram.

HENTAI — Japanese word that has come to mean anime and manga pornography.

HYPEBEAST — Someone who is obsessed with acquiring fashionable clothing, particularly streetwear. Sometimes used derogatively to mean a person who is obsessed with following trends.

IRL — In real life, as opposed to online, often used in a digital context.

METATAGS — Snippets of text describing a website's content that don't actually appear on the web page itself. They help search engines determine what a page is about and who will be interested in it.

MLM — Multi-level marketing scheme. A multi-level marketing scheme's strategy is similar to that of a pyramid scheme: its sales force gain income from selling products and recruiting more salespeople. Salespeople usually have to buy the products they are selling themselves, so even if they cannot sell their stock, the scheme does not lose money. MLMs are notorious for drawing people in with the promise of flexible working hours and the opportunity to earn lots of income, but, more often than not, workers lose money.

MUKBANG — A video in which someone eats a large quantity of food while talking to their audience. These are often livestreamed. The name originated in South Korea as a portmanteau of the words 'eating' (*meongneun*) and 'broadcast' (*bangsong*).

NFT — Non-fungible token. A unit of data stored on a blockchain that represents an object, such as a piece of art. It cannot be copied, so it certifies the authenticity and ownership of the asset it represents.

NOOB — A person who displays a lack of skill, is a novice or inexperienced in something, particularly on the internet, for example, at playing a video game.

NSFW — Not Safe for Work. Internet slang to mark explicit content that the person may not want to be seen looking at in public.

PARASOCIAL RELATIONSHIP — The psychological relationship experienced by an audience member in their mediated interactions with celebrities and internet personalities. The viewer feels attached to and is invested in the lives of these celebrities. They feel as though they know them, as if they are friends, while the celebrities have no idea of their existence.

POGCHAMP/POGCHAMP EMOTES — An emoticon used on Twitch to mean excitement or shock, based on streamer Ryan 'Gootecks' Gutierrez.

REDDIT/SUBREDDIT/R//R/ALL — A social news website and forum. Content is created and curated by site members who can post on the site and vote on content they like. Posts with more votes will be shown first. It is formed of subreddits (interest-based sub-forums) that can be found by typing r/ and then the name of the subreddit at the end of reddit's url. r/all curates content across the whole website.

SHADOWBAN — When a user is blocked or partially blocked from a social media platform by the platform without their knowledge. They can still post but their posts will be hidden from others and may have lower engagement rates.

SHADE — An idiom with roots in the Black and Hispanic LGBTQ+ community meaning to snub or slight. Expressing contempt for another person can be called 'throwing shade'.

SHELL ACCOUNTS — A shell account refers to an account run by a computer bot rather than a person.

SLACK — A communication platform primarily used by businesses to enable employees to virtually chat to each other.

SOCK PUPPET ACCOUNTS — An account created by a user to deceive or manipulate people online anonymously.

SPONCON/#SPON/#SPONNING — Used to mark a post as containing paid advertising material.

STAN — An extremely devoted, obsessive fan, often part of a self-identified group or fandom.

STREAMING — Simultaneously filming and broadcasting continuous video to be watched live.

SWIPE UP — A feature on Instagram that users only acquire once they have reached a certain number of followers that allows them to link to other websites or products to purchase.

THE GREAT FIREWALL/FIREWALL — A term that refers to the various legislative and technological ways through which China blocks its citizens' access to certain websites.

TEA — Gossip. The term has its roots in the Black LGBTQ+ community.

UNBOXING VIDEOS — A popular genre on YouTube: people record themselves opening packaged products and often reviewing them. Especially popular with tech items and toys.

VANITY METRICS — Social media metrics such as follower count that may, on the surface, make an influencer appear successful, but are ultimately unreliable as they can be manipulated or skewed, for example, by purchasing views or likes.

VINE — A defunct video-sharing app enabling users to upload looping videos of up to 6 seconds. Vine was extremely successful and helped to launch the careers of many high-profile creators, but this success did not last long and the app was discontinued in 2016.

NOTES

PREFACE

1 Kevin Roose, 'Don't Scoff at Influencers. They're Taking Over the World.',
   The New York Times (16 July 2019), https://www.nytimes.com/2019/07/16/
   technology/vidcon-social-media-influencers.html

CHAPTER 1 – THE MILLION-FOLLOWER POLICY

1 Christina Newberry, '44 Instagram Stats That Matter to Marketers in 2021',
   Hootsuite (6 January 2021), https://blog.hootsuite.com/instagram-statistics/
2 Paris Martineau, 'Inside the Weird, and Booming, Industry of Online Influence',
   WIRED (22 April 2019), https://www.wired.com/story/inside-the-industry-
   social-media-influence/
3 A. Guttmann, 'Number of brand sponsored influencer posts on Instagram
   from 2016 to 2020', *Statista* (30 June 2020), https://www.statista.com/
   statistics/693775/instagram-sponsored-influencer-content/
4 'Instagram SHOPPING', *Instagram*, https://business.instagram.com/shopping
5 Yuanling Yuan and Josh Constine, 'SignalFire's Economy Market Map',
   SignalFire, https://www.signalfire.com/blog/creator-economy
6 'Followers', *Mention*, https://mention.com/en/reports/instagram/followers/
7 'How much does Kylie Jenner earn on Instagram?', *BBC* (26 July 2019), https://
   www.bbc.co.uk/newsround/49124484
8 Matt Perez, 'Top-Earning Video Gamers: The Ten Highest-Paid Players
   Pocketed More Than $120 Million In 2019', *Forbes* (29 January 2020), https://
   www.forbes.com/sites/mattperez/2020/01/29/top-earning-video-gamers-the-
   ten-highest-paid-players-pocketed-more-than-120-million-in-2019/
9 @JeffreeStar, *Twitter* (1 November 2019), https://twitter.com/JeffreeStar/

status/1190314552757374976

10   Daniel McIntyre, 'Move over Kylie! YouTube star Shane Dawson breaks the internet and earns $35 million in seconds as he launches Conspiracy Collection makeup range with pal Jeffree Star', *Daily Mail* (14 November 2019), https://www.dailymail.co.uk/femail/article-7682541/Shane-Dawson-Jeffree-Star-makeup-collaboration-earns-35-million-seconds.html

11   'Nine-year-old earns €24m as the highest-paid YouTuber of 2020', *The Irish Times*, (28 December 2020), https://www.irishtimes.com/culture/tv-radio-web/nine-year-old-earns-24m-as-the-highest-paid-youtuber-of-2020-1.4446443

12   Natalie Mortimer, 'Oreo Youtube ad banned after BBC raises concerns over native ad transparency', *The Drum* (26 November 2014), https://www.thedrum.com/news/2014/11/26/oreo-youtube-ad-banned-after-bbc-raises-concerns-over-native-ad-transparency

13   'FTC Staff Reminds Influencers and Brands to Clearly Disclose Relationship', *Federal Trade Commission* (19 April 2017), https://www.ftc.gov/news-events/press-releases/2017/04/ftc-staff-reminds-influencers-brands-clearly-disclose

14   James Purtill, 'Instafamous must reveal #ads under new transparency rules', *ABC News* (1 March 2017), https://www.abc.net.au/triplej/programs/hack/social-influencers-must-reveal-ad-under-new-transparency-rules/8315962

15   Sarah Perez, 'U.S. Consumers Now Spend More Time In Apps Than Watching TV', *Tech Crunch* (10 September 2015), https://techcrunch.com/2015/09/10/us-consumers-now-spend-more-time-in-apps-than-watching-tv/

16   John B. Horrigan and Maeve Duggan, 'Home Broadband 2015', *PEW Research Center* (21 December 2015), https://www.pewresearch.org/internet/2015/12/21/home-broadband-2015/

17   'Internet Advertising', *PwC*, https://www.pwc.com/gx/en/entertainment-media/pdf/outlook-internet-advertising-2016.pdf

18   'Newspapers and Magazines', *PwC*, https://www.pwc.com/gx/en/entertainment-media/pdf/newspapers-and-magazines-outlook-article.pdf

19   Anna Collinson, 'Zoella's book Girl Online outsells JK Rowling', *BBC* (3 December 2014), https://www.bbc.co.uk/news/newsbeat-30305855

20   Ewan Moore, 'KSI Reminds Fans To Vote, Causing Massive Surge In Young Voter Registration', *Gaming Bible* (26 November 2019), https://www.gamingbible.co.uk/news/games-politics-ksi-reminds-fans-to-vote-causing-massive-surge-in-voter-registration-20191126

21   Yuanling Yuan and Josh Constine, 'SignalFire's Creative Economy Market Map', *SignalFire*, www.signalfire.com/blog/creator-economy

22   Alicia Adejobi, 'Government "spent £63k" on Love Island reality stars and celebrities on promote NHS Test and Trace', *Metro* (14 January 2021), https://metro.co.uk/2021/01/14/government-spent-63k-on-celebrities-promoting-nhs-test-and-trace-13903482/

23   Li Jin, 'The Passion Economy and the Future of Work', *Andreesseen Horowitz*, https://a16z.com/2019/10/08/passion-economy/

24   Lena Young, 'Woman Dominate Influencer Marketing But Still Earn Less Than Men', *Klear* (5 March 2020) https://klear.com/blog/paygap-influencer-

marketing/

25   Yuanling Yuan and Josh Constine, SignalFire's Creative Economy Market Map, SignalFire, www.signalfire.com/blog/creator-economy

26   eMarketer Editors, 'What's the Difference Between a KOL and a Wanghong?', *eMarketer* (2 August 2018, https://www.emarketer.com/content/what-s-the-difference-between-a-kol-and-a-wanghong

27   Haneen Dajani, 'UAE's paid social media influencers will need licence under new media rules', *The National News* (8 March 2018), www.thenational.ae/uae/uae-s-paid-social-media-influencers-will-need-licence-under-new-media-rules-1.710664

28   Bryan Burrough, 'FYRE FESTIVAL: ANATOMY OF A MILLENNIAL MARKETING FIASCO WAITING TO HAPPEN', *Vanity Fair* (29 July 2017), https://www.vanityfair.com/news/2017/06/fyre-festival-billy-mcfarland-millennial-marketing-fiasco

CHAPTER 2 – THE 'INFLUENCER' FACTOR

1   Marcello Mari, 'What has Yahoo! Actually Acquired: A Snapshot of Tumblr in Q1 2013', *GWI* (21 May 2013), https://blog.globalwebindex.com/chart-of-the-day/what-has-yahoo-actually-acquired-a-snapshot-of-tumblr-in-q1-2013

2   Anthony Cuthbertson, 'TUMBLR PORN BAD: ONE-FIFTH OF USERS HAVE DESERTED SITE SINCE IT REMOVED ALL ADULT CONTENT', *Independent* (11 March 2019), https://www.independent.co.uk/life-style/gadgets-and-tech/news/tumblr-porn-ban-nsfw-verizon-yahoo-adult-content-a8817546.html

3   Rachel Sklar, '"Fuck Yeah" on Tumblr', *Medium* (22 May 2013), https://medium.com/@rachelsklar/fuck-yeah-on-tumblr-d41546137466

4   'X Factor final ratings at 10-year low', *BBC* (14 December 2014), https://www.bbc.co.uk/news/entertainment-arts-30470600

5   'More votes in reality TV than the general election?', *Good Morning Britain* (23 February 2015), https://www.itv.com/goodmorningbritain/articles/more-votes-in-reality-tv-than-the-general-election

6   Julia Stoll, 'Average time per day spent watching Broadcast TV in the United Kingdom (UK) from 2010 to 2019, by age', *Statista* (12 January 2021), https://www.statista.com/statistics/269918/daily-tv-viewing-time-in-the-uk-by-age/

7   'Adults' media use and attitudes', *Ofcom* (June 2017), https://www.ofcom.org.uk/__data/assets/pdf_file/0020/102755/adults-media-use-attitudes-2017.pdf

8   'Online Nation', *Ofcom* (30 May 2019), https://www.ofcom.org.uk/__data/assets/pdf_file/0024/149253/online-nation-summary.pdf

9   Bryony Jewell, 'Love Island's Molly-Mae Hague "can rake in £13K and Dani Dyer could charge £8K PER Instagram post as they lead the villa stars making a fortune on social media"', *Daily Mail* (9 June 2021), https://www.dailymail.co.uk/tvshowbiz/article-9668675/Love-Island-Molly-Mae-Hague-rake-13K-Instagram-post-villa-stars-make-fortune-online.html

10   MollyMae, 'ANSWERING YOUR JUICY ASSUMPTIONS! PLANNING A BABY? BROKEN FRIENDSHIPS? MONEY£££? | MOLLY-MAE, *YouTube* (17

11 'Ratings! The Wall Beats The X Factor Celebrity as first live show hits new low', *TellyMix* (27 October 2019), https://tellymix.co.uk/ratings/421858-ratings-the-wall-beats-the-x-factor-celebrity-as-first-live-show-hits-new-low.html

12 Carla Marshall, 'How-to Make a Living From YouTube's Partner Earnings', *Tubular Insights* (23 October 2013), https://tubularinsights.com/youtube-partner-earnings/

13 H. Tankovska, 'Facebook's advertising revenue worldwide from 2009 to 2020', *Statista* (5 February 2021), https://www.statista.com/statistics/271258/facebooks-advertising-revenue-worldwide/

14 Emily Bell, 'Facebook is eating the world', *Columbia Journalism Review* (7 March 2016), https://www.cjr.org/analysis/facebook_and_media.php

15 'Youtuber James Charles Speaks Out After Being Trolled Over 'Influencer Representation' Comment After Met Gala Debut', *Capital FM* (8 May 2019), https://www.capitalfm.com/news/james-charles-met-gala-2019/

16 jamescharles, *Instagram* (1 November 2020), https://www.instagram.com/p/CHDuavQpCAT/

17 'Vogue Portugal', *Condé Nast*, https://www.condenast.com/brands/vogue#Portugal

18 'Millennials' pay "scarred" by the 2008 banking crisis', *BBC* (3 February 2019), https://www.bbc.co.uk/news/business-47106711

19 Alexandra Mondalek, 'The New Four Ps of DTC Marketing — Download the Case Study', *Business of Fashion* (11 March 2021), https://www.businessoffashion.com/case-studies/marketing-pr/the-new-four-ps-of-dtc-marketing-download-the-case-study

20 Sam Hall, 'Gymshark founder Ben Francis set to become UK's richest self-made person under 30', *iNews* 14 August 2020), https://inews.co.uk/news/uk/gymshark-founder-ben-francis-uk-richest-self-made-person-under-30-580157

21 Rachel Gee, 'A third of Instagram users have bought an item of clothing they saw on the social network', *MarketingWeek* (6 September 2016), https://www.marketingweek.com/why-brands-with-a-fashion-focus-are-most-likely-to-boost-sales-on-instagram/

22 Anne Helen Peterson, 'How Millennials Became The Burnout Generation', *BuzzFeed News* 5 January 2019), https://www.buzzfeednews.com/article/annehelenpetersen/millennials-burnout-generation-debt-work

23 Jamie Ballard, 'Millennials are the loneliest generation', *YouGovAmerica* (30 July 2019), https://today.yougov.com/topics/lifestyle/articles-reports/2019/07/30/loneliness-friendship-new-friends-poll-survey

24 Celie O'Neil-Hart and Howard Blumenstein, 'Why YouTube stars are more influential than traditional celebrities', *Think with Google* (July 2019), https://www.thinkwithgoogle.com/marketing-strategies/video/youtube-stars-influence/

25 Joele Forrester, 18-25 year Olds Influenced More by Social Media Influencers Than Family and Friends', *Talking Influence* (10 April 2019), https://talkinginfluence.com/2019/04/10/18-25-year-olds-influenced-more-by-social-

media-influencers-than-family-and-friends.

26   Stephanie McNeal and Ryan Broderick, 'Lifestyle Influencers Are Now
      Sharing Some Bogus Far-Right Conspiracy Theories About The Coronavirus
      On Instagram', *BuzzFeed News* (4 April 2020), https://www.buzzfeednews.
      com/article/stephaniemcneal/coronavirus-lifestyle-influencers-sharing-
      conspiracy-qanon?fbclid=IwAR3oX_2RsGFTejfSwhZOOQkzx-
      EcFsDmbhe4gRlveM7eFmI8-LfFgoLx4oM

27   Art Swift, 'American's Trust in Mass Media Sinks to New Low', *Gallup* (14
      September 2016), https://news.gallup.com/poll/195542/americans-trust-mass-
      media-sinks-new-low.aspx

28   Henry Mance, 'Britain has had enough of experts, says Gove', *Financial
      Times* (3 June 2016), https://www.ft.com/content/3be49734-29cb-11e6-83e4-
      abc22d5d108c

29   'Two-Thirds of Consumers Worldwide Now Buy on Beliefs', *Edelman* (2
      October 2018), https://www.edelman.com/news-awards/two-thirds-consumers-
      worldwide-now-buy-beliefs

30   Rachel Sugar, 'Steak-umm's new marketing strategy: millennial angst with
      a side of meat puns', *Vox* (28 September 2018), https://www.vox.com/the-
      goods/2018/9/28/17910462/steak-umm-viral-tweet-authenticity-angst

31   Fnr Tigg, Sunny D Becomes a Meme After Randomly Tweeting 'I Can't Do This
      Anymore', *Complex* (4 February 2019), https://www.complex.com/life/2019/02/
      sunny-d-becomes-a-meme-after-randomly-tweeting-i-cant-do-this-anymore

CHAPTER 3 – EXTREMELY ONLINE

1   Chloe Taylor, 'Kids now dream of being professional YouTubers rather
      than astronauts, study finds', *CNBC* (19 July 2019), https://www.cnbc.
      com/2019/07/19/more-children-dream-of-being-youtubers-than-astronauts-
      lego-says.html

2   Brooke Auxier, Monica Anderson, Andrew Perrin, and Erica Turner, 'Parental
      views about YouTube', *PEW Research Center* (28 July 2020), https://www.
      pewresearch.org/internet/2020/07/28/parental-views-about-youtube/

3   Mansoor Iqbal, 'YouTube Revenue and Usage Statistics (2021)', *Business of Apps*
      (14 May 2021), https://www.businessofapps.com/data/youtube-statistics/

4   Mansoor Iqbal, 'Twitch Revenue and Usage Statistics (2021)', *Business of Apps*
      (29 March 2021), https://www.businessofapps.com/data/twitch-statistics/

5   Sean Czarnecki, 'Study: PewDiePie is YouTube's highest earner at $8m a month',
      PRWeek (6 August 2019), https://www.prweek.com/article/1593191/study-
      pewdiepie-youtubes-highest-earner-8m-month.

6   Ben Gilbert, 'Ninja just signed a multi-year contract that keeps him exclusive
      to Amazon-owned Twitch (11 September 2020), https://www.businessinsider.
      com/ninja-signs-multi-year-exclusivity-contract-with-amazon-twitch-2020.

7   H. Tankovska, 'Average time spent by children daily on TikTok, Instagram,
      Snapchat and YouTube in the United Kingdom (UK), as of February 2020',
      Statista (8 April 2021), https://www.statista.com/statistics/1124962/time-spent-
      by-children-on-social-media-uk/

8   Kristen Rogers, 'US teens use screens more than seven hours a day on average
     — and that's not included school work', *CNN* (29 October 2019), https://edition.
     cnn.com/2019/10/29/health/common-sense-kids-media-use-report-wellness/
     index.html

9   Michael Grothaus, '96.5% of YouTube creators don't make above the
     U.S. poverty line', *Fast Company* (28 February 2018), www.fastcompany.
     com/40537244/96-5-of-youtube-creators-dont-make-above-the-u-s-poverty-
     line

10   abbyroberts, *TikTok* (30 June 2019), https://www.tiktok.com/@abbyroberts/
     video/6708449161286520070

11   Sophie Bishop, 'Why the 'Ideal' Influencer Looks Like… That', *PaperMag* (12
     August 2019), https://www.papermag.com/top-beauty-influencers-2639784604.
     html

12   Jia Tolentino, 'The Age of Instagram Face', *The New Yorker* (12 December 2019),
     https://www.newyorker.com/culture/decade-in-review/the-age-of-instagram-
     face

13   Adebola Lamuye and Barney Davis, 'Please stop "influencing" on our
     doorsteps, Notting Hill residents tell "unapologetic" Instagrammers', *Evening
     Standard* (28 February 2019), https://www.standard.co.uk/news/london/please-
     stop-influencing-on-our-doorsteps-notting-hill-residents-tell-unapologetic-
     social-media-bloggers-a4078806.html

14   Louise France, 'Is TikTok star Holly H the most influential 23-year-old in
     Britain?', *The Times* (2 November 2019), https://www.thetimes.co.uk/article/is-
     tiktok-star-holly-h-the-most-influential-23-year-old-in-britain-9ts35ksfn

CHAPTER 4 – HYPE HOUSES, #RELATIONSHIPGOALS, AND KIDFLUENCERS

1   'Comber Retreat', *Luxury Home Rental*, http://luxuryhomerental.com/
     properties/315-comber-retreat/

2   Jackson Ryan, 'Inside the $15 million YouTube House, where it's all work and
     no play', *CNET* (12 October 2018), https://www.cnet.com/news/inside-the-15-
     million-youtube-house-where-its-all-work-and-no-play-fortnite/

3   James Hale, 'Fanbytes Launches ByteHouse, TikTok's First U.K.-Based Creator
     Collective', *Tubefilter* (21 May 2020), https://www.tubefilter.com/2020/05/21/
     fanbytes-bytehouse-tiktok-creator-collective/

4   Daisuke Wakabayashi, 'Inside the Hollywood Home of Social Media's Stars.
     (Don't be Shy.)', *The New York Times* (30 December 2017), https://www.nytimes.
     com/2017/12/30/business/hollywood-apartment-social-media.html

5   Joe Cortez, 'The Average Net Worth In America [2021 Edition]',
     CommonCentsMom (23 January 2021), https://www.groovewallet.com/ksi-net-
     worth/

6   Hanna Lustig, 'A power struggle and trademark dispute are rocking TikTok's
     Hype House as the influencer collective finds fame and fortune', *Insider* (7
     March 2020), https://www.insider.com/tiktok-hype-house-facing-power-
     struggle-legal-dispute-2020-3

7   Taylor Lorenz, 'An Influencer House Wouldn't Stop Partying, So L.A. Cut Its Power', *The New York Times* (19 August 2020), https://www.nytimes.com/2020/08/19/style/la-party-power-cut-tiktok.html

8   Dan Whateley, 'An LA landlord is suing a TikTok influencer group after months of conflict about unpaid rent, pandemic partying, and TV show production', *Insider* (7 January 2021), https://www.businessinsider.com/tiktok-stars-of-collab-house-drip-crib-sued-by-landlord-2020-12

9   @defnoodles, *Twitter* (22 August 2020), https://twitter.com/defnoodles/status/1297218800316686336

10   The Drip Crib, 'Drip Crib LA TV show Demo', *YouTube* (7 August 2020), https://www.youtube.com/watch?v=o-jyqBTQ8qo&ab_channel=TheDripCrib

11   Eloise Fouladgar, 'why i left the wave house', *YouTube* (17 December 2020), https://www.youtube.com/watch?v=YxVPDlR3YM8&ab_channel=EloiseFouladgar

12   'U.S. Employees Working More Hours During COVID-19 Pandemic', *Business Facilities* (23 March 2020), https://businessfacilities.com/2020/03/u-s-employees-working-more-hours-during-covid-19-pandemic/

13   The Mystery Hour, 'Instagram Husband', *YouTube* (8 December 2015), https://www.youtube.com/watch?v=fFzKi-o4rHw&ab_channel=TheMysteryHour

14   daniausten, *Instagram* (5 August 2019), https://www.instagram.com/p/B0w0-GpATUi/

15   daniausten, *Instagram* (23 October 2020), https://www.instagram.com/p/CGqs-EKg9h2/

16   'UK BLOGGERS SURVEY 2019', *Vuelio* (2019), https://www.vuelio.com/uk/wp-content/uploads/2019/03/UK-Bloggers-Survey-2019-Vuelio.pdf

17   'Mommy', *Intellifluence*, https://intellifluence.com/mommy-parenting

18   Brooke Auxier, Monica Anderson, Andrew Perrin, and Erica Turner, 'Parents' attitudes — and experiences — related to digital technology', *PEW Research Center* (28 July 2020), www.pewresearch.org/internet/2020/07/28/parents-attitudes-and-experiences-related-to-digital-technology

19   'Top 10 highest paid child YouTubers of 2020 so far', *Pound Toy* (31 July 2020), https://www.poundtoy.com/blogs/news/top-10-highest-paid-child-youtubers-of-2020-so-far

20   Crystal Abidin, '#familygoals: Family Influencers, Calibrated Amateurism, and Justifying Young Digital Labor', *Sage* (5 June 2017), https://journals.sagepub.com/doi/pdf/10.1177/2056305117707191

21   Brooke Auxier, Monica Anderson, Andrew Perrin, and Erica Turner, 'Parents' attitudes — and experiences — related to digital technology', *PEW Research Center* (28 July 2020), https://www.pewresearch.org/internet/2020/07/28/parents-attitudes-and-experiences-related-to-digital-technology/

22   Ideas Desk, 'Kids to Parents: Stop Sharing Pictures of Us on Social Media', *Time* (10 March 2016), https://time.com/4253207/parents-social-media/

23   Ruth Graham, 'Myka Stauffer and the Aggressively Inspirational World of "Adoption Influencers"', *Slate* (4 June 2020), https://slate.com/human-interest/2020/06/myka-stauffer-adoption-influencers.html

24 FinallyAnonymous6, 'AITA? My mom is an influencer. I am sick of being a part of it, I had "NO PHOTOS" hoodies printed for me and my little sister', *Reddit* (2020), https://www.reddit.com/r/AmItheAsshole/comments/evqd98/aita_my_mom_is_an_influencer_i_am_sick_of_being_a/

25 Crystal Abidin, '#familygoals: Family Influencers, Calibrated Amateurism, and Justifying Young Digital Labor', *Sage* (5 June 2017), https://journals.sagepub.com/doi/full/10.1177/2056305117707191

26 'France passes new law to protect child influencers', *BBC* (7 October 2020), https://www.bbc.co.uk/news/world-europe-54447491

CHAPTER 5 – CREATOR ECONOMICS

1 Jill Goldsmith, 'VidCon's Flagship Anaheim Event Will Return Live This October', *Deadline* (23 March 2021), https://deadline.com/2021/03/vidcon-anaheim-live-event-1234719760/

2 Sam Gutelle, 'It's Official: Viacom Announces Its Acquisition of VidCon', *Tubefilter* (7 February 2018), https://www.tubefilter.com/2018/02/07/viacom-officially-acquires-vidcon/

3 hankschannel, 'VidCon Update', *YouTube* (7 February 2018), https://www.youtube.com/watch?v=c62AURJz6oA

4 Nick Statt, 'YouTube is a $15 billion-a-year business, Google reveals for the first time', *The Verge* (3 February 2020), https://www.theverge.com/2020/2/3/21121207/youtube-google-alphabet-earnings-revenue-first-time-reveal-q4-2019

5 Ians, 'YouTube paid $30 bn to creators, artists in the last 3 years: CEO Wojcicki', *Business Standard* (27 January 2021), https://www.business-standard.com/article/technology/youtube-paid-30-bn-to-creators-artists-in-last-3-years-ceo-wojcicki-121012700267_1.html

6 Adam Fitch, 'How does MrBeast make money? Breaking down the youTube star's net worth', *Dexerto* (20 January 2021), https://www.dexerto.com/entertainment/how-mrbeast-makes-money-1497316/

7 Sarah Rendell, 'Logan Paul net worth: How much has YouTube star earned in his career?', *Independent* (7 June 2021), https://www.independent.co.uk/sport/boxing/logan-paul-net-worth-career-earnings-b1858248.html

8 'MrBeast says he lost $800,000 after scrapping a YouTube video series', *Yahoo! Life* (15 December 2020), https://www.yahoo.com/lifestyle/mrbeast-says-lost-800-000-205226682.html

9 MrBeast, 'Videos I could not upload', *YouTube* (1 May 2020), https://www.youtube.com/watch?v=gsWPpE4Rid0.

10 'THE INFLUENCER MARKETING INDUSTRY GLOBAL AD SPEND: A $5-$10 BILLION MARKET BY 2020 [CHART]', *Mediakix* (6 March 2018), https://mediakix.com/blog/influencer-marketing-industry-ad-spend-chart/

11 A. Guttmann, 'Number of brand sponsored influencer posts on Instagram from 2016 to 2020', *Statista* (30 June 2020), https://www.statista.com/statistics/693775/instagram-sponsored-influencer-content/

12 Werner Geyser, 'The State of Influencer Marketing 2019: Benchmark Report

[+Infographic]', *Influencer Marketing Hub* (14 February 2021), https://influencermarketinghub.com/influencer-marketing-2019-benchmark-report/

13   Hugo Amsellem, 'Mapping the Creator Economy' *Arm The Creators* (3 December 2020), https://www.armthecreators.com/mapping-the-creator-economy/

14   Ken Tenbarge, 'A family vlogger who recently built a $10-million mansion said that fans should have to pay to watch his videos and he's getting ripped to shreds', *Insider* (29 December 2019), https://www.insider.com/austin-mcbroom-ace-family-complains-people-should-pay-youtube-videos-2019-12

15   glamazontay, 'WHY IM ON ONLYFANS? | GRWM CHAT', *YouTube* (13 May 2020), https://www.youtube.com/watch?v=2bGa4EWL-x0&ab_channel=glamazontay

16   Taylor Lorenz, 'Snapchat Wants You to Post. It's Willing to Pay Millions.', *The New York Times* (15 January 2021), https://www.nytimes.com/2021/01/15/style/snapchat-spotlight.html

17   Creator Economics, 'Should Influencers Choose Equity or Cash???', *YouTube* (14 October 2020), https://www.youtube.com/watch?v=BhD8UeN5I6E&feature=youtu.be&ab_channel=CreatorEconomics

18   Chris Stokel-Walker, 'Instagram: beware of bad influencers…', *The Observer* (3 February 2019), https://www.theguardian.com/technology/2019/feb/03/instagram-beware-bad-influencers-product-twitter-snapchat-fyre-kendall-jenner-bella-hadid

19   Imogen Watson, 'Grey and YouGov find 96% of people in the UK do not trust what influencers say', *The Drum* (31 October 2019), https://www.thedrum.com/news/2019/10/31/grey-and-yougov-find-96-people-the-uk-do-not-trust-what-influencers-say

20   Rachel Hosie, 'An Instagram star with 2 million followers couldn't sell 36 T-shirts, and a marketing expert says her case isn't rare', *Insider* (30 May 2019), https://www.insider.com/instagrammer-arii-2-million-followers-cannot-sell-36-t-shirts-2019-5

21   'Influencer Marketing: Social media influencer market stats and research for 2021', *Business Insider* (6 January 2021), https://www.businessinsider.com/influencer-marketing-report

22   'The World's Influencer Marketing Platform Industry is Projected to Grow to USD 24.1 Billion by 2025, at a CAGR of 32%', *PR Newswire* (6 January 2021), https://www.prnewswire.com/news-releases/the-worlds-influencer-marketing-platform-industry-is-projected-to-grow-to-usd-24-1-billion-by-2025--at-a-cagr-of-32-301201952.html

CHAPTER 6 – SPILLING THE TEA

1   Bianca London, 'American student's fairytale life in Cambridge enchants Instagram: 300,000 people following student's photos of carefree days of dreaming spires, black-tie balls and Champagne on the river', *Daily Mail* (25 March 2015), dailymail.co.uk/femail/article-3010757/US-student-s-enchanting-Instagram-photos-reveal-fairytale

2   Abby Jitendra, 'The Tab meets … Caroline Calloway', *The Tab* (2015), thetab.
        com/uk/cambridge/2015/02/01/tab-meets-caroline-calloway-45726

3   Harling Ross, 'Was Caroline Calloway the First Instagram Influencer?', *Repeller*
        20 June 2018), https://repeller.com/caroline-calloway-interview/

4   Kate Taylor, 'More Parents Plead Guilty in College Admissions Scandal', *The
        New York Times* (21 October 2019), https://www.nytimes.com/2019/10/21/us/
        college-admissions-scandal.html

5   Kayleigh Donaldson, 'The Empty Mason Jar of the Influence Economy: The
        Case of Caroline Calloway and her Creativity Workshop Tour', *Pajiba* (18
        January 2019), pajiba.com/web_culture/the-case-of-caroline-calloway-and-her-
        creativity-workshop-tour.php

6   'Sali Hughes #3 Weak dilutes & boiled piss, if only! I invented the aubergine
        penis emoji', *Tattle Life* (12 September 2019), tattle.life/threads/sali-hughes-3-
        weak-dilutes-boiled-piss-if-only-i-invented-the-aubergine-penis-emoji

7   'Bitch Eating Crackers', *Urban Dictionary* (16 December 2015), https://www.
        urbandictionary.com/define.php?term=Bitch%20Eating%20Crackers

8   Andreea Cristina Bolbea and Sirin Kale, 'The Relentless Horror of Being
        Stalked as an Instagram Star', *Vice* (19 November 2018), https://www.vice.com/
        en/article/j5zeb4/andreea-cristina-instagram-stalker-blog

9   Taylor Pettaway, 'Man arrested after allegedly stalking, threatening to kill a San
        Antonio social media influencer', *Express News* (10 February 2021), https://
        www.expressnews.com/news/local/article/Man-arrested-after-allegedly-
        stalking-and-15939757.php

10   Jason Murdock, 'Instagram Influencers Are Using Black Lives Matter for Self-
        Promotion, and Being Caught in the Act', *Newsweek* (11 June 2020), https://
        www.newsweek.com/instagram-influencers-wild-george-resch-black-lives-
        matter-protests-twitter-exposed-social-media-1510144

11   Influencersinthewild, *Twitter* (10 June 2020), https://twitter.com/influencersitw/
        status/1270521188406702082

12   Kat Tenbarge, 'Jeffree Star accuses say the makeup mogul has a history of
        sexual assault, physical violence, and hush-money offers', *Insider* (1 October
        2020), https://www.insider.com/jeffree-star-sexual-assault-allegations-violence-
        accused-predator-myspace-payments-2020-9

13   Joe Price, 'Logan Paul Gained 80,000 Subscribers Following Controversial
        "Suicide Forest" Video', *Complex* (6 January 2018), https://www.complex.com/
        life/2018/01/logan-paul-subscribers

14   Lindsay Dodgson, 'Jake Paul and Tana Mongeau's break-up was worth more
        than $600 million in media value — here's how their careers benefited from the
        whirlwind romance', *Insider* (10 February 2020), https://www.insider.com/what-
        tana-mongeau-and-jake-paul-relationship-worth-to-careers-2020-2

15   897203 views across videos as of 24/5/2020

16   Zoe Haylock, 'Welcome to the Circus: 19 moments that defined YouTube
        drama's economy … and then destroyed it.' *Vulture* (2 March 2021), https://
        www.vulture.com/article/youtube-drama-channels-guide.html

CHAPTER 7 – PLATFORMS VS THE PEOPLE

1   'A billion likes for the Influencer Awards', *Monaco Now*, https://monaconow.com/a-billion-likes-for-the-influencer-awards/

2   Katie Warren, 'A third of the people in this European country are millionaires', *Business Insider* (26 May 2019), https://www.businessinsider.com/third-of-population-in-european-country-are-millionaires-2019-5?r=US&IR=T

3   'Monaco: Opening its luxurious doors to Instagram stars', *BBC* (8 June 2020), https://www.bbc.co.uk/news/av/stories-52938402

4   'The one and only INFLUENCER Awards #IAMMONACO', *Influencer Awards Monaco*, https://www.influencerawardsmonaco.com/

5   Agence France-Presse, 'Harry and Meghan break record with Royal Sussex Instagram account', *The Guardian* (4 April 2019), https://www.theguardian.com/uk-news/2019/apr/04/harry-and-meghan-break-record-with-royal-sussex-instagram-account

6   'Inside Monaco: Playground of the Rich', *BBC iPlayer* (8 June 2020), https://www.bbc.co.uk/iplayer/episodes/m000jykc/inside-monaco-playground-of-the-rich

7   'Revolutionary MDL Beast Festival United a Generation of Progressive Saudi Talent' (13 December 2019), https://www.prnewswire.com/news-releases/revolutionary-mdl-beast-festival-unites-a-generation-of-progressive-saudi-talent-300974271.html

8   'Saudi Arabia: "Image Laundering" Conceals Abuses', *Human Rights Watch* (2 October 2020), https://www.hrw.org/news/2020/10/02/saudi-arabia-image-laundering-conceals-abuses

9   'Saudi Arabia', *Freedom House*, https://freedomhouse.org/country/saudi-arabia/freedom-world/2020

10   Anton Troianovski, '"You Know Your Audience": Russia's Internet Stars Turn Away From Putin', *The New York Times* (30 June 2020), https://www.nytimes.com/2020/06/30/world/europe/russia-internet-putin-referendum.html

11   Concha Pérez-Curiel and Pilar Limon Naharro, 'Political influencers. A study of Donald Trump's personal brand on Twitter and its impact on the media and users', *Communication & Society* (12 September 2018), https://revistas.unav.edu/index.php/communication-and-society/article/view/37815/32043

12   'How Britain Killed its computing Industry w/ Mar Hicks', *The Tech Won't Save Us with Paris Marx* (18 March 2021), https://podcasts.apple.com/gb/podcast/how-britain-killed-its-computing-industry-w-mar-hicks/id1507621076?i=1000513548246

13   Brooke Erin Duffy, '(Not) Getting Paid to Do What You Love', *Yale University Press* (27 June 2017), https://yalebooks.yale.edu/book/9780300218176/not-getting-paid-do-what-you-love

14   Jessica Schiffer, 'Influencer marketing, long lacking diversity, faces a reckoning', *Vogue Business* (19 June 2020), www.voguebusiness.com/companies/influencer-marketing-long-lacking-diversity-faces-a-reckoning

15   Lena Young, 'Women Dominate Influencer Marketing But Still Earn Less Than Men', *Klear* (5 March 2020), https://klear.com/blog/paygap-influencer-

marketing/

16 Kat Tenbarge, 'Jeffree Star accusers say the makeup mogul has a history of sexual assault, physical violence, and hush-money offers', *Insider* (1 October 2020), https://www.insider.com/jeffree-star-sexual-assault-allegations-violence-accused-predator-myspace-payments-2020-9

17 Julia Alexander, 'LGBTQ YouTubers are suing YouTube over alleged discrimination', *The Verge* (14 August 2019), https://www.theverge.com/2019/8/14/20805283/lgbtq-youtuber-lawsuit-discrimination-alleged-video-recommendations-demonetization

18 EJ Dickson, 'Inside LGBTQ Vloggers' Class-Action "Censorship" Suit Against YouTube', *Rolling Stone* (14 November 2019), https://www.rollingstone.com/culture/culture-features/lgbtq-youtube-lawsuit-censorship-877919/

19 Rachael Tatman, 'Gender and Dialect Bias in YouTube's Automatic Caption', *University of Washington Linguistics Department* (4 April 2017), https://www.aclweb.org/anthology/W17-1606.pdf

20 Ibid.

21 Casey Newton, 'BODIES IN SEATS', *The Verge* (19 July 2019), https://www.theverge.com/2019/6/19/18681845/facebook-moderator-interviews-video-trauma-ptsd-cognizant-tampa

22 Elena Botella, 'TikTok Admits It Suppressed Videos by Disabled, Queer, and Fat Creators', *Slate* (4 December 2019), https://slate.com/technology/2019/12/tiktok-disabled-users-videos-suppressed.html

23 Sam Biddle, Paulo Victor, and Tatiana Dias, 'Invisible Censorship', *The Intercept* (16 March 2020), https://theintercept.com/2020/03/16/tiktok-app-moderators-users-discrimination/

24 Ibid.

25 Alex Hern, 'TikTok "tried to filter out videos from ugly, poor, or disabled users"', *The Guardian* (17 March 2020), https://www.theguardian.com/technology/2020/mar/17/tiktok-tried-to-filter-out-videos-from-ugly-poor-or-disabled-users

26 Rebecca Lewis, 'ALTERNATIVE INFLUENCE: Broadcasting the Reactionary Right on YouTube', *Data & Society* (18 September 2018), https://datasociety.net/library/alternative-influence/

27 Alex Gekker, et al., 'Slicing BreadTube', *Digital Methods Summer School*, https://wiki.digitalmethods.net/pub/Dmi/SummerSchool2019/BreadTube%20Report%20%E2%80%93%20Digital%20Methods%20Summer%20School%202019.pdf

28 Shivali Best, 'Instagram influencers need just 42,000 followers to earn the average UK salary', *Mirror* (12 December 2019), https://www.mirror.co.uk/tech/instagram-influencers-need-just-42000-21082268

29 Gaby Dunn, 'Get Rich or Die Vlogging: The Sad Economics of Internet Fame', *Splinter* (14 December 2015), https://splinternews.com/get-rich-or-die-vlogging-the-sad-economics-of-internet-1793853578

30 Sissi Cao, 'Here's Why Becoming a Lucrative YouTube Star Keeps Getting Harder', *Observer* (28 February 2018), https://observer.com/2018/02/study-

youtube-stars-earnings-us-median-income/

31 Li Jin, 'The Creator Economy Needs a Middle Class', *Harvard Business Review* (17 December 2020), https://hbr.org/2020/12/the-creator-economy-needs-a-middle-class

32 Ibid.

33 'THE AIC OFFICIALLY LAUNCHES', *American Influences Council* (30 June 2020), https://www.americaninfluencercouncil.com/aic-member-memo/aic-officially-launches-on-the-10th-anniversary-of-social-media-day

34 Geoff Weiss, 'Hank Green's Internet Creators Guild To Shutter, Citing No "Path To Financial Stability"', *Tubefilter* (10 July 2020), https://www.tubefilter.com/2019/07/10/internet-creators-guild-to-shutter/

35 Piper Thomson, 'Understanding YouTube Demonetization and the Adpocalypse', *Learn Hub* (14 June 2019), https://learn.g2.com/youtube-demonetization

36 Rob Horning, 'I Write the Songs', *Real Life Mag* (2 September 2020), https://reallifemag.com/i-write-the-songs/

CHAPTER 8 – LOGGING OFF

1 Daniel Frankel, 'YouTube Controls 16% of PandemicTraffic Globally: Sandvine', *Next TV* (7 May 2020), https://www.nexttv.com/news/youtube-controls-16-of-pandemic-traffic-globally-sandvine

2 Geoff Weiss, 'TikTok Added 12 Million Unique U.S. Visitors In March, As Watch-Time Surges In Quarantine (Report)', *Tubefilter* (28 April 2020), https://www.tubefilter.com/2020/04/28/tiktok-added-12-million-unique-us-visitors-in-march/

3 Paige Leskin, 'TikTok surpasses 2 billion downloads and sets a record for app installs in a single quarter', *Business Insider* (20 April 2020), https://www.businessinsider.com/tiktok-app-2-billion-downloads-record-setting-q1-sensor-tower-2020

4 Helen Pidd and Amy Walker, '"Why are people buying book tubes": fashion workers' anger at owners and consumers', *The Guardian* (3 April 2020), https://www.theguardian.com/business/2020/apr/03/why-are-people-buying-boob-tubes

5 'Asos adds three million customers as profits soar amid pandemic', *BBC* (14 October 2020), https://www.bbc.co.uk/news/business-54535775

6 Elizabeth Crawford, 'Soup-to-Nuts Podcast: Social media influencers offer economical access to consumers during pandemic', *Food Navigator USA* (19 August 2020), https://www.foodnavigator-usa.com/Article/2020/07/27/Soup-to-Nuts-Podcast-Social-media-influencers-offer-economical-access-to-consumers-during-pandemic

7 Amanda Perelli, Dan Whateley, and Sydney Bradley, 'How the coronavirus is changing the influencer business, according to marketers and top creators on Instagram and YouTube', *Business Insider* (1 September 2020), https://www.businessinsider.com/how-coronavirus-is-changing-influencer-marketing-creator-industry-2020-3?r=US&IR=T

8   Siobhan Freegard, 'Why Micro-Influencers Are Seeing Big Growth During Lockdown', *Talking Influence* (5 May 2020), https://talkinginfluence.com/2020/05/05/micro-influencers-growth-lockdown/

9   'Watching the Pandemic', *YouTube Culture & Trends*, https://www.youtube.com/trends/articles/covid-impact/

10   Abram Brown, 'Coronavirus: The World Health Organization Is Becoming The Planet's Most Important Social Media Influencer', (16 March 2020), https://www.forbes.com/sites/abrambrown/2020/03/16/coronavirus-the-world-health-organization-is-becoming-the-worlds-most-important-social-media-influencer/?sh=5aaf6d7a5321

11   Sophie Ross, *Twitter* (30 March 2020), https://twitter.com/SophRossss/status/1244757242001457153

12   Bill Bostock, 'The fashion influencer who fled NYC for the Hamptons while infected with COVID-19 received up to $350,000 in government PPP loans, report says', *Business Insider* (29 July 2020), https://www.businessinsider.com/arielle-charnas-influecner-something-navy-received-ppp-loans-nypost-2020-7?r=US&IR=T

13   Kat Tenbarge, 'The era of A-list YouTube celebrities is over. Now the people cancelling them are on top', *Business Insider* (21 October 2020), https://www.insider.com/dangelo-wallace-interview-youtube-shane-jeffree-tati-drama-channels-2020-9

14   'YouTuber Jenna Marbles quits over blackface', *BBC* (26 June 2020), https://www.bbc.co.uk/news/newsbeat-53192702

15   Rupert Neate, 'Billionaires' wealth rises to $10.2 trillion amid Covid crisis', *The Guardian* (7 October 2020), https://www.theguardian.com/business/2020/oct/07/covid-19-crisis-boosts-the-fortunes-of-worlds-billionaires

16   Rachel Kraus, 'Everything that happened at the Big Tech antitrust hearing', *Mashable* (29 July 2020), https://mashable.com/article/biggest-moments-from-big-tech-anti-trust-hearing/?europe=true

17   Kevin Roose, 'Social Media Giants Support Racial Justice. Their Products Undermine It', *The New York Times* (19 June 2020), https://www.nytimes.com/2020/06/19/technology/facebook-youtube-twitter-black-lives-matter.html

18   Mireille Charper, *Instagram* (30 May 2020), https://www.instagram.com/p/CA04VKDAyjb/